SRI LANKA

Paradise Lost
Paradise Regained

SRI LANKA

Paradise Lost
Paradise Regained

Michael Naseby
The Rt Hon. the Lord Naseby, PC

UNICORN

First published by Unicorn
an imprint of the Unicorn Publishing Group LLP, 2020
5 Newburgh Street
London W1F 7RG

www.unicornpublishing.org

10 9 8 7 6 5 4 3 2 1

ISBN 978-1-912690-74-9

Cover design Unicorn Publishing Group
Typeset by Vivian@Bookscribe

All photographs from the author's collection unless stated otherwise.
Front cover photograph iStock Tom de Waart / Globetravelphotography.

Printed and bound in Malta by Jellyfish

Paradise Lost and *Paradise Regained*
(John Milton, 1608–74)
England's leading poet in the Civil War

Recollections from over fifty years of a unique friendship
between a British politician and the people of Sri Lanka

Michael Morris, MP
The Rt Hon. the Lord Naseby, PC

CONTENTS

COGITO · ERGO · SUM

The Armorial Ensigns of
MICHAEL WOLFGANG LAURENCE
BARON NASEBY
One of Her Majesty's Most Honourable Privy Council

College of Arms
London

Garter Principal King of Arms

FOREWORD

I have some knowledge of Sri Lanka as Michael Morris MP approached me in 1975 to be Vice Chairman of the All Party Parliamentary Group on Sri Lanka that he was setting up. I also went on a formal CPA Parliamentary visit led by Michael in 1984 and on numerous occasions visited friends there.

I was elected Speaker in 1992 and was delighted when the House of Commons chose Michael to be my senior Deputy and Chairman of Ways and Means. He is still remembered by colleagues from all sides of the House for his sensitive handling of the highly controversial Maastricht Bill. Feelings running high; Government had a wafer thin majority but with care and understanding the Bill progressed through 25 days of debates to become law. A 'tour de force' by any yardstick.

Michael spent time visiting the Island almost every year, interviewing those in public life. He became involved in every aspect of Sri Lanka life. He saw and knew everyone of importance. He learned the aspirations of those in markets, the countryside and the fishing villages.

I know from experience there is no British politician more knowledgeable, more trusted by the people of Sri Lanka than Michael Morris.

In the UK he campaigned objectively for a better understanding of Sri Lanka's needs to combat the attempts to achieve a separate State by force through the Tamil Tiger Terrorists.

I know Lord Naseby, as he now is, has been careful never to side with any political party or ethnic group and has never had any business relationships.

In 2005 he was honoured by the Government of Sri Lanka with the highest award for foreigners: 'The Sri Lanka Ratna (Titular)'. In February 2015 he was invited by the new President Sirisena to attend the National Celebrations and was given pride of place on the dais ahead of any Diplomat. In 2018 he was elected Winner of the 'Outstanding Friend to the British Sri Lankan Community'.

I have found this book a real insight to Sri Lanka: carefully researched but written with fluidity that makes a good read.

The Right Honourable Baroness Boothroyd, OM PC
House of Lords

Author in full Sri Lanka Ratna (titular) regalia with family friend Mrs Veena Talwatte

FOREWORD

I have much pleasure in writing a Foreword for this book for the Rt. Hon. The Lord Naseby.

The book of Lord Naseby's experiences of Sri Lanka over six decades promises to be most interesting. Michael Morris, the Lord Naseby, has had a wide experience of Sri Lanka, first as a representative of an International Company and thereafter as a member of both Houses of Parliament, whence he continued a close relationship with my country as well as many Sri Lankans.

His deep love and concern for Sri Lanka led him to assume the post of Chairman of the All Party British Sri Lanka Parliamentary Group. He has been a true friend of Sri Lanka, taking on many responsibilities to assist the country not only in its relationships with the UK Governments, but also at times of crisis such as the three-decade long civil war in Sri Lanka and the Tsunami disaster.

His deep commitment, as well as his wide knowledge of the country and its peoples and the numerous friendships and trust he built with his genial and candid manner has, I believe, helped him to conduct whatever responsibilities he took on for Sri Lanka with success.

We appreciate his non-partisan approach when dealing with Sri Lankan issues as well as his steadfast decision to refrain from involvement in business matters.

In addition to his national and international political interests, Lord Naseby is a keen sportsman and a lover of the Arts. I am aware that he has a great love for tennis and cricket, both very British sports, which figure among the better and pleasanter aspects of our colonial inheritance.

I had the pleasure of awarding the Presidential Honour of the *Sri Lanka Ratna* – the highest honour awarded to foreigners by the President of Sri Lanka, in recognition of Lord Naseby's long and dedicated service to Sri Lanka and its peoples.

I take this opportunity to wish my friend Lord Naseby and his dear wife Dr Ann Morris, good health and happiness.

H.E. Chandrika Bandaraneuka Kumaratunga
President of Sri Lanka: 1994–2005

Maps reproduced from *Total Destruction of the Tamil Tigers* by Paul Moorcraft, published by Pen & Sword Military.

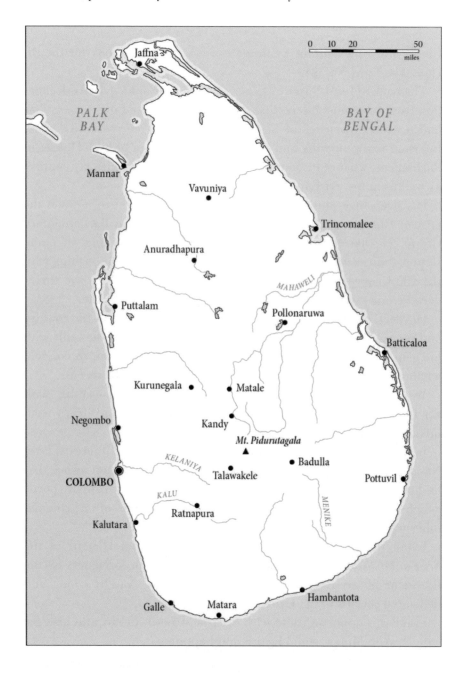

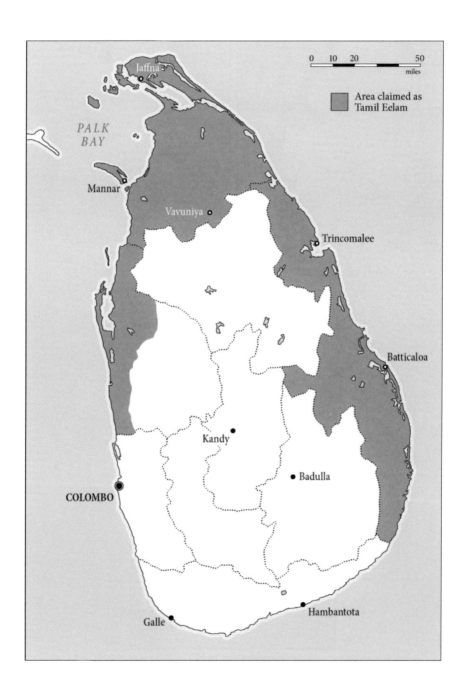

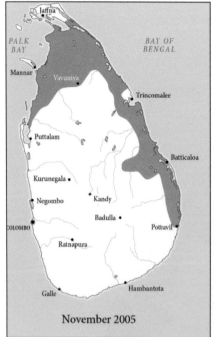

November 2005

February 2007

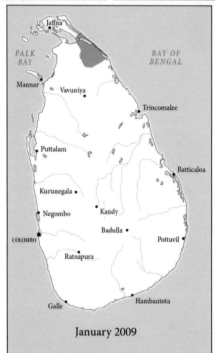

January 2009

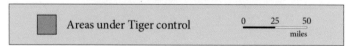

Areas under Tiger control

0   25   50
             miles

14

NASEBY 1645

Lt.Gen.Cromwell's Letter

For the Honourable Willian Lenthall, speaker of the Commons House of Parliament: these.

Sir,

Being commanded by you to this service, I think myself bound to acquaint you with the good hand of God towards you and us.

We marched yesterday after the King, who went before us from Daventry to Harborough; and quartered about six miles from him. This day we marched towards him. He drew out to meet us; both armies engaged. We, after three hours fight very doubtful, at last routed his army; killed and took about 5,000, very many officers, but of what quality we yet know not. We took about 200 carriages, all he had; and all his guns, being 12 in number, whereof two were demi-cannon, two demi-culverins, and (I think) the rest sackers. We persued the enemy from three miles short of Harborough to nine beyond, even to sight of Leicester, whither the King fled.

Sir, this is none other but the hand of God; and to Him alone belongs the glory, wherein none are to share with Him. The General served you with all faithfulness and honour; and the best commendations I can give him is, that I dare say he attributes all to God, and would rather perish than assume to himself. Which is an honest and a thriving way, and yet as much for bravery may be given to him, in this action, as to a man. Honest men served you faithfully in this action. Sir, they are trusty; I beseech you in the name of God, not to discourage them. I wish this action may beget thankfulness and humility in all that are concerned in it. He that ventures his life for the liberty of his country, I wish he trust God for the liberty of his conscience, and you for the liberty he fights for.

In this he rests, who is

Your most humble servant

OLIVER CROMWELL

Haverbrowe
14 June 1645

A far cry from today with the addition of 'Colombo Port City'. Even so the original port remains a major stopover for cruise liners, transshipment to the rest of South & S.E. Asia as well as a destination for the growing economy of Sri Lanka.

CHAPTER
One

Sri Lanka – Ceylon – Serendip – Taprobane

Some may wonder at the relevance of the subtitle *Paradise Lost and Paradise Regained*, referring of course, to John Milton's great epic poems. Milton is entirely relevant to my story, as he lived through the English Civil War, fought on the side of Parliament and I am certain that had I lived in those times, I too would have been on the same side. Northampton South, my constituency, supported the Parliamentarians and the Battle of Naseby on 14 June 1645 was the turning point in the First Civil War against Charles I. The wounded from both sides were taken to the churches in Northampton, hence the reason I chose Naseby as my name in the House of Lords.

So, one civil war sowed some of the seeds of my wishing to enter Parliament but the remainder of the seeds did not germinate until I travelled to the East – and specifically South Asia – to visit my parents in Lahore, Pakistan in 1955.

I was always fascinated by the East in general and in India in particular.

As a young boy I collected stamps and had an interesting collection of pre- and post-Partition editions, as well as some from the colonies such as Ceylon. I also read about India, principally Kipling but not exclusively, as well as fiction and non-fiction. Then there were the Wolf Cubs (the younger section of the Boy Scouts) where we were told about Mowgli and others under the guidance of Akela, but only after we had done whatever 'badge challenge' we were engaged in at the time. I remember there were twelve badges. I was pretty keen and Hey Presto! I got all twelve!

However, there were really two main influences. First, as Head of House at Sandersons, Bedford School, I shared my study with an Indian boy, Kit Srinivasan. We were both boarders. Bedford School had extensive historical links with the Raj at a time when young boys were sent to England to board at the age of seven and their parents, when they retired, moved to Bedford or its environs, finding the area very agreeable and far less expensive than London or south of the river.

As two young men sharing a study, we talked a great deal about our own lives and I remember listening in rapture to Kit's tales about his home in India. I do not know which of us set up the creative tension but more seeds were sowed at school because later in life Kit became Foreign Secretary in the Indian Civil Service at the same time that I was elected Chairman of The Ways and Means Committee.

The second influence was my dear father who, after World War II, had set up as an architect, having previously served at the Ministry of Works advising how to handle bomb damage. He quickly discovered that a country needs about ten years to get back to normality (a fact that the West and the Tamil diaspora have failed to understand), so, to feed his family he decided to work overseas. In early 1955, he was appointed architect to the Punjab Government based in Lahore. My brothers and I visited our parents that summer. It was my mother with whom I had a good rapport and who made sure I was educated about Partition and all the local customs.

The Pakistani Government had a policy to encourage its young civil servants to learn to fly, a sort of discreet military training, I think. Whatever, as an eighteen-year-old son of a civil servant I was eligible to receive the training. I have to thank my dear father for this opportunity which in itself led to me becoming an RAF pilot during my National Service. It turned out to be the adventure of a lifetime and just two years later I was a fully qualified RAF pilot with both RAF and NATO wings. At the Lahore Flying Club, on 26 August 1955, after just five hours and twenty-five minutes' flying time, and only ten days after first sitting in an aircraft, I went solo in an Auster Aiglet. What a wonderful summer of flying! I flew to Rawalpindi, Peshawar, Multan, Jacobabad and Karachi. I clocked up thirty-eight hours' flying in just five weeks. I still vividly remember flying along part of the Pakistan-Afghan border and looking down at the inhospitable mountainous terrain below.

The East did not feature again in my life until my last year at St Catharine's College, Cambridge where I was reading Economics. I had fallen in love with a girl who I had met at Miss Harding's dancing classes whilst at school. After much difficulty with my prospective father-in-law, who did not rate an Economics degree at all – even an Upper Second – and did not welcome any diversions for his dear daughter and her medical studies, my fiancée Ann and I realised we would be on our own, financially speaking. I had very little money, just a few hundred pounds saved from my flying pay and I had spent £75 on an engagement ring. I decided we should look for a good British company with the opportunity to work in the East because the salary would be better and accommodation would be provided, which might enable us to save a little or at least sufficient for a deposit on a house if we decided to return to the UK. My choice was Reckitt & Colman (Overseas) Ltd trading in India as Atlantis East Ltd now a part of the Reckitt Benckiser Group.

After fifteen months of training in the UK, I was posted with my family to Calcutta, arriving in January 1962. My position was as Assistant Sales Manager Eastern India, and I was responsible for West Bengal, Orissa, Bihar, Uttar Pradesh and the Hill Country surrounding Darjeeling. In today's terms a population of 440 million! My boss was an Indian accountant called Mr Joseph who taught me all the tricks of the trade for market dealing in the East. However, even he could not have anticipated the invasion of north-east India by the Chinese in 1963. My company's *godown* (warehouse) was wrecked by the Chinese who absconded with several cases of company goods. I hope that was my first and last experience of having to make a claim for war losses.

Then on Monday 10 May 1963, at 9.00 am, as I was sitting at my desk outside the air-conditioned offices under the *punkuh* (fan) the Budha Sahib's (CEO) secretary came over and asked me to go immediately to his office. Mr Tom Leveritt was a large man who was well-seasoned in international trading for the Reckitt & Colman group. 'Michael,' he said, 'You have done well in your time with us in terms of work – travelling to get to know your vast area, learning Hindi and above all raising the standard of all our company's sporting teams' (we used to have inter-company tournaments in many sports on Wednesday afternoons). 'I have good news and bad. Today, you are promoted to Marketing Manager, Ceylon. The bad news is you and the family must fly down to Colombo on Friday. You will be in charge, as the Budha Sahib, Mr Alexander, is on leave and the current Marketing Manager has just been accused of alleged illegal gem dealing.'

On hearing the news, my wife was no more distressed than myself, as we had both found Calcutta challenging in every respect. She had been working on her two six-month placements as a trainee House Officer doctor at the world-respected SSKM Hospital under A.K. Basu. In addition, she had given birth to our son, Julian, just four months before our arrival in India. We had both heard how much more appealing Colombo was than Calcutta.

So, on Friday 14 May, just four days after my meeting with Mr Leveritt, we set off from Dum Dum Airport to fly in an Indian Airlines Vickers Viscount to Ratmalana Airport on the outskirts of Colombo. I say 'we', as not only were we a family of three, but we also had a little dog called Twinkle and there was an aged shotgun in my hand luggage as well. Even though I had all the approved papers for the gun, seasoned travellers will know a firearm is a wonderful distraction to Customs the world over, and so it was in Colombo. All our other luggage sailed through, although it was common knowledge that Ceylon Customs levied duty on almost all Western goods.

The air was warm and the sun shining as we were whisked off to the famous Galle Face Hotel, kissed by the soothing sea breezes of the ocean. What a memorable day it turned out to be for me at the age of twenty-six.

CHAPTER
Two

Marketing Manager for Reckitt & Colman, Ceylon

After the excitement of transferring from Calcutta, the reality of life in a new country that neither my wife nor I knew, soon hit us. This was despite the trouble the company took to settle us in.

No one had mentioned the monsoon season, of course, when buckets of rain fell nearly every day. The Galle Face Hotel was probably the best on the island but it was not exactly geared up to servicing the needs of an eighteen-month-old baby. We were waiting to take on the Marketing Manager's flat and I consoled my wife that it would be only for a couple of weeks until he returned to England. Little did I know that he appeared to be waging a rear-guard action to resist being sent back. The stay in the hotel dragged on and on until I put my foot down and after six weeks we were found a bungalow, which was fine but not terribly clean. Indeed, my wife recollects it took three days to remove the cockroaches, let alone the dirt. We did eventually move into the intended accommodation once it had been vacated by the outgoing executive about three months after our arrival. It was a nice flat in Turret Road overlooking Victoria Park. I have two fond memories of that flat: first, I used to have my hair cut by the travelling barber on the veranda, and second, when it came to launch the 'Goya' range of fragrances (Reckitt's had bought the company in the UK), I decided to have the PR launch at home: Ann put on a wonderful show.

The challenges of settling in did not end with the domestic side of life. Our offices were just inside the Colombo Fort area and belonged to our import agents E.B. Creasy. I arrived on the Monday morning full of the joys of promotion. The Office Manager showed me into a really nice office but stated I could not begin using it until the outgoing executive had departed (and I was also to share his secretary until she could eventually become mine). In the meantime, I could use the desk just outside the office, but without the benefit of air-conditioning.

In a new country one often has to get a work visa. An appointment

I am by profession a marketing man. The key to success is to understand your market. The picture reflects life in Ceylon in 1963: the colour, heat, excitement – all creating an impact never to be forgotten.

was arranged for me to go just around the corner to the visa office, in the company of our visa specialist. He had with him two half bottles of Scotch whisky, which he assured me was the currency for an urgent visa application, as mine was. However, the visa was valid for only six months and when I went to renew it again, this time with no urgency, the liquid currency element had not changed. I also gently checked if the same procedure would apply to my wife, a doctor, as she hoped to practice, at least part-time. The answer was not encouraging: I was told Ceylon had more than enough of its own doctors and did not need any white doctors. Needless to say, this did not go down well at home. Thankfully, a little later Ann was introduced to a Dr Siva Chinnatamby who was doing some of the early Pill birth-control trials, who asked Ann if she would help her, which she did, but unpaid of course.

My trials with the very slow-departing executive continued. I later discovered he had told our HQ in Hull that he must stay on to show me round the island so that I understood the markets which, he alleged, were very different from India. They were not. In fact, they were a good deal more straightforward, with little counterfeiting, fewer stock losses and all round more trustworthy personnel. My colleague decided we should go on two separate tours, each lasting about a week, with a week in between to prepare a report and to catch-up on other matters affecting the business. I telephoned Mr Leveritt in Calcutta to ask what was going on with my colleague. He was most sympathetic, apologised and said he would leave no later than the week following our second tour. Much to my relief, this actually happened.

Tour number one was down the south-west coast as far as the Yala Game Reserve, after which we retraced our steps to the road going north with an overnight stay at Belihuloya, across to Batticaloa on the east coast, continuing up the coast to Trincomalee along the A6, visiting the now World Heritage sites of Polonnaruwa and the rock fortress of Sigiriya, then the Hill Country with its tea estates and a final run back to Colombo via the Gem City of Ratnapura. The vehicle available for this grand tour was a totally unsuitable Ford Anglia, with just two doors, and we had to accommodate a driver. I made it quite clear that under no circumstances would I sit in the back and that I expected to be driven! My colleague took it on the chin: 'Fine,' he said. He would drive and the driver would sit in the back and navigate. Thus, arranged, we set off.

At that time, there were no hotels available so one had to stay in either a rest house, open to non-government travellers who could afford the cost, or the circuit bungalows primarily used by travelling government officials. Our company had contracts with the government to sell Dettol, Disprin and other pharmaceuticals, so we were classified as government officials.

I still have vivid memories of that initial tour, which provided a most marvellous introduction to the breath-taking beauty of the Sri Lanka countryside: from the coast, with its perfect sandy beaches and palm trees, up into the foothills, with the plantations of spices, palm and rubber trees, and then finally to the tea plantations. It was quite a stunning backdrop to the challenges of touring on business.

I remember the first night at Bentota Rest House situated at the apex of sea and river. I had a really nice room overlooking the sea, with basic facilities of a bed with good mosquito nets and with the legs standing in water bowls to deter the ants.

Each evening we would meet with our own area sales person, wholesaler and best retailers at the local market. First of all, we would hire a bicycle rickshaw; primarily because it was the only way to travel around and also, much like a London cabby, the owner would know everyone, plus all the local tittle-tattle of who was trading well and who was in difficulties, and so on. Next came the welcome sign, 'Ayubowan', followed by sitting on stools, handing over business cards and discussing trade, offering new or existing products on special deal in my honour. The business was always followed by refreshments in the form of tea laced with sugar or Coca Cola or Fanta with local delicacies or cashew nuts. I had decided in India to live on Fanta and cashew nuts. For me, Sri Lankan cashew nuts, especially roasted ones, are one of the world's greatest delights. By 7.00 pm we had concluded our business and returned to the rest house. Of course, there were a couple of incidents on that first evening in the market. Bicycle rickshaws are for two, rather than three adults, as we were. My colleague merely paid extra as the poor fellow tried to pedal his Raleigh pride and joy with the extra passenger. I also had a short argument that evening with my colleague about offering a special discount in my honour, a trick learned in India. I pointed out I was in charge and it was I who would return and not he; after that there was no more trouble.

The evening brought time to enjoy a large bottle of lager brewed under licence usually from Holland, *Three Coins or Lion Lager*, as well as time to read the *Daily News*, a government-owned newspaper (with all that means about objectivity in the press) that continues to this day. The evening meal was either fish curry, if one was on the coastal road, or chicken curry, if up country. The following day began with a cooked breakfast and no hurry to set off: thankfully, driving on the left, avoiding the tuk-tuks (motorised three-wheeler rickshaws) and still to this day the epitome of travel throughout the island. Add to this the huge long Nagula carts pulled by two bullocks, which have almost disappeared today, a few cars and the ever-colourful lorries: what a challenge but at least the road was tarmac and well signposted, unlike in India.

Our first stop was Galle, one of the finest Dutch-inspired towns with a magnificent walled fort protecting the port. We parked the car at the rest house, set off in our rickshaw, carried out our business, returned to the rest house for a light lunch and then were back on the road, heading down the coast through Matara. We stopped again to meet a few key traders and to take tea before moving off again for the Tangalle Rest House. As dusk set in we could see the stick fishermen climbing on to their stakes with a branch at a right-angle so they could cast their baited line into the sea swirling around them. This must be a unique sight anywhere in the world. I sat with my *Three Coins* beer, totally captivated for over an hour. Dinner: yes, fish curry, clearly the freshest possible.

Next day, further along the coast to Hambantota (the hometown of former President Rajapaksa) we almost made it to the fascinating game reserve of Yala but for an actual visit I had to wait for over a decade as there was certainly no time on a business tour. We retraced our steps to Ambalantota and headed north on the A18 to stay the night at the well-known Belihuloya Rest House. The temperature was cooler and the building nestled alongside a clear free-flowing stream, as it is today, some fifty years later.

We made an early start, as we had a long day ahead covering markets en route at Monaragala, Ampara and across to the coast at Batticaloa, the then capital of the Eastern Region. The language had changed to Tamil, reflecting the Tamil invasion in the third century from South India. Actually, the majority of the shopkeepers were Muslim and they were the largest ethnic group, followed by the Tamils and finally the Sinhalese. Even then, although not the least bit involved in politics, I could see very little to link the Eastern Province with the Northern, Tamil-dominated region.

We made our proverbial calls in the market in Batticaloa and then travelled north to Trincomalee to arrive at the rest house in time for a short break. I sat on the veranda, surrounded by the most beautiful Bougainvillea, which I can still visualise to this day. We looked down on the huge natural harbour, so vital to the allies in World War II; sought after and watched by both India and China and so nearly lost to the Tamil Tigers but for the bravery of the Sri Lanka Navy in March 2003. Since both my colleague and I had been in the armed forces, we were welcomed into the Officers' Mess for lunch. I felt quite nostalgic as a former RAF pilot. I do not think my colleague had anywhere near as interesting a National Service as I had.

After lunch we were back on the road, calling at some of the villages to check if they stocked Disprin analgesic tablets and Dettol.

The afternoon was dedicated to culture, as we wanted to see the ruins of Polonnaruwa. I walked round with a local guide who spoke good English. It was he who pointed out to me my first cobra, fast asleep on a wall in the sunshine. My guide poked him with a long stick and just like a trained circus animal the cobra's neck shot up with fangs displayed ready to strike. We moved on, giving him a wide berth.

Today Polonnaruwa is a beautifully kept World Heritage Site with an interesting museum. Nearby is another rest house alongside a 'tank'. This is, in effect, a manmade reservoir, dating from the third century, which provided irrigation for the paddy fields. We did not spend much time there, as we wanted to get to another World Heritage Site: Sigiriya.

We arrived just as dusk fell at the Sigiriya Rest House, nestled beneath the sixth-century rock fortress. I wanted a quick swim in the pool to cool down, and I dive in to find myself accompanied by every frog in the local area – quite a sight as I came up for breath and hurriedly got out! We turned in early that night, as we needed to start climbing the fortress by 6.00 am at the latest before the sun became too strong. I was a fit twenty-six-year-old but the pathway up was really steep. Halfway up are some amazing frescoes, paintings of attractive young women from the Court of the then king, King Kasyapa (reigned 473 to 495AD). We pushed on, as it was beginning to get warm. As we continued our climb and daylight arrived, the track turned to the right and came to an end at two statues carved out of rock called the 'Lions Claws'. The citadel was still nearly 200 feet above us. Now it was a case of climbing with both hands and feet, as there was no stairway. At the top, the fortress is flat with a manmade tank hewed out of rock and the ruins of the palace that once stood in isolated splendour. Now only the outlines of the walls remain.

As we looked down upon the vista before us, it took our breath away: acres and acres of paddy fields disappearing into infinity with seemingly tiny people working in them. This truly is, for me, one of the wonders of the world. Visitors today will find it all organised much more efficiently, with a pathway to the top complete with iron railings. However, I would argue that it does not give quite the same experience as having to climb it as we did. We descended at speed to a well-earned breakfast, as we had another day of challenging driving ahead.

Sigiriya is on a side road, so we made for Matale to get to Kandy in time for lunch at the Queen's Hotel, whilst continuing to drop in on traders en route. Kandy was the last capital of the indigenous Sinhalese, eventually conquered by the British in 1815. It was also the headquarters of Mountbatten's South East Asia Command in World War II. It is a busy, bustling city. I was introduced to our key contacts there but we still had a journey ahead to Nuwara Eliya at the pinnacle of the Hill Country covered in tea estates all the way up. We reached the Hill Club at dusk.

The temperature was pretty cool, as we were 4,000 feet up. As I looked around, I marvelled at what seemed to be a little piece of England. There was a stone hot water bottle in my bed but I did not retire until I had a game of snooker with the steward, who was far too good for me.

In the morning, we visited the market and I made a mental note that I must return and explore. Little did I know then that one day in 2009 I would be looking for the Naseby Tea Estate and would indeed find it. To this day, I do not know why a Scot, James Taylor, would call it Naseby. I wonder if his forebears were at the Battle of Naseby on 14 June 1645. If they were, then they must have been on the side of Parliament, for it was this battle that decided the Civil War.

We set off again down the winding road to Ratnapura, the gem capital of Sri Lanka, with stunning vistas en route. We again met our most important traders, one of whom insisted we visit the gem pit famous for Sri Lanka's blue sapphires. 'Pit' is the right word, for the miners, wearing little more than loin cloths, descended into a dark world to work their trade. This was not something I ever wished to know more about.

After a cup of tea we set off for Colombo, about 70 miles away, and I reached our hotel in time for dinner. It is difficult to describe how I felt: thrilled and awestruck at what I had seen and experienced, with a vow to share it with my wife Ann on a journey of our own. As life turned out we did the whole visit some years later when we were on holiday. In addition, Ratnapura continued to be etched in my mind and, years later when I was a politician I was an official observer of two elections there.

The eventual departure of the over-staying colleague came to be and it was like a monsoon cloud had lifted; I had tried to be calm and enthusiastic at his extended stay but it had not been easy. However, the day finally came and I went to the office in the fort, took possession of my air-conditioned office and reflected that I was now in charge.

I had already thought out a broad strategy for my remaining six months. Clearly it was not long enough to do anything dramatic, which in any case would have had to be cleared with HQ in Hull. My up-country tours had convinced me we had a team of good salesmen who had achieved some remarkable distribution in depth. However, there did not seem to be any coherent communication strategy to market our range of brands. I decided to ask our two advertising agencies to do a formal presentation on the Ceylon market in general and then specifically about the brands they handled.

The bulk of our advertising was handled by the oldest and number one agency in the world: J. Walter Thompson (JWT), which in 1987 became a key component of WPP and continues to be a world-leader in advertising today. The director responsible for our account was the Chief Executive himself, who said in his own words: 'I personally handle the agency's three biggest clients and this includes Reckitt & Colman.' His name was one of the tongue-twisting names only Sri Lanka can produce: Ananda de Tissa de Alwis. We became life-long friends but more of that later.

JWT's presentation on the economy had me riveted and I thanked my lucky stars that I had a good degree in Economics from Cambridge.

I reflected what a fortunate coincidence it had been that Professor Walt Rostow from the USA was on a two-term visiting professorship to my college, St Catharine's, to launch his book, *The Stages of Growth for Developing Countries*. The pitch from JWT was brutally frank: the country was virtually broke and suffered from rampant inflation, high taxes and shortages of basic food such as rice as well as spare parts for any machinery, let alone the normal Western foods such as butter, jam or coffee. Jokingly, he said it was little wonder that sales of Disprin were rocketing, as so many people needed analgesics.

The end result of this morning's work was a marketing plan for each of the primary brands, fully costed but with the objective of dominating certain media and not just spending on every brand we had. It did not take long to put together; a recommendation which went to HQ with a courtesy copy to Mr Leveritt in Calcutta. Hull responded quickly, wishing me all success.

The second agency was a relatively new creative hot shop, which seemed to me to be a good fit for the launch of the Goya fragrances. The budget was not huge but enough to get them interested and motivated. I was keen to investigate interesting and arresting merchandising ideas. It was in this context that I suggested the PR launch at my apartment. It would be novel and, as I suspected, every media person in town wanted to see the Englishman's apartment and meet his doctor wife.

The launch was a success. I liked the two key directors and, indeed, the distributors, the Lalvani Brothers in the Pettah. I should explain that the Pettah was the Colombo wholesale market for all the key products: gems, furniture, consumer goods – frankly almost everything legal and some smuggled goods too! Even today it is a nest of tiny roads with some buildings dating back to the Dutch period. It is bounded on the west by the Fort, to the north by the harbour and to the south by the fish market. Although I am no longer involved in commerce, I always visit the Pettah, particularly to see my favourite jeweller, Mr Hassan, at New Central Jewellery Stores, 212 Main Street. Sadly, he died in 2018. All these marketing presentations sound straightforward but they contained a great deal of written material which had to be typed up, and this was carried out by my excellent secretary who was Tamil. One day when we were less busy I asked her about the Tamil people, as I sensed there was an issue there. She explained how she saw matters. Under the British rule, which was, in effect, until 1948, the civil service had a significant number of Tamils in all the senior- and middle-ranking positions. According to her, this was done as a conscious policy because the Tamils were the largest minority party who would give faithful service to the British in exchange for their favour. In addition, the Tamils were well educated and many went to university. By contrast, the Sinhalese had led the Independence Movement and apart from their highest castes they were generally not so well educated. Once Independence was granted, the Sinhalese took over, and resenting the best jobs going to Tamils, took to changing the entry system to university from selection on ability to selection in proportion to national percentage shares of the population. Add to this mix the very different religions between Buddhists, Hindus and Muslims and the other deeply emotive issue of language. Prior to Independence all three languages of Sinhalese, Tamil and English were used. However, under Mrs Sirimavo Bandaranaike (Sri Lanka's Prime Minister from 1960–65, 1970–77), Sinhalese was made the official language with English acceptable for commercial work, but not Tamil. This meant applications for anything official had to be in Sinhalese, quite a challenge for those Tamils who only spoke their own language. Whilst under the British rule the tensions bubbled below the surface, but once gone, these tensions inevitably came to the surface and the distrust between the groups began to grow. Thinking back now to my secretary, an educated Tamil, her thoughts were perceptive. She was a little younger than me; I wonder if she is still alive.

Although I was the Marketing Manager, it transpired that I ended up being in charge of almost every aspect of the business. One day the Factory Manager, Peter Crisp, came to see me to explain that a new tableting machine for Disprin was coming from the UK and was due in the next week. Perhaps I should like to see where it was to be placed in the factory at Ratmalana, next to one of Colombo's cricket grounds?

This particular incident reminds me of the BBC's now retired cricket commentator 'Blowers', whose repartee, besides pigeons, usually involved London's red double-decker buses. He would have had a feast in Colombo watching Ceylon Transport's red double-deckers trundling along the Galle Road carrying not just the legal fifty-six passengers but at least eighty if not more. These red double-decker buses had been bought from London Transport, supposedly at the end of their useful life. Far from it. Eastern mechanics are absolute wizards at keeping vehicles on the road, machining spares or whatever. I went to the factory, duly admired where the new plant was going to be and thought no more of it. Five days later I received a phone call from Mr Crisp stating the machinery had arrived safely but there was a snag: our forklift truck was not powerful enough to lift it into the factory building and nor were any of the neighbours' forklifts. Intended as a joke, I said, 'Get an elephant,' as I had seen elephants dragging massive teak trees up country.

'I am not joking,' said Mr Crisp.

'Nor am I,' said I, on reflection. In fact, I remembered in the presentation from the agency launching the Goya fragrances that we had talked about hiring an elephant, suitably garlanded. I rang the agency, got the telephone number of the *mahout* (elephant man) and gave it to Mr Crisp. My only condition was that I was present when the elephant came.

The *mahout* duly arrived the next day with a large elephant. He was shown where the tableting machine had to go. He had his kit of variable chain lengths, which were tied to the pallet. The elephant received his command and slowly dragged the machinery through the door, just missing the lintel and then continued until the pallet was within seemingly an inch of where it was to go. Chains undone, the elephant gratefully received his bananas and trundled away, job done.

After the weeks of challenge with a baby at the Galle Face Hotel and our short stay in the bungalow, we moved into the company apartment in Turret Road overlooking Victoria Park and began to enjoy our new home and its surrounds. We had joined the swimming club on Galle Road to be able to have a cool swim. Additionally, I had joined Queen's Club so that I could play good tennis. Following our experience of being founder members of the Barrackpore Yacht Club on the Hooghly River about 20 miles outside Calcutta, we decided to join the Ceylon Yacht Club on Beira Lake. It was not quite the same success, as members could not bring an *ayah* (nanny), which we found a challenge. The sailing was quite good and my wife was very popular as crew, however we pulled out. Instead, we went down the coast with friends every weekend to a chalet at Hikkaduwa, a safe beach with excellent swimming and a rest house next door for food and drink. We even managed to supplement the swimming in the late afternoon during the week by going to a tiny bay just below the Mount Lavinia Hotel.

Whilst I was very happy in my job, I knew Ann wanted to work as a doctor back in the UK. Indeed, we both thought the extra income would help. I myself was coming up to four years with the Reckitt Group and felt ready for a change. I particularly wanted to have some experience on the other side of marketing with an advertising agency. We talked at length about how to make it happen. Our joint decision was that Ann would return to the UK with baby Julian in order to apply for a trainee GP post. She departed in early October, waiting until Julian had just turned two, and thereby eligible for his own seat on BOAC, calling in at Karachi to stay with friends. Meanwhile I would stay in Ceylon until the end of my contract, which meant returning just before Christmas. I would take my three months' leave which every overseas posting received, resign once safely back in the UK and then apply to advertising agencies.

In reality, the daytime of my remaining three months was not really very different from before. A number of friends took pity and invited me to supper. The weekends were not really a challenge as I swam, played tennis and visited a bachelor friend of mine, Chris Woosnam-Mills, who was in charge of the Partmore Tea Estate, Agrapatna, in the Hill Country. We would sit on his veranda putting the world to rights and marvelling at the vista of endless tea estates below. After dinner we retired to the Scalextrics room. By this I mean a large room in which Chris had built a double-track racetrack with two hairpin bends. Two of his staff were strategically positioned, one at each hairpin. Racing took well over an hour, with the boys putting the cars back on the track when they skidded off. I still have vivid memories of the cries of excitement. Sadly, that life was already under pressure as visas were not being extended to ex-pat staff on the tea estates and nationalisation with minimal compensation was just around the corner.

One other stroke of luck was a telephone call from Ananda de Tissa de Alwis, the head of JWT. He told me he was standing for Parliament as a UNP (United National Party) candidate at the next general election and invited me to dinner to talk through a few ideas. He was a bachelor but, in the best traditions of the East, his mother ran the lovely house, so all meals were prepared to suit Ananda's lifestyle.

Both of us found the evening a really stimulating experience as we bounced ideas off each other, so much so that we arranged to meet every Tuesday evening to talk politics and electioneering. Towards the end of my stay he said: 'Michael you should think of entering UK politics as you clearly have quite a lot to offer.' My response was that I enjoyed advertising too much and, in any case, I had little money. Looking back, I think I can fairly say that it was almost Ananda's fault that I did go into politics. However, I also blame my wife for inviting to our first dinner party at our flat in Hackney, above her surgery, her former anatomy lecturer who was organising the Conservative candidates in the GLC election. He pointed out that I had time to spare, being on leave, and he needed help and so why did I not join in? And, of course, I did.

Back in Sri Lanka, Ananda was elected to Parliament and years later became Speaker of the Parliament. I only made First Deputy Speaker and Chairman of Ways and Means, thwarted in my quest to succeed Betty Boothroyd as Speaker by losing my seat in Northampton South in the tidal wave defeat of 1997. In my case this was primarily due to the intervention of Jimmy Goldsmith's Referendum Party who took 2.5 per cent (or 1,405 votes), nearly all my right-wing supporters, letting in Labour with a majority of 744.

What joy if we had both made Speaker, although sadly Ananda had died before 1997. Still, I owe him a huge thank you for sowing the seed that eventually germinated on 28 February 1974 when I was elected MP for Northampton South with a majority of 179.

A typical river scene of the early 1970s. Two young boys probably sieving for semi-precious stones.

CHAPTER
Three

Return to Sri Lanka: Halcyon Days

It would be ten years before the seed sown in Colombo in 1963 began to germinate.

On returning to England my family and I lived in Islington, North London. We were part of a nucleus of young couples wanting to have our own home and we were prepared to put time, effort and money into restoring attractive early Victorian houses. These were houses neglected since World War II, primarily due to rent controls, which made it totally uneconomical for any landlord to keep his property in repair. It was not unusual to have houses with only one cold tap and sometimes a WC in the yard. We restored two such houses: one at 6 Gerrard Road where we lived from 1964 until 1970 when we moved into a Georgian house with great potential at 49 Duncan Terrace, which we also restored.

Islington at that time was not just about gentrification: it was a hotbed of young families, working professionals, easy mixers, full of life who wanted to help improve society and the environment, not just their own four walls. This inevitably led to clashes with the local council, which was solidly Labour of the *old school*.

I had decided almost immediately on my return from Sri Lanka that I wanted to try to become an MP. I contacted Central Office and found that candidate selection was controlled by Jim Prior, MP, who later was to be a stalwart of Margaret Thatcher's Cabinet. He interviewed me and asked about my experience in the Party, which was virtually none except for helping in the GLC Election, but he found my Sri Lanka experience enthralling so I was put on the approved list of candidates. This was late in 1964. I tried for a few seats but then, all of a sudden, Islington North became available in 1965 because the Conservative candidate had pulled out. So I applied, along with the usual eighty or so others, but I was the only one who could claim to be local. The seat was described as a 'dead loss' seat because this was Labour heartland, as it is still today. In fact, today (at the time of writing) it is the seat of the Leader of the Labour Party, Jeremy Corbyn, MP. I was selected to be the Conservative Party candidate, I fought the seat and lost but I learned a good deal about campaigning. My knowledge of the advertising and marketing worlds helped me greatly.

Harold Wilson won the election easily but it was not long before his popularity waned. The group of young professional activists then looked to me with hope that I might stand in the forthcoming council election due in May 1968. Nationally I was looking for a winnable, marginal seat but I thought a bit of campaigning and being the driving force of the Islington Conservative team would do me no harm. We got really well organised and found candidates for every ward except one where we did a deal with a community-type group of three Independents. We fought well, communicated exceedingly well and had positive proposals for Islington, which included stopping the destruction of its historic (and potentially lovely) residential squares. By this time Wilson's Government was in deep trouble and highly unpopular. Lo and behold, we won fifty-seven out of sixty seats, the remaining three being the Independents with whom we had done a deal not to stand. The next three years were wonderful and we achieved a great deal: squares were saved, new decent high-density, low-level council housing was built, people were encouraged to come in and restore the Victorian houses and even the Almeida Theatre was saved by my wife as Chairman of the Arts & Recreation Committee. Ann made a specific visit on Local Election Day with the official in charge and a decision in principle was agreed not to demolish it. What a joy it is to attend this avant-garde theatre today and for Ann to be one of its patrons.

I reflect on 1968 with great pride: we achieved the biggest swing in London, made life-long friends and created a stimulating and attractive environment bristling with energetic creativity which continues to this day. This just shows what can be done in three years when a catalyst is created. Not bad to be the only Conservative Administration in the last century to win Islington. Of course, at the next council election three years later in 1971 we lost every seat as Labour was not to be caught napping again.

For the Morris family it was time to move on. In late 1972 I was selected by the Conservative Party to fight the new seat of Northampton

South, viewed as a long-shot marginal by the Party. My wife and I decided that ten years in London was probably enough, as by this time we had three young children. So, we looked at properties in a radius of about 50 miles north of London, with good connections to the capital, as I was a director in a large and well-respected American advertising agency, Benton & Bowles. By chance, one Tuesday afternoon on her day off as a GP in London, Ann visited her mother in Bedford. On the way back she called in to see a property, an attractive early Victorian villa, again in much need of modernisation. It also had extensive grounds plus a 200-yard long driveway bordered by rhododendrons. I visited it on my way to Northampton on the following Friday, a beautiful day, when the rhododendrons were in full bloom.

We negotiated the sale with the owner, who turned out to be The Rt Hon. Francis Pym, MP. The deal was done and we moved in July 1973 and look forward to celebrating fifty years in our home in 2023. Ironically, we soon discovered that the house had a history of involvement with Parliament and the Indian subcontinent. The house was originally built for John Peel, the fourth son of Prime Minister Robert Peel. His brother William died at Cawnpore in the Indian Mutiny. It was subsequently purchased by the Pym family in 1866 and lived in by Guy Pym, MP for Bedford from 1894 to 1918. In the 1930s it was let to Sir Frederick Liddell, Clerk to the House of Commons and finally it was let to the Heeley family who originally owned the Brewery in Islington: such are the quirks of life.

Once settled, I turned my attentions to focus on my seat as the prospective parliamentary candidate. My half of Northampton was not huge: just 44,000 electorate in six wards. In terms of potential political support this was one good, two middling and three poor. However, I had things going for me. Northampton was an industrial town so as a marketing/advertising man I knew the benefits of making factory visits. There was a daily paper, the *Chronicle & Echo*, that was eager for copy and news. Above all, I soon discovered there was a small but hard-working Bangladeshi community of about 6,000. I sought out the community leaders and having worked in Calcutta there was an immediate rapport. Sadly, I did not speak much Bengali but far more than anyone else plus my Hindi held me in good stead.

The General Election came: we had good leaflets – targeted – and with one set in Bengali plus support from the community leaders. It was not an easy election for Ted Heath's Conservatives after the three-day week. Heath was defeated and we failed to win Northampton North – the supposed easier seat to win. However, the count in the Town Hall for Northampton South became tenser by the hour. On the first count, I lost by about 200 votes. We challenged and someone tipped me off to 'check the bundles'. I briefed my people to make sure that every bundle of twenty-five Conservative votes should be collected into four bundles of twenty-five. It appeared some of our 'twenty-fives' were hidden inside three Labour bundles and counted as one hundred votes for Labour by mistake! On the second count we won by a tiny margin and so the Labour Candidate asked for another count. The same procedure was undertaken with really careful checking. I won by 179 votes. On reflection, without the Bengali votes I would not have won, so once again I was indebted to the East.

I was now the Member of Parliament for Northampton South. I awaited my summons and at the end of February took my seat. However, storm clouds were gathering because Harold Wilson did not have a working majority so we all knew that another election was not far off. In fact, it was just seven short months before the second election was called for October 1974.

Most of my time was spent campaigning, raising issue after issue in the Commons and organising marches. My one diversion was to join both the All-Party India and Pakistan Parliamentary Groups, not least for the excellent curry lunch briefings at India House. I also met the then High Commissioner for Sri Lanka, Sir George Corea. Memories of my time there came flowing back, not least of Ananda de Tissa de Alwis who turned out to be a mutual friend of both of ours. I voiced my thoughts about whether there should be an All-Party British Sri Lanka Group. However, by September we were campaigning again as it was clear that the Conservatives were going to lose seats. With thanks to a wonderful friend, Graham Underwood, an estate agent who said he would trace every Conservative who had moved from the area and get them a postal vote, coupled with good campaigning, and much to the chagrin of the same Labour Candidate, the election came and I won by 142 votes. I was returned to Westminster, albeit in Opposition. I decided to re-activate my thoughts about an All-Party British Sri Lanka Group. Thoughts are one thing but the doing is quite another. I learned I needed five MPs or Lords to make a group: two in Government, two in Opposition and one other. The task was not easy for a new boy and it was not obvious who might be interested. At the time, Sri Lanka itself appeared to be going through difficulties under Mrs Bandaranaike, which did not help. Truth be told, there was very little news about Sri Lanka in the English media at all, which I found strange. However, persistence paid off and in June 1975 I put the inaugural meeting of the All-Party British Sri Lanka Parliamentary Group on the Whip. Six colleagues turned up. At their behest I was voted Chairman, as the only one who had ever been to Sri Lanka.

The group was set up and now we faced the challenge of getting matters moving in terms of briefings. We invited Sir George Corea to tea, who welcomed the formation of the group but was fairly hesitant about what was happening on the ground in Sri Lanka, except to emphasise how important UK aid would be, particularly for the power project on the Mahaweli Ganga. I arranged a meeting with the Secretary of State for Overseas Development, Judith Hart, MP, who was impressive, clearly dedicated to her task and enthusiastic to help Sri Lanka over the dam project. Thankfully, in those days aid could be tied to British companies doing the construction. I write this as Brexit is taking place. Whatever happens I suspect some aid will once again be tied to help British companies with overseas capital projects.

My strategy was to try hard to get an official CPA (Commonwealth Parliamentary Association) visit to Sri Lanka. It was explained to me by UK officials that the invitation had to come from the host country but there seemed to be a strange reluctance on the part of the Sri Lanka High Commissioner to offer the invitation.

Only some years later did I really understand why, when a subsequent High Commissioner, General Cyril Ranatunga, explained a particular event of 1971 which had contributed to Sri Lanka's increasingly challenging political landscape. Since my leaving Sri Lanka, the country had been through quite a lot, politically speaking, and there was a lot of information to absorb.

In Sri Lanka in 1971, there was an extremist Marxist Party led by Rohana Wijeweera called the Janatha Vimukthi Peramuna (People's Liberation Front) known as the JVP. Wijeweera had been to university in Moscow and organised the party to adhere to Marxist ideals: central committees, coordinating committees, districts and secretaries to lead a revolution as part of the class struggle. The party's communications and propaganda were hard-hitting, extensive and persuasive against a background of a depressed economy, particularly with ordinary people suffering from rice rationing, heavy unemployment and rural poverty. There had been rumours of an uprising but the reality was more like a whirlwind: in the early hours of 5 April 1971, ninety-three police stations in seven of the nine national provinces were attacked. It is thought to have involved 16,000 JVP youths of which over 90 per cent were Sinhalese. They were on the rampage and the government had to call in the army to quash the uprising, which it did by the end of April when an amnesty was issued, to be effective from 29 April until 4.00 pm on 3 May. The uprising cost the lives of between sixty and eighty police and soldiers, with another 300 injured. Surprisingly, between 13,000 and 14,000 JVP rebels responded to the amnesty offered by the government, of which all but 4,200 were released from custody after interrogation. No one seems to know exactly how many JVP members or their Sinhalese youth followers were killed or went missing but it seems it must have been several thousand. Indeed, the really alarming figures of between 30,000 and 60,000 were quoted by General Cyril Ranatunga in his book *From Peace To War, Insurgency To Terrorism*. He gave me a signed copy when I saw him in Colombo in March 2012, with the inscription: 'To Rt Hon the Lord Naseby & Lady Naseby in appreciation of being true friends of Sri Lanka. From General (retd) Cyril & Mrs Myrtle Ranatunga'. General Ranatunga was recognised as a caring military man with a keen foresight of the challenges facing the army when he was in charge. Later he was a distinguished High Commissioner for Sri Lanka in London, where I got to know him really well.

By any international yardstick this was a huge internal rebellion by the youth of the dominant ethnic group. Although I did not know any of this in depth when I set up the Parliamentary Group, it is just one example of the deep distrust many Sri Lankans felt towards 'Mrs B's'

(Mrs Sirimavo Bandaranaike, the then Prime Minister) policies. Her government had brought in the nationalisation of the tea estates and compulsory confiscation of all domestic property for owners who had more than two houses, as well as other land ownership restrictions. There had been earlier flare-ups, including an attempted coup in 1961, which I did know about because one of my sales staff at Reckitt & Colman had a relative who had been involved. It had been Mrs B. who, in 1970, decided on the name change from Ceylon to the Democratic Socialist Republic of Sri Lanka, (although it was not implemented until 1972), and she also declared Buddhism the state religion and designated Sinhala the official language. Add to this the new Republican Constitution, which would alienate Tamils even further by changing the method of entry into university. It does still mystify me how little of all this got out into the international media allied to how little comment the UK government made.

Looking back to the time when I was Parliamentary Private Secretary to the two Ministers of State in Northern Ireland for the years 1979 to 1981, I now fully appreciate the volatility of the various ethnic, caste and religious factions in Sri Lanka, which make Northern Ireland seem quite straightforward. Looking forward, it makes me realise how difficult it is for any government of Sri Lanka to make progress when these discriminatory actions have taken place. Of course, most of them have now been removed as we shall see but memories of them do not fade easily and trust is doubly difficult.

Back to the present and to Sri Lanka, in the parliamentary session prior to the 1978 General Election a new Constitution had been passed into law creating the post of Executive President (similar to France) with the Prime Minister downgraded to number two. The now Executive President, J.R. Jayawardene, knew of an impending invitation for the All-Party Group to visit and was delighted to formally authorise it. Specifically, the UK CPA was invited to send a delegation to Sri Lanka from 8–16 December. I was asked if I was free to go. The answer was an emphatic yes.

Picture of former Parliament Building in Colombo.

CHAPTER
Four

Executive President J.R. Jayawardene
1978–83 and 1983–9

On Thursday 8 December 1977, four of my fellow parliamentarians and I took off on an Air Lanka flight from Heathrow in one of those wonderfully long-range Lockheed TriStar planes, comfortably seated in Club Class and looked after by the ever-efficient Anthony.

The leader of the delegation was Richard Buchanan, JP and the others were Baroness Doris Fisher, John Hunt, MP, James Kilfedder, MP and me, by far the most junior parliamentarian but of course the only one who knew anything about Sri Lanka. We arrived in the early morning of the 9th and were taken to the Hotel Taprobane overlooking the harbour port. After recovering, we had a briefing from our hosts and during early evening drinks we received another briefing from the UK High Commissioner, Sir John Nicholas, an experienced Foreign Office hand who had served in a wide variety of posts and was now on his last tour. He and I warmed to each other, perhaps because I had worked for two years in South Asia.

In the following ten days we did a lot of travelling around the country visiting Kandy, the Hill Country, Nuwara Eliya, Sigiriya and Anuradhapura before heading north to Jaffna. This gave us a feel for the country, its culture and its people. In addition, we had excellent briefings from a variety of ministers and spent over an hour with President Jayawardene (also known as J.R.) himself. I found 'J.R.' a fascinating man. He was immaculate in starched white national dress, and an erudite man with a deep knowledge of Shakespeare, which he used to quote liberally, and, as he would chortle 'to test my English friends'. At the meeting he had some of his junior ministers in attendance, two of whom were young, well educated, thorough and dynamic. They were Gamini Dissanayake and Lalith Athulathmudali. Both became fervent friends in the years ahead until they were assassinated by the LTTE (Liberation Tigers of Tamil Eelam).

There were two key issues on our agenda, which we explored with the President: the economy and ethnic tension.

The economy was the 'easier', relatively speaking, of the two issues: President Jayawardene had inherited an economy in dire straits due to the socialistic policies of Mrs Bandaranaike. However, he and his team had worked hard to see it turned around by encouraging the private sector to invest and generate business. This had almost magical results and it was certainly clear to us visiting politicians that the economy was growing again, with unemployment falling and rationing had ended completely. People felt much better.

The issue of ethnic tension was altogether more complicated and none of us had fully understood what a tinderbox Sri Lanka had become. The President reminded us that he had brought in the reforms to the electoral system by dropping the 'first past the post' system and replacing it with proportional representation to make it easier for minorities to be elected. This was in part to counter the marginalisation of the Tamil communities under Mrs Bandaranaike due to some of the disastrous policies her government had implemented. As a result of the election reforms, the TULF (Tamil United Liberation Front) had won sixteen seats. The President soon realised on coming to power that these issues had to be tackled and acted upon by making both Tamil and English the national languages. On the surface this might have been seen to be the answer but half a cake is rarely successful for emotive issues, which this clearly was. It was not until Mahinda Rajapaksa came to power that all three languages were made official but it takes time to implement change on the ground and for it to become fully accepted.

The President also blamed the British for the way the Tamils had been left after Independence.

First, there were the Tamils in the Hill Country who had been brought in under the British Rule from India to work the tea estates but were then left stateless – no less than 975,000. Mrs Bandaranaike signed an agreement that 600,000 should be returned to India, leaving the balance of 375,000 in Sri Lanka. In addition, and as my secretary back at Reckitt & Colman in Colombo had explained, the British had followed their usual practice of promoting the minority ethnic group into key civil service positions. This brought trust for the British, as the Tamils were well educated and spoke good English, but resentment from the majority Sinhalese. However, once Independence was granted in 1948, it did not take long for the majority ethnic group, the Sinhalese, to want key positions and a much fairer entry system into the Civil Service. This was understandable and somewhat reluctantly accepted. However, this whole issue was totally undermined when Mrs Bandaranaike made Sinhalese the official language and Buddhism the state religion. This upset just about every group: the Tamil Hindus (many of whom did not speak Sinhalese), the Muslims and other faith groups too, including the Christians. Looking back there is little doubt these two actions of Mrs Bandaranaike inflamed the situation and certainly caused huge tension between the Tamil leaders and other parliamentarians.

Two members of my group and I decided we wanted to meet the leader of the Tamils to find out more about their cause, over and above what we had been able to do in Parliament. So, we asked to see him at his home near the racecourse, to which he agreed. Appapillai Amirthalingam, in broad terms, was a moderate but he was determined to get devolution for the Northern and Eastern Provinces.

A quick history lesson will reveal how this tinderbox had come to be. First, a Marxist hartal in 1953, then in 1957 the anti-Sri campaign organised by the Federal Party, an extremist Tamil party objecting to the new system of allocating letters and numbers for the registration of vehicles, claiming that the word 'Sri' was discriminatory against the Tamils. There were further communal riots in Ampara in 1958. The cause this time was a so-called colonisation scheme in Gal Oya, increasing the number of Sinhalese, which was rather similar to the objections I received as the new MP for Northampton South when a new Development Corporation was set up to move Londoners to Northampton! Add to this the attempted police coup in 1961 and even worse the JVP uprising in 1971. There were even issues in the north. In the 1970s the army was engaged in trying to prevent smuggling and illicit immigration which was rife as the Palk Strait was only 40 miles wide – about one hour by speed boat. Initially, spices and coconut oil were exchanged for Indian consumer products but during the 1960s the trade had gradually changed and the radicalisation of some of the Tamil youth began to take place. Young people began to get used to going to Tamil Nadu for military training.

Hastened by the arrival of the DMK (Dravida Munnetra Kazhagam – Dravidian Progressive Conference) Government in Tamil Nadu in 1967, which then stepped up the anti-Sri Lanka Government propaganda, the seeds were sown for the foundation of the LTTE. Even Mrs Bandaranaike was concerned and she visited Jaffna in 1970 to meet with the mayor. Mrs Bandaranaike was quite popular with the ordinary people and the Tamil farmers for her promotion of Jaffna onions. A plea was made by the mayor to release forty-two Tamil youths who had been arrested for violence, bank robberies and murders. Mrs Bandaranaike reflected on this and decided they could be released, as they were probably just nice young boys who had fallen in with the wrong crowd. Sadly, that wrong crowd turned out to be the LTTE and the youths went on to become its core members. We quizzed Mr Amirthalingam about all of this. He was charm itself, explaining that this was normal youth excesses. All three of us left wondering: was it just youthful excess or something more sinister?

On the day we left, I nipped into the Pettah to visit my jeweller friend Mr Hassan at the 'New Central Jewellery' and bought a present for my wife. We arrived back in the UK tired but satisfied we had done a thorough job, believing that Sri Lanka was well on the way to recovery following its somewhat turbulent recent past. It was 20 December and so the House of Commons had risen, which meant there was no opportunity to report back. Indeed, to this day, I do not know if a report was ever made. I suspect it was, at best, just a verbal briefing to the relevant minister. Thankfully, I kept my own notes.

Thinking back about the visit at the end of 1977 I can see it rekindled my interest in the country and the challenges it clearly faced, and I knew I could not just leave it as a fascinating visit. Nevertheless, back to the jobs at home. I had a marginal seat to fight with a majority of only 142 and I was still an active director at the advertising agency, Benton & Bowles.

However, once Mrs Thatcher and the Conservatives had won a huge majority in the May 1979 General Election I found I could pick up the tabs. Well, it was not quite as straightforward as that. I was very close to Airey Neave, MP, the man who masterminded Mrs Thatcher's rise to power in defeating Heath for the leadership of the Conservative Party in late 1975. I had been his unofficial bag carrier. We had discussed the forthcoming election. He said to me he would do his best to persuade Mrs Thatcher, if we won, to appoint me as a Junior Minister. Between the election and Parliament sitting, Airey was blown up by an IRA bomb. Then, Hugh Rossi, MP, who was about to be appointed Minister of Housing and Local Government, said he would ask for me to be his Junior, so I thought I was back on track. The fates were not on my side for suddenly the government planners realised they needed a Catholic in Northern Ireland and Hugh Rossi was the only one available. He asked me to help him in Northern Ireland but only as his PPS (Parliamentary Private Secretary) rather than as part of the official government. I was hugely disappointed but decided to accept, as I had nothing else planned. I did the job for two years, which gave me an insight into the troubles in Northern Ireland and a great appreciation of the need for patience. This was so vital in later years and gave me a better understanding of Sri Lanka's challenges.

During this time, I did not ignore Sri Lanka. Pretty soon after taking power, Mrs Thatcher was advised by some party, allegedly the Foreign Office, to pull out of the Victoria Dam project. I asked her a question at Prime Minister's Question Time and as a result she invited me to Number 10 to explain why the UK should continue with this very expensive project which had been initiated by Labour's Judith Hart, MP. I was not in marketing and advertising for nothing: I made my case, was listened to by the PM and thanked with the words: 'Well done – you have convinced me.'

All seemed set fair in 1981 to make another visit to Sri Lanka. This time I was leader of the group and was accompanied by colleagues including Betty Boothroyd, MP, later to become Speaker of the UK Parliament with myself as her Chairman of Ways and Means and First Deputy Speaker. We had a superb visit from 30 September to 22 October. Sri Lanka was doing well economically and on the whole things seemed better in the north as well. There were, however, repeated reports of killings of moderate Tamils who had crossed swords with a faction of the Tamil youth organised and led by the then little-known Velupillai Prabhakaran.

Although Sri Lanka was relatively quiet in 1982 – politically speaking – the UK certainly was not, with the impending Argentinian invasion of the Falklands. One evening I was asked to see Douglas Hurd, who had just taken over as Foreign Secretary. He pointed out that there was a key vote coming up in the United Nations where the UK was trying to persuade our potential friends to vote for us rather than for the Argentines. Douglas said: 'You know President Jayawardene well, could you telephone him and try to persuade him to instruct his Foreign Minister Hameed to vote for the UK rather than join the non-aligned?' I reflected on the request and decided to talk it over with my Vice Chairman, Betty Boothroyd, MP. We both agreed it was a reasonable request and so the next day I telephoned the President, warning him it was an All-Party request. He questioned me a bit further and then said, yes, he would do his very best. The result was that Sri Lanka was just one of seven countries that supported the UK. There can be no better case history for a successful All-Party Group getting to know the leading politicians in their country of interest and then calling on that relationship when needed. What a contrast with the Hague/Cameron era. They never wanted to share anything with the All-Party Sri Lanka Group. Indeed, they did the very opposite by undermining us, particularly by consulting with and often taking up the cause of the Tamil diaspora groups.

In January 1983, Ann and I decided to have a break in the Maldives and to link it with a visit to Sri Lanka. This was primarily to keep in touch with the key political figures there but also to check on the Victoria Dam project and to help the promotion of the country as a tourist destination alongside more inward investment. I do fondly remember one wonderful evening when the President gave a dinner in our honour in the grounds of his official residence in the Fort. Cigars were passed round, which I declined as I have never smoked. President J.R. retorted: 'Does your father smoke cigars?'

I answered: 'Yes sir'.

'Right, I shall give him a box complete with humidifier. Don't worry, Castro sends me such a box once a week.' My dear father was amazed and thrilled, although he did mention later they were so strong he had to cut them in half, which seemed sacrilegious to me.

They say a week is a long time in politics but nothing could have prepared me for what followed later that year. My wife and I were watching *News at Ten* on Monday 25 July 1983 when we heard the word 'Colombo'. Our attention grabbed, we saw images on our television screen of smoke billowing out over the city. The narrative that followed the pictures chilled me to the bone. The story was that thirteen army personnel had been killed in Jaffna by landmines on Saturday 23 July. Their bodies were being transported to Colombo for the nation to mourn their death. Traditionally, the bodies would have been sent to their home village or town but someone, presumably with President Jayawardene's permission, felt a statement had to made and that these soldiers, killed by terrorists, should be given a national common funeral at the General Cemetery in Kanatte. The reaction in Colombo and indeed elsewhere on the island was an explosion of anger against the Tamil community because the perpetrators of the atrocity were the Tamil LTTE, and in particular one Prabhakaran. At the cemetery an angry crowd had congregated. In an attempt to resolve the situation, the President agreed that the funeral should be called off and the bodies sent to the next of kin. The crowd reacted almost immediately and set off on a rampage, in retaliation, in search of Tamils.

More of the same harrowing pictures of smoke billowing out from the city dominated our television screen for another three days, with reports that Tamil shops, offices and homes were being torched, many killed and thousands more fleeing for their lives. At last on the Thursday the news came that a curfew had been imposed. I had already telephoned the High Commissioner Mr A.T. Moorty, to ask why the curfew had not been imposed immediately but he could make no comment. Why President Jayawardene did not impose such a curfew only he knows. For the Sri Lankan President it might have been a difficult and bold decision which would have upset some, but still, he should have acted.

The failure to act meant that the whole situation spiralled out of control island-wide. Wherever there were Tamils, violence took place. The incentive to riot was not immediately obvious as none of the rioters had any relationship to the dead army personnel. Indeed, to this day no one knows exactly who started it or what contributed to the spread of it. I merely observe that the Tottenham riots in the UK in 2014 spread like a bush fire and even with immediate response from the authorities the damage was huge.

What we do know is that it was election time and there were electoral lists in circulation – for canvassing – something we have in the UK. Those lists would have made Tamils easily identifiable, just by their name, in addition to the visual identifier of the red spot on the forehead of the women. Once rioting starts it attracts 'bees to the honeypot', with all sorts of people joining in to loot, seek revenge or just get taken along with the crowd. Add to this the heat of Colombo and looted alcohol in circulation and a heady cocktail is created which is a fuel to rioting. Critics said the army should have responded but the reality is it will only deploy if the police seek help, which they failed to do. With the curfew in place the rioting subsided but then rumours began to spread that the Tamil Tigers were about to attack Colombo. This time the President did act quickly and the army was ordered in. The consequences of all this was a nationwide tragedy of monumental proportions for almost all Tamils.

Four hundred and seventy-one people were reported killed in Colombo but it was later estimated that a truer figure may be as high as 1,500. Thousands were wounded, women were molested and countless numbers of homes, shops and offices torched, not just in Colombo but also in the Hill Country where stateless Tamils were living and working. In parts of Colombo the blitzed shops are still visible today, like bomb damage in London from the war. Some Tamils fled north to Jaffna, others escaped in ships sent by India. Those who could not escape either stayed with relatives and even Sinhalese friends, frightened beyond belief. Others, numbering 65,000, became refugees. Remarkably, accommodation was quickly found in schools, temples, churches, warehouses and any space the government could house them safely. One can be critical about the lack of action to quell the riots but equally I have only praise at how quickly the civil servants and charities swung into action to look after the refugees. A friend of mine, a senior civil servant, Bradman Weerakoon took Ann and me around a number of buildings in January 1984 to see for ourselves how the government was trying to look after these people. Conditions were crowded, of course, but nevertheless the places were very clean with decent supplies of food, access to proper medical attention and each family had its own space. Although it took time to resettle the displaced, it seems that about 16,000 had been settled in Colombo, leaving a rump of about 2,000 left when we visited.

The other somewhat inevitable element of this tragedy was that the better-off Tamils moved abroad in large numbers to Canada, Australia, England and some to the USA, Holland, and the Nordic countries: anywhere where English was spoken. As displaced Sri Lankans who had witnessed such terrible atrocities, a significant number of these families became the core of the diaspora who later funded the Tamil Tigers in their cause of Eelam – the proposed independent Tamil state, separate from Sri Lanka. Many of them became very successful businessmen, making huge donations to the cause as their wealth grew.

Black Friday (as the events of July 1983 quickly became known) had left an indelible scar on every Tamil and those abroad created a powerful lobby against Sri Lanka to justify separatism or Eelam. The effects of these events continued to grow across the country. In Jaffna and elsewhere numbers in Tamil Youth gangs mushroomed with a constant flow of new recruits egged on by the emotions of Tamil aspirations.

It is a sad irony that prior to these unfortunate events relations between Tamils and the other communities had been good, with most living happily alongside each other. I can surmise that young Prabhakaran must have sat back in early August thinking to himself what a huge success he had achieved from just one land mine that had killed the thirteen soldiers, which started this whole sorry episode. It is known he did the deed allegedly in retaliation for an assault on three Tamil women but he later admitted it was in revenge for the death of his close associate Charles Anthony.

It was not just the rioting that has left its mark on me to this day but the extraordinary tactics that the President used to get re-elected. 1983 was the year of local elections island-wide along with eighteen parliamentary by-elections. The UNP (United National Party), the President's own party, did very well so the President announced that instead of having an election for President he would save money as it was clear he would have been elected with a huge majority. This is probably the only argument we ever had face-to-face, as I made clear to him this was not democracy and a proper election would have given him a powerful mandate.

Victoria Dam, photograph courtesy of Rehman Abubakr

CHAPTER
Five

1984: A Year of True Friendship

I could not get out of mind the horrific events of July 1983 and the effects it must have had on every Sri Lankan family regardless of ethnicity, race or religion. For the Tamil community it was horrendous, paralleling Kristallnacht in 1938 Germany, except that was a planned attack by Hitler and his youth movement whereas this was an involuntary response to the killing of thirteen Sinhalese soldiers trying to keep the peace in Jaffna. What I did understand, however, and probably due to the amount of time I had spent in Sri Lanka, was that it was really just one group of Tamils who wanted a devolution of power from the main state (which was understandable) and who wanted to go far, far further and have a separate state of their own, linked in some form to Tamil Nadu – the Indian Tamil state in nearby south India. At the other end of the spectrum was the Sinhalese majority, with a population of about 12 million, who saw themselves as a tiny cog in the vast states of South Asia and must have been left wondering what would happen to them if Eelam – the Tamil state – was created.

I came to the conclusion that if the All-Party Group was worth its salt then a broad range of parliamentarians should try to get out to Sri Lanka to see if we could build bridges and be a catalyst for progress. My wife and I had already booked to go to the Maldives for a break in January and were then to fly to Nepal to be briefed on that country of which I knew a little. I decided that we should make a stopover in Colombo to prepare the ground for a parliamentarians' visit, which I was hoping to organise later in the year.

The idea found favour so we arrived in Colombo on 7 January at no cost to the Sri Lanka Government at all. We had an audience with the President on the Monday, during which I raised the question of a visit. He was enthusiastic about the idea, which pleased me. We also discussed the tragic cancellation of his planned official State Visit to the UK, which was to have followed on from his visit to the USA to meet President Reagan. President Jayawardene had given President Reagan a baby elephant. The visit to England was cancelled because of the after effects of the July 1983 riots. J.R. told me the baby elephant had died on exactly the same day as he was to have arrived in the UK, so clearly the visit would not have been auspicious.

Following the excellent session with J.R. I met the Prime Minister Premadasa. I was pleased we could discuss in some detail the refugee challenges and find out what was happening in the north. My impressions were of a thoroughly practical and down to earth politician.

Both the Minister of Foreign Affairs, the Hon. A.C. Hameed and his deputy, Tyronne Fernando, MP hosted dinners for me on the following days so I could meet a cross-section of people and try to understand what was happening on the devolution plans and the security situation. The British High Commission responded as well and I attended a lunch, on the 10th, with a wide range of backbench parliamentarians, NGOs (non-governmental organisations) and other movers and shakers. I decided in the short time available to visit at least one refugee camp – and try to visit without notice.

We visited Kotahena (in the suburbs of Colombo) accompanied by Bradman Weerakoon, the President's right-hand civil servant and trouble-shooter. I have seldom seen a more competent civil servant at work. There was a combination of humanity and efficiency about him that made things happen in a confident and humane manner. We have become close friends since that visit. We found the camp to be well run and took particular care to visit parts not on the schedule and in her capacity as a doctor my wife went to the medical centre. No one would ever claim it was any fun living in a refugee camp but the people were safe here; indeed, for some poor souls it was probably better than what they had endured previously. We had an in-depth debrief with Mr Weerakoon. Time did not allow for a trip to Jaffna but on advice I made a note to visit the Gurunagar and Kaithady camps on my next visit and to do so unannounced.

Finally, as a politician I was thrilled to make a formal visit to the new parliamentary building out at Kotte, funded by the Japanese. I had a stimulating discourse with the Speaker and also called on my dear friend Ananda de Tissa de Alwis, MP who, after all, was the catalyst for my going into politics in the first place. He had suffered a stroke so was not, at that time, the dynamic, erudite politician I knew. However, he did later make a complete recovery and eventually become Speaker. My thank you letter summed up my feelings and I quote:

> All in all, I think this was the most interesting tour I have ever made to Sri Lanka. Visits to the refugee camp had a salutary effect on one, it just seemed so alien to the way of life in Sri Lanka that people could just for a few days, be at each other's throats.
>
> You all face a daunting task in the months ahead, as the wound has gone very deep. All your friends in the UK are praying that the party talks will find a solution although the initial omens do not seem too good.

As a former senior marketing man, I had always understood that one of my key responsibilities was to help business and commerce between the two countries, although I was very strict and never got involved financially, not even buying any stock. Around this time there were four areas of policy in which I believe I helped ease the wheels.

First, I had been asked, at the request of David Veitch, the General Sales Manager of Air Lanka to provide advice on how to handle landing rights both at London Heathrow and Manchester Airport. The All-Party Group lobbied the UK authorities, which advanced the negotiations.

The second issue I took up concerned ECGD (Export Credit Guarantee Department) cover for UK companies exporting to Sri Lanka. This had been raised by Mr N. Wijewardane, Chairman of the Bank of Ceylon. I duly wrote to Jack Gill, Secretary to the ECGD, questioning what appeared to be a restriction of facilities. On 9 March 1984, Mr Gill replied: 'I hope I can allay your fears by confirming that the full range of ECGD facilities is available to UK companies exporting to this market.' I reflected that it did no harm that I, together with two other Bow Group friends (Conservative Think Tank) had written a pamphlet entitled *Helping the Exporter*. On 22 March Mr Wijewardane wrote: 'I am very grateful for the kind interest you are taking to ensure that Sri Lanka continues to get facilities from institutions such as the ECGD.'

Thirdly, prior to my departure on this trip, I had had a meeting in London with a Mr John Edwards concerning a pitch by Cable & Wireless for a contract to improve and upgrade telecommunications in Sri Lanka. When I met President Jayawardene, I was therefore able to reassure him that I knew the company and that it was highly respected. I understand that Cable & Wireless was appointed.

Fourthly, I was asked by the Parliamentary Under-Secretary of State, Ray Whitney, MP to follow up the question of possible British aid for the improvement of English language teaching which I had raised with the Sri Lanka Government the previous year. I was told that the ODA (Overseas Development Agency) officials were able to reach agreement in principle with Ranil Wickremesginhe for a six-year period, the officer in charge of English Language teaching in Sri Lanka. I certainly did raise it and believe it went through, although there were certainly storm clouds approaching as the Minister for ODA, Timothy Raison, put in a letter to me after I had sent him a copy of my report. He wrote: 'We had intended to send a project identification mission to Sri Lanka about now [28 Feb 1984] to consider what we should do after the completion of the Victoria Dam: but the outlook for the Country is so uncertain.'

Part of the joy of my visits to Sri Lanka was that we worked hard, at the end of which we could usually enjoy a few days' rest. This trip was a little different: not much beach but almost two days at Yala, the country's biggest and best endowed wild animal park. Our good friends Robin and Veena Talwatte had organised for the four of us to stay in the President's bungalow on the inside edge of the park. It all sounded very grand until we discovered that poor Veena had to bring all the bed linen, food and drink, etc! We got up early on 19 January, at about 5.00 am, and were soon out on the trail. It was quite superb: we spotted six leopards, one of which was just 30 feet away and a rogue elephant. Mention of the elephant reminds me of the true story of how elephants stamped the ground at the time of the 2004 Indian Ocean earthquake and tsunami, thereby giving the signal to all the animals to move inland. And they went: snakes, monkeys, deer and even big cats. Truly amazing. I was not surprised to read of two factors in an article by Christine Kennedy fairly soon after the tsunami: first, that the animals probably heard the quake before the tsunami hit landfall, and secondly the likelihood of ground vibration. All truly fascinating.

There was a final formal dinner and then the next day we were to catch the plane to Nepal on flight RA216. However, the trip to the airport was not smooth, as I explained in my letter of thanks to Robin and Veena at the time:

As you will have heard, the car broke down opposite the Pettah and near the docks. I despatched your man in search of a taxi and waited. Initially there were a few helpers but before long it has increased to about thirty. It was fine until we came to go when they wanted payment for pushing the car. In the pushing mass we had to abandon your driver and depart smartly. I was not able to thank him adequately and hope the mob didn't set on him or steal the car!

I finished the letter: 'Thank you once again for a really superb week, would life had more weeks like that one.' Readers should be reassured that the driver was OK.

Here we were just a few weeks into 1984, the year of George Orwell's awful prognostications for the world, but for me it will remain etched in my memory as one of the years when I felt I made a significant contribution to Sri Lanka in general and particularly British-Sri Lanka relations, culminating in the opening of the Victoria Dam, the following spring, on 12 April 1985 by the Prime Minister of the UK, The Rt Hon. Margaret Thatcher, MP.

I get ahead of myself. On my return to the UK I produced the usual report, sent it to the Foreign Secretary and to the minister in charge of our aid programme at the Overseas Development Agency. My covering letter highlighted two key points and I quote:

On the question of the official opening of the Victoria Dam, I understand from Balfour Beatty that Princess Anne has been approached informally. My own thoughts, and indeed recommendation is that our Prime Minister might like to consider it as part of a goodwill South East Asia tour (Sri Lanka, Malaysia, Singapore and Indonesia). You know she really would have a rapturous welcome.

(What a contrast to Cameron's disgraceful performance when he went to CHOGM (Commonwealth Heads of Government Meeting) in 2014.)

In the following paragraph I wrote: 'I have been asked by the President to lead an All-Party Group of MPs (about 10) sometime in April/May/June.' Our minister's response was enthusiastic, saying 'such a visit could only be of benefit'. My report did also suggest that President Jayawardene's State Visit should be reinstated but it never was, although he was made hugely welcome when he made a private visit later that summer.

The challenge for me was to set about organising ten colleagues to agree to go to Sri Lanka and then agree on the dates. In the end I got my ten and they were:

Michael Morris, MP (Con) Leader and Chairman of the CPA All-Party British Sri Lanka Parliamentary Group
Betty Boothroyd, MP (Lab) Deputy Leader and Vice Chairman
James Hill, MP (Con)
Eric Deakins, MP (Lab)
Mark Fisher, MP (Lab)
Lord Kaberry of Adel (Con)
Andrew Mackay, MP (Con)
Gareth Wardell, MP (Lab)
Alec Woodall, MP (Lab)

Actually, we should have been more but both David Madel, MP and Robert Maclennan, MP were taken ill before departure and David Nellist, MP declined the invitation.

Our itinerary was busy: Colombo on 31 May, 1 June and again on 4 June; Jaffna on 2 June, Trincomalee on 3 June; Kandy on 5 and 6 June and then returning to Colombo to give a press conference on 6 June.

The objectives of the visit were to see for ourselves what the situations were in regard to Eelam, the Tamil areas, Human Rights, state security and the role of India. Although inevitably we reviewed the past, our objective was to look to the present and more especially the future. It would be impertinent for foreign MPs to make formal recommendations, but we believed it might be helpful if we spoke frankly of our fears, doubts and anxieties to all we met, irrespective of rank or position of those with whom we had discussions.

Looming in the background was the problem of the two different minorities: 1,871,535 Tamils as well as 400,000 Indian Hill Country Tamils both looking to their ethnic links with the 50 million+ living in Tamil Nadu. In contrast, 74 per cent of the population were Sinhalese, the majority race on the island, but in terms of the vast Indian Subcontinent, they had nowhere else to go. We wrote:

> The communal violence of July/August 1983 went very deep. We met Tamils who lost family and homes in the rioting; we also met Sinhalese who had befriended Tamils, often at great personal risk to themselves. [*We noted there had been no authoritative report on the tragedy nor exactly what happened at Welikada gaol*]... We still feel it would be helpful if there were, even now, a public independent judicial enquiry set up which would publish its report. It cannot help Sri Lanka to allow this deep wound to fester on rumour, allegation and counter allegation.

As we looked to the future, the issue of the moment was the call for Eelam, the creation of an independent Tamil-speaking sovereign state comprising the present Northern and Eastern Provinces of Sri Lanka. I reflect that there is still the same hope today but now it is mostly the cause of the diaspora/LTTE living abroad and thankfully most Tamils accept it is unrealistic in a unitary state, although they yearn for more devolution. To quote:

> We still found the call for Eelam to be totally unrealistic with only 41% of the total Eastern Region being Tamil. We met the Muslim Leaders who told us the whole concept of Eelam was totally alien to them.

We also commented:

> Those Tamils living abroad who actively or passively support the call for Eelam would do more for their people by concentrating

their help and abilities in highlighting the areas of discrimination and discontent and in pressing for a solution through devolution of power within a viable unitary state.

We looked at Jaffna and reported:

It seemed to us that the situation particularly in Jaffna Peninsula was acute in terms of lack of investment going back over many years and that some form of devolved government needed to be set up as a matter of urgency in both regions.

We looked closely at the Prevention of Terrorism Act and the Emergency Regulations. There were parallels with the UK but equally there were disparities, which we highlighted. We called for the legislation itself to be open to annual parliamentary review. We soon found in our discussions with the President, the Minister of National Security and the Minister of Defence that these issues needed addressing.

We made some helpful recommendations on policing Jaffna, based on our experience of Northern Ireland. A number of us knew India quite well – certainly I did having worked there for nearly two years of my life. All of us respected and in many ways admired India but although we understood the close ties between Tamil Nadu and Sri Lanka Tamils, we stated as forcefully as we could and I quote:

There can be no excuse for one member of the Commonwealth to harbour and nurture terrorists whose aim is the destabilisation of a neighbouring Commonwealth nation. We made it clear to the Sri Lanka Tamils that they have grievances which cannot be ignored but neither is their dependence on Tamil Nadu helpful to a solution.

Our final, departing comment was that we hoped our talks with them and the representations we had made, coming from friends, helped crystallise their thinking. As we departed from Sri Lanka, the changes that were announced certainly indicated that we had been listened to, and were welcomed by us. I cannot resist the observation that if the same considered approach had even been tried by the Cameron/Hague team, then the tension of recent years and the meaningless UNHCR (United Nations High Commission for Refugees) Geneva hearings would have been unnecessary.

I was proud of my colleagues, who were as good a cross-section of the UK Parliament as anyone could wish. We worked hard, spoke frankly without fear or favour and went wherever we wished. In return, the Sri Lanka Government responded in every possible way. It is therefore appropriate to quote our conclusion in full:

A few impressions like this cannot hope to encompass more than strands of common thought. We believe our visit was thorough, objective and submitted by Members of Parliament who have friends in all the ethnic communities of Sri Lanka.

We left hoping the All-Party Conference would succeed and that those who had chosen not to take part would rejoin; it seemed to us that this was not a time for scoring party political points. Conciliation from both sides is imperative. The Government is in a position to take an initiative to ensure local devolved democracy is implemented speedily in the North and East. The TULF in their turn have to use their undoubted energies and talents to obtain a realistic and fair deal for their people.

Sri Lanka is an integral part of the Commonwealth. She has pioneered democracy and we believe the President to be sincere when he stated to us that democracy was precious to everyone in Sri Lanka. However democracy is a delicate plant that needs nurturing. In the case of Sri Lanka the Government and the Sinhala people have to give a lead and find a way forward that will give dignity to all its people.

On our last day we held a press conference and delivered our report to the media. The report was well-received and good coverage appeared the next day in all the English-language and leading Sinhalese Sri Lanka press, even though by then we were back in the UK.

I sent copies of the report to the Foreign & Commonwealth Office and the Overseas Development Agency. The report was welcomed, given in-depth consideration and to quote just one line from the Minister of State at the ODA:

> This was obviously a most interesting and informative visit. The South Asian Department would also be interested to see the background material which you have on the refugee problem.

It also appeared to be well received in Colombo. I quote from Sir John Nicholas's letter, our High Commissioner, to me:

> We found the report most interesting and agree with its main thrust without exception. As seen from here, the delegation was a great success and we were most impressed with the way the delegation acted as a whole under your leadership. It all gave an excellent impression.

Indeed, we were asked for so many copies of the report, with one party asking for a dozen, that we decided to print it as a booklet entitled: *Some Impressions of Sri Lanka – A report by three MPs recently returned from the Country – Betty Boothroyd, James Hill, Michael Morris.*

The pace of activity did not really stop, as I was informed that the President of Sri Lanka would be making a visit to the UK to discuss policy, help and the forthcoming opening of the Victoria Dam. He had mentioned to me privately that he was contemplating asking Mrs Thatcher to open it. Once it was public knowledge that he had in fact asked the Prime Minister to open the dam, I wrote to her and I quote:

> I understand the President [of Sri Lanka] has invited you to open the Victoria Dam which is, as you know, the single biggest British aid project undertaken. In my report to Sir Geoffrey Howe in January I recommended that you should be approached about the opening, particularly if it could be included as part of a tour of other parts of South East Asia such as Malaysia, Singapore and Indonesia.

This was a delightful surprise to everyone. I myself thought it might happen as I had sowed the seed some years prior with Balfour Beatty, the main construction company, and had carefully nurtured it each time I visited, and particularly on my visit in January. Additionally, this visit was to be followed by a visit from my friend Lalith Athulathmudali, Minister for Security. I remember thinking to myself what a good thing it was that we had our general election in 1983 before all this activity.

The President came, had tea with Her Majesty the Queen and talks with Sonny Ramphal, Commonwealth Secretary General. He had a meeting with MPs and Lords in one of the Committee Rooms in the Commons and what a rousing welcome he received with the banging of desks and clapping. To round it all off, on 27 June, he was Guest of Honour at a dinner at Number 10 to which Ann and I were also invited. I sat next to the Hon. Ronnie de Mel, MP, probably Sri Lanka's most successful Finance Minister. A few days later there was another dinner for Lalith Athulathmudali but not at Number 10. Meanwhile, the Tamil community had been carrying out a silent vigil outside the offices of the High Commission.

The summer recess for Parliament was looming, so I thought I would ask one last written question of the BBC External Services, which read: 'Mr Michael Morris asked the Secretary of State for Foreign and Commonwealth Affairs if he will estimate the cost of providing the same level of output by the BBC external service in Sinhalese to Sri Lanka as is currently broadcast in Tamil.' The reply was: 'The cost would be approximately £74,000.' My reason for the question was that I had been told by Tamil friends that the BBC service in Tamil was biased in favour of Eelam and often attacked the Jayawardene Government. Sadly, the new service never happened. So much for the impartiality of the BBC.

The recess arrived and, joy of joys, I could now watch cricket. The summer of 1984 was to be no ordinary summer. At last I was to have the privilege to watch Sri Lanka play its first Test Match in England at Lord's Cricket Ground, the home of the MCC. However, I get ahead of myself because the journey to get Sri Lanka into the ICC had started in the late 1970s when my friend Gamini Dissanayake and I sat down to work out a strategy of how to get Sri Lanka elected. We divided the task with Gamini as Chairman of the Sri Lanka Cricket board tackling India, Pakistan, Australia and New Zealand whilst I agreed to lobby the MCC – the guardians of the game of cricket – the Minister of Sport and all the High Commissioners in London whose country played Test cricket.

Between us we must have done a good job for it was announced in 1981 that Sri Lanka was elected to full Test status.

At 11.00 am on 23 August 1984 my eldest son Julian and I were seated in the MCC Chairman's Box, along with the Sri Lanka High Commissioner and other dignitaries, about to witness a unique game of cricket, namely Sri Lanka's first Test Match at Lord's, the home of cricket. If I am honest, most people thought Sri Lanka would put on a spirited show but they would be beaten on the fourth day or maybe just make the fifth and final day. How wrong we were. The match was a draw but so nearly won by Sri Lanka thanks to an immaculate opening century innings by Sidath Wittemuny (with Duleep Mendis), scoring 190, a record score for any Sri Lankan batsman and his 628 minutes innings remains the longest Test innings at Lords. This was no single hero event, as he was supported by Jeevan Mendis who made 111 and in the second innings by S.A.R. Silva 102 Not Out. Indeed, by the whole talented team.

I am a member of the MCC, as well as being President of Northamptonshire County Cricket. At a Test Match in the summer of 2018 I walked through the hallowed Pavilion at Lords, marvelled at the commemorative boards in the Visitors' Dressing Room with names of these three talented young cricketers, their centuries recorded for posterity from this first ever Test for Sri Lanka in England. I felt so moved that later I asked the MCC Library if I could see the scorebook of that memorable match.

On 11 October I arrived at 4.00 pm to find not just the scorebook but all the memorabilia of that wonderful match. I turned the pages of Bill Frindall's scorebook, slowly noting his copperplate precision writing. To me it was like opening the most exciting Christmas present. I sat there with eyes wide open, totally enthralled, fascinated at how the figures could so easily mesmerise me. Reflecting on the experience, I asked who had the copyright and how could I get permission to reprint the opening page in my book. The answer from Mr Neil Robinson, Head Librarian, was that the copyright rested with the widow, Mrs Debbie Gregory. The procedure was for me to write through the MCC, which I duly did. I received a letter from the librarian a couple of weeks later that permission was granted. What happy days which might never have happened but for the friendship of two politicians oceans apart but joined by their love of cricket.

The MCC Score Book of the first day's play of the first Test between England and Sri Lanka. The copyright has been released. It will be available to be photographed immediately after the Ashes Test on August 18th.

On New Year's Day 1985 I reflected on all that had happened in Sri Lanka over the past decade since I had started the All-Party Group and looked forward to the exciting potential opening of the Victoria Dam. I reflected to myself that when I went to see Mrs Thatcher about the Mahaweli Ganga project and specifically the Victoria Dam element so soon after her election as Prime Minister in 1979 I was none too sure if she would continue the project as it was the largest aid project the UK had ever given. But she did. I remember thinking to myself that I needed to keep behind this to ensure the British company already partially involved would become the prime contractor and in an ideal world the UK's Prime Minister should be invited to open it. In some ways the challenge was a classic case history for a marketing man but clearly it worked.

On 12 March 1985 I received a telegram from Colombo, specifically from the Honourable Minister of Mahaweli Development Sri Lanka, Gamini Dissanayake, which read:

YOU ARE CORDIALLY INVITED FOR VICTORIA COMMISSIONING ON 12TH APRIL TRAVEL ARRANGEMENTS WILL BE MADE FORMAL INVITATION FOLLOWS.

I still have the telegram. Maybe I am old-fashioned but telegrams had an urgency and impact that the digital world has lost. A letter followed, dated 8 March, stating that:

The ceremonial inauguration of the Victoria multi-purpose Project would be undertaken by His Excellency J.R. Jayawardene and the Rt. Hon Mrs Thatcher, you are cordially invited to grace this occasion with your wife. An official invitation will be forwarded to you in due course. If you are able to attend the ceremonial opening, I shall send prepaid air tickets for both of you and arrange for you to be taken round as a guest of my Ministry, to see the development works completed in the Island during the past eight years.

I responded on 19 March, thanking Gamini for the invitation, accepting for myself but regretting that my wife was not free to come for the celebrations of this wonderful achievement.

I still have in my possession the formal invitation; the First Day cover with the two stamps Rps 7 and Rps 0.60 perfectly franked; the schedule of events starting at 8.50 am and concluding at 11.25 am with the National Anthem. In between, Mrs Thatcher unveiled the Monolith, together with the President, and I quote from a wonderful booklet produced for the occasion, 'to the throbbing of Magulbera'. At 10.45 am Mrs Thatcher gave a ten-minute speech and finally at 11.05 am, she, the President and Gamini Dissanayake undertook the formal commissioning of the Victoria Reservoir Project to the chanting of Buddhist Seth Pirith; a spiritual prayer to bless the outcome from a particularly important event or occasion. In this case it was long and built up to a high, even hectic, emotional chant reflecting the massive importance of the Victoria Dam Project to the nation.

As one would expect there was massive media coverage the next day, particularly in the Sri Lanka newspapers with headlines such as: 'Victoria-Never in history has one country gifted' ... 'Lasting monument to British Lanka friendship: Thatcher' ... 'No arms for Tamil terrorists from UK – Maggie'. I even have a copy of the *Daily News* with a strap round it: 'Your personal copy of the special issue of today's *Daily News* with the compliments of the Mahaweli Authority.'

Anyone reading this may well wonder at the significance of this project and whether it was anything more than a dam with a reservoir, so I think a little piece of history would not be out of place. A booklet entitled, *Mahaweli: a moving story*, was produced covering the history of the region. I shall quote from parts of it.

THE MAHAWELI is a moving story. It's a saga of Sri Lankans moving in search of their ancient heartland, lying way north from the central hills. To that extent it is a story of the Sri Lankans returning home. It began when the Father of the Nation, Sri Lanka's first Prime Minister after Independence, The late Rt. Hon. D.S. Senanayake commenced restoring the ancient irrigation works in the Rajarata way back in the 1930's. The Rajarata as the name connotes, is King's Country, lying in the plains towards the north which flourished during the Anuradhapura and Polonnaruwa civilisations – two eras spanning nearly two millennia, from

6th Century BC to the 13th Century AD. During this period Sri Lanka's ancient kings painstakingly built an intricate irrigation network mingling a complex system of inter-related dams, canals and reservoirs, to become the nerve centres of ancient Sri Lanka heartland. Alas in the 13th Century AD in the face of incessant invasion and pestilence the people left the Rajarata and retreated to the hills and Kandy.

The long march back to the Rajarata started way back in the 1930s. The Accelerated Mahaweli Programme, which is the quintessence of the Mahaweli Master Plan – drawn up by the UN-FAO and Sri Lanka experts – has quickened the pace giving it momentum. Some 1.5 million people, nearly one in ten of the Sri Lankan population are retracing their steps to the land their forebears evacuated. And when they get there they are quickly in their element and instinctively feel their way to disused tanks and reservoirs and inevitable dagobas and ruins of temples. It is a voyage of rediscovery ending in finding their roots and awakening to their ethos.

Underpinning this whole exercise is the UK grant-aided Victoria multi-purpose project in the misty Dumbara Valley.

Margaret Thatcher's visit and her commitment to making the project a success for both countries was evident from the instant her plane touched down until she departed. In this time she commissioned the opening of the Victoria Dam, attended and spoke at a formal dinner, and addressed Parliament on Saturday 13 April with passion, understanding and a commitment to Sri Lanka. It was my privilege to accompany her at all stages. Indeed, as I write this chapter I have in front of me the final copy of her speech to them of the new Parliament at Kotte. I was there and listened to all twenty-eight pages of it intently. This was no genuflection to tradition but a speech that demanded attention, beckoned careful study and was delivered with a warmth and understanding that only Margaret could achieve. She did not shirk addressing the challenging and difficult issues Sri Lanka faced but she offered the hand of practical encouragement, friendship and understanding so sadly lacking in nearly all her successors in Number 10 Downing Street, finishing with Mr Cameron.

Of course she highlighted the huge grant of £110 million for the Victoria Dam, Britain's biggest ever grant at that time and rightly highlighting the successful British companies who helped to build it: Balfour Beatty, Costain, Edward Nuttall together with Whessoe Boving, Hawker Siddeley, NEI, Reyrolle, BICC, GEC and the consulting engineers Sir Alexander Gibbs and partners. For once we had a prime minister prepared to show our real support for British companies by using public money to pay for a project sponsored by the aid budget.

It would be invidious of me to try to summarise Mrs Thatcher's speech, so I have decided to print it in full as an appendix (see Appendix I). I would just highlight the references to the on-going ties between Sri Lanka and Britain: the common commitment to democracy, economic freedoms and facing up to terrorists, be they the IRA or the Tamil Tigers. Although I played no part in the writing of the speech my views were well known to the Foreign Office and the Prime Minister's advisers: I could not help but recognise certain key phrases, which pleased me.

On reflection the whole visit might all seem rather formal but it had its lighter moments. After the formal opening of the dam we moved to the old Governor General's Residence in Kandy for a light lunch. The President had arranged for Sri Lanka's best-known tusker elephant to be on parade

Victoria Dam commemorative plate – 12 April 1985 by The Rt. Hon. Mrs Margaret Thatcher MP. Prime Minister of The United Kingdom

in full regalia to pay his respects to the visiting dignitary. I was sitting at the same table as Mrs Thatcher and her husband Denis, along with the President and certain other Sri Lankans. The President suggested to Denis that he might like to feed the elephant with a bunch of bananas, which were on the table. Sri Lanka bananas are small and very tasty. Denis got up with the bananas and approached the elephant, who was standing still with his trunk swinging. As the trunk swung down Denis stuffed the bananas into the opening of the trunk through which the elephant breathes. Mrs T., as ever on the ball, yelled out: 'Denis, not the trunk you idiot but the mouth!' Too late. Rajah could not breathe, blasted out a cry through the trunk resulting in the bunch of bananas being shot into the air as if they were cannon balls. The squashy remains landed on our table and those of our neighbours. Everyone collapsed with laughter. Rajah did a bended knee salute and departed with what I am sure was a twinkle in his eye.

A symbol of tension in Sri Lanka in this period created the need for armed protection whether it be for the Author or with parliamentary colleagues.

CHAPTER
Six

Reality Strikes

The euphoria of Mrs Thatcher's visit in April 1985 and the hopes of the All-Party Peace Conference were inevitably going to be punctured somewhere.

In fact, it was the systematic and frequent killings by the Tamil Tigers of both moderate Tamils and innocent Sinhalese civilians, coupled with rising tensions in the Eastern Province where violence and murders were becoming more frequent between the Muslim community and other Tamil Youth movements. The security forces, tasked with trying to keep the peace, responded, but inevitably sometimes they overacted with a force and viciousness that only inflamed the situation.

I used to get the Sri Lanka English-language newspapers, particularly the *Island* and the *Sunday Times*, both of which I viewed as balanced. A later issue, of 25 February 2005, gives a good example of the heights and arbitrary nature that the violence reached in Sri Lanka with the headline: 'GA killed, body found near tank'. The report said the government agent of Mullaitivu was taken off a Jaffna-bound bus by a group of machine-gun toting terrorists. The GA concerned was the most senior civil servant killed to date. There seemed to be no specific reason for his murder, just that he was a symbol of the government. In all the years I have been associated with Sri Lanka I cannot but marvel at the dedication and professionalism of these senior civil servants. The ultimate challenge was how these men and women maintained the running of basic government services through all the troubles, right up to the end of the war on 19 May 2009. This covered every aspect of daily life, including the running of schools and hospitals and the provision of food and kerosene supplies. It is easy to forget that they were still at their desks trying to provide all these local services, including back-up emergency food in warehouses with terrorist activities and, later on, the war raging around them. To me they are the real heroes of Sri Lanka society.

One of the results of the tension and the killings, estimated in May 1985 to have been as high as 300 from all ethnic groups, was that many of the better-off Tamil families had decided to leave Sri Lanka. Significant numbers had already gone following the troubles in 1983: indeed, it is estimated that maybe as many as 100,000 fled to the sanctuary of India's Tamil Nadu. What was not known was what proportion of these were young Tamils going for terrorist training. However, what was known was the impact on the UK as more and more Tamils came to Britain to seek asylum.

This, in turn, resulted in questions being asked of the UK Government by backbenchers, but not all the questions were asked with pure altruism at heart, seeking explanations for the cause of the arrival of these people. There were those on the Left who wanted to undermine Mrs Thatcher's visit to Sri Lanka. This manifested itself in the Early Day Motions that began to appear in January 1985 (EDM 332). The architect of these EDMs on Sri Lanka was Mr Dave Nellist, MP who was a thorn in my side all the time he was an MP from June 1983 until he lost his seat in April 1992. Interestingly, the other prominent signatory was the man to be Leader of the Labour Party some thirty-one years later, Jeremy Corbyn, MP. One of the coincidences of life is that I fought the 1966 General Election in Islington North, which was to become Mr Corbyn's seat. Even as I write this the Boundary Commission is recommending that the electorate of Islington North be subsumed into a neighbouring seat, thus maybe spelling the end of Islington North.

There had been three EDMs before Mrs Thatcher departed for Sri Lanka: on 30 January, 25 February and 5 March 1985. Two alleged that terror was being unleashed by Sri Lanka armed forces on Tamil civilians, resulting in a lack of basic food, transport and health facilities. There was no mention of the action of the terrorists themselves. The third called on the UK Government to have 'an exceptional policy to grant leave to remain in the UK to Tamils who express a fear to return to Sri Lanka'.

Once returned from Sri Lanka, it was not long before the MPs took up the cause with Mrs Thatcher once again, but this time with written questions. Mr Maples, a Conservative, asked on 20 May 1985: 'What is the policy towards the return of Sri Lanka Tamils from the UK to Sri Lanka?' Interestingly, the Home Secretary, the Rt Hon. Leon Brittan,

MP, himself answered. He said there were about 900 Sri Lanka Tamils who had expressed a fear to return and their departure had not been implemented. Although he did not see the need for a blanket approach, he said Tamils who had made a claim would be allowed to stay for twelve months whilst the details were investigated and the policy would apply to new and recent arrivals.

The press picked up the story and it continued to run: another EDM followed which, in essence, described the killings in Sri Lanka as indiscriminate. There followed another written question on 24 May. I began to wonder how many more parliamentary initiatives the Overseas Tamil Movement would think up. Clearly I had no control over this but I began to think what I, as Chairman of the All-Party Group, could do to help Sri Lanka. I spoke to colleagues in the Home Office and asked them to consider making a statement or some official announcement to acknowledge and address the situation before it became untenable.

I was really pleased when it was announced that a statement would be made on Monday 3 June 1985. (Mondays have the benefit that not all MPs are present!) The announcement of the statement went on the screen just after noon and it was to be made by the Home Secretary.

The Secretary of State for the Home Department (the Rt Hon. Leon Brittan, MP) rose at 5.34 pm (ref: Col 52 in Hansard), it lasted for thirty minutes with questions from thirteen colleagues. The gist of the statement was as follows:

On 20 May I announced my future policy towards Sri Lanka Tamils who expressed a fear to return to Sri Lanka. In the week following that statement more than 500 Tamils arrived here seeking asylum. I decided that further measures were necessary to reduce the influx and, after consultation with the Secretary of State for Foreign and Commonwealth Affairs, I announced on 29 May the imposition of a visa requirement for Sri Lanka citizens, to come into effect the following day. The need for such a measure was demonstrated by the fact that 244 Tamils arrived on 29 May – a further 76 arrived shortly after the visas requirement came into effect.

He went on to say that if a Tamil failed the normal visa rules then he/she would only be granted a visa if they could demonstrate 'he is suffering severe hardship or through family links'.

The first Opposition Member questioned the departure from two important traditions, namely for the first time restrictions on a Commonwealth citizen and secondly a breach of the concept of asylum. Mr Brittan rejected the Commonwealth argument on the grounds that at least four Commonwealth countries, including India, required British subjects to have visas. On the question of asylum, Mr Brittan made the case that it was far better to have checks and interviews in Sri Lanka than having hundreds of people arriving daily in the UK. He then pointed out that no less than 1,260 Tamils had arrived in a four-week period between 1 and 28 May 1985.

The second questioner, Roger Sims, MP, Conservative was interesting. He, together with a Labour colleague, had been on a fact-finding mission to Sri Lanka to look at Human Rights issues in February that year. Their report was pretty scathing but the key paragraph stated:

> The proposals put forward in December 1984 appear to provide, if not a feasible solution, a very practical basis for negotiation. We deplore the precipitate manner in which they were rejected by the Tamil United Liberation Front.

I knew both these colleagues well and respected their findings but as Mr Sims highlighted to the Home Secretary, this was a serious and worrying internal problem and it would not be solved by us opening our doors to anything up to 3 million Tamils. The remaining questioners did not shed much new light on the subject except for Sir John Page who congratulated his many Tamil constituents in Harrow who had kept calm during the escalation of the troubles in their homeland.

My neighbour in Northampton North asked a further set of written questions on 12 June. Two facts of major consequence came out. First, India had admitted 100,000 Tamils from Sri Lanka but of course we do not know how many of those going to Tamil Nadu were young Tamils belonging to one of the terrorist groups to be given training. The other key point was that the Foreign Minister replying said: 'On 31 May President Jayawardene gave the UK High Commissioner in Colombo a formal assurance that no Tamils returning to Sri Lanka would be harassed or persecuted in any way.'

Reflecting on this whole issue today, I am confident Leon Brittan was correct in the actions he took.

During the summer recess I decided I would try to organise an All-Party visit to Sri Lanka for those who really did take an interest. As it happened my wife and I had already agreed to visit the Maldives in February 1986 and to spend four days' holiday at Bentota, so it was not too difficult to extend the trip by a few days to go to Colombo. I was privileged to have an hour-long session with President Jayawardene. We discussed how the UK Government and friendly parliamentarians could assist Sri Lanka in the challenges the country faced. Much of what we discussed was carried in a long interview covering nearly a page in the *Island* newspaper on 3 February.

Having returned home to the UK, I continued to watch developments with increasing concern as I did not want to see the Government of Sri Lanka, who was trying so hard to keep the peace, to be undermined. However, at the same time I also did not want to see large numbers of Tamils descending on the UK who were, in effect, economic migrants and who would put a strain on the UK immigration controls.

At the end of September, with Parliament back from summer recess, I had discussions with the High Commissioner Monerawela. I had been unable to put together a team in the time available so I agreed to go out to Sri Lanka on my own in mid-October on a short fact-finding visit. At around the same time, I was able to put some colour into the speech that the Rt Hon. Sir Geoffrey Howe, QC, MP made to the UN General Assembly on 23 September 1986. He had asked to see me when preparing his speech. I think he found our discussions helpful. He covered Sri Lanka on page 33 in a wide-ranging speech, which I felt showed Sri Lanka trying hard to move forward.

I then went on my short visit to Sri Lanka and, as always, worked hard and put in the hours. I met the President and key ministers and was fully briefed on the Political Parties Conference which had been just been held in Colombo. The basic objective of this conference was to bring together five committees to amend the Constitution to set up Provincial/ District Councils with an elected Chief Executive who would have the power of a minister over those agreed powers of devolution. The five committees could not agree. I was also brought up to date on India's policy towards Sri Lanka under Rajiv Gandhi. I had a positive discussion with Ronnie de Mel over his success in securing extra aid money which would enable the Samanalawewa power scheme to begin, and which would involve the UK contractor Balfour Beatty. I had a briefing on the second round of the talks between the Sri Lanka Government and the TULF.

Sadly, even in 2016, seven years after the war had ended, there were still Tamils trying to avoid the visa restrictions and claim asylum as economic migrants. Once the war was over Tamils who had their asylum rejected were sent back to Sri Lanka. The UK Government took particular care to make sure the High Commission in Colombo knew who was being returned and when they would arrive back in Sri Lanka. Despite all this there is still a steady number of Tamils trying to circumvent the UK's immigration rules, even going to the extent of self-harming, particularly with burns and thus claiming torture carried out in Sri Lanka. Claims of torture by the Sri Lanka authorities are regularly being made by Tamils seeking asylum in the UK. I have checked on this on my last three visits, the most recent being in 2017. On each occasion I have asked the Head of ICRC (International Committee of the Red Cross) if it had any evidence at all of torture as defined by the Geneva Convention and each time, despite the answer coming from a different person, the answer was the same and emphatic: 'No evidence of torture although some instances of heavy-handling.' Add to this the fact that those Tamils who are refused entry to the UK are each given a contact telephone number with the British High Commission if they face difficulty or harassment – no calls have been made as far as I am aware.

There is no better symbol of Sinhalese heritage than the Rock Fortress of Sigiriya. It has stood majestically through the centuries. Picture taken by the author from Sigiriya Rest House symbolising the beauty and tranquillity of the Rock Fortress.

CHAPTER
Seven

Peace Talks

Whilst questions were being asked and debated in the British Government and press throughout 1985 and 1986, the officials and the government in Sri Lanka were doing their best to navigate the events that were the cause of these debates. India, as the major regional power, had long viewed Sri Lanka as part of her sphere of influence, sometimes taking direct action that was perceived as helpful but at other times unhelpful. Mrs Indira Gandhi fell into the unhelpful category. She appears to have thought that the Tamils under Mrs Bandaranaike's Government were being discriminated against and in this she was correct. The result was that she would quietly, and under the radar, do all in her power to help the underdog, not least with the acceptance of the various Tamil Youth movements, including militant groups which by 1987 had expanded to six. They were: LTTE (Liberation Tigers of Tamil Eelam), TELO (Tamil Eelam Liberation Organisation), PLOTE (People's Liberation Organisation of Tamil Eelam), EROS (Eelam Revolutionary Organisation of Students), EPRLF Eelam's People's Revolutionary Liberation Front) and TELA (Tamil Eelam Liberation Army). Of course, there was a spin-off benefit to Mrs Gandhi's support that the 60 million population in Tamil Nadu would look to her party with favour at any general election.

Mrs Gandhi was assassinated in October 1984 by her own bodyguards. Rajiv Gandhi, her son, came to power and was a little more subtle. He was sworn in as Prime Minister the same day and elected as Leader of the Congress party a few days later. In December 1984 he led the Congress Party to a landside victory in the elections to the Lok Sabha. He made sure the Tamil groups being trained in India were monitored and, in a sense, kept under control. At the same time, he knew it was in no one's interest to have a broken state next door. Having viewed the success of the Victoria Dam opening alongside ever-escalating violence on the ground, India decided, in mid-1985, to broker talks with Sri Lanka, and in early July talks were held in India between President J.R. Jayawardene and Prime Minister Rajiv Gandhi.

These were quickly followed by four Sri Lanka lawyers, under the leadership of Dr Harry Jayawardene, QC, brother of the President, going to Delhi allied to which J.R.'s special envoy went to Madras where all the separatists had their headquarters. The next stage was to agree a ceasefire with the five key Tamil guerrilla groups which was achieved, coming into force on 31 July aided by the government stating their armed forces would be confined to barracks.

The location for the initial talks had been Thimphu, Bhutan in early July. They became known as The Thimphu Talks. On 13 July the Tamil delegation issued what became known as THE THIMPHU DECLARATION 1985, which had for the Tamil team four key elements:

1. Recognition of the Tamils as a nation.
2. Recognition of the existence of an identified homeland for the Tamils in Sri Lanka.
3. Recognition of the right of self-determination of the Tamil nation.
4. Recognition of the right of citizenship and the fundamental rights of all Tamils who look upon the island as their country.

It is interesting to read the opening statement made by Dr Jayawardene on 12 August. It runs to nine pages and goes into the issues raised in great depth and supported by facts and figures. I can see I have annotated my copy in places. Not surprisingly, the first three points were rejected as being incompatible with the Constitution of Sri Lanka or unrealistic as between one ethnic group and another. There was, however, acceptance of the fourth. Jayawardene went on to say there must be a complete renunciation of all forms of militant action, including the closing down of military camps. He concluded, and I quote from the copy I have had all these years in my possession: 'This is the only basis on which any settlement reached here can be implemented and peace restored to our country.'

After two rounds of discussion the talks broke down and the conflict restarted.

By now the Sri Lanka Government was slowly recognising that if it was not really careful it would be facing disaster. Earlier that year, in February 1985, President Jayawardene had established a new anti-terrorist unit and, more importantly, had agreed to a Joint Operations Command (JOC) to coordinate the activities of the army, navy and air force. To any of us who have served in the forces it seemed an obvious and logical objective, especially when dealing with terrorists, but it is one thing to set up a JOC but quite another to find someone to successfully run it with leadership and inspiration. Thankfully someone did have inspiration: the newly promoted Lieutenant General Cyril Ranatunga, later to become a close friend of mine. It was not just co-ordination that was needed but modern equipment was vital as well.

The UK and other Western nations were approached to supply equipment to the Sri Lanka Government. They had supplied considerable quantities in the past, albeit to a relatively small army. However, once again, as has so often happened, the Western nations shied away because of the previous riots and pressure from the diaspora. In the end Sri Lanka soon found out there were only three nations willing to help: China, Pakistan and Israel.

In his book, *From Peace to War, Insurgency to Terrorism*, General Ranatunga quotes from a meeting between J.R.'s son, Ravi Jayawardene, and Shimon Peres, Prime Minister of Israel. It had come to light that some of the Sri Lankan terrorists were being trained by the PLO (Palestine Liberation Organisation). Peres's response was that Israel and Sri Lanka had things in common: terrorists being trained by the same group and therefore the two countries had a shared enemy. Peres then instructed that Sri Lanka be given all possible help and this arrived in the form of Dvora attack boats, and later, aircraft. The same willingness to help came from the Chinese who, when asked, quickly sent armoured cars, tanks and T56 assault rifles.

General Ranatunga introduced two other initiatives that were important. He set up a school for officers and troops to learn Tamil. He must have been one of the first to recognise that Human Rights were an aspect of the law of war, even if terrorists ignore them. The mention of language training brings back happy memories of my days in Calcutta where five days a week I went with about six other young executives to learn Hindi from the *munshi* (teacher). Would that our Foreign Office was equally enlightened today. Secondly, he was the first Head of the Armed Forces to set up a 'Joint Operations Command' structure covering the Navy, Army and Air Force, leading to Operation Liberation One in 1987.

Slowly but surely the Sri Lanka armed forces were growing in numbers. By 1987 the army had increased its size to 1,740 officers and 24,913 other ranks. (In 1978 these figures were 496 officers and 8,489 other ranks.) And they were needed because the LTTE, now the dominant terrorist group, was ever more active. General Ranatunga writes in his book that his strategy to deal with the LTTE would require a full-scale assault with crack troops and a huge element of surprise. So, arose Vadamarachchi: Operation Liberation – ONE. A huge amount of intelligence-gathering was carried out, not least as Vadamarachchi was tucked away in the northern tip of the Jaffna Peninsula and was not only the LTTE Leader, Prabhakaran's, birthplace but also the headquarters for all the significant terrorist units including what was later to become the TULF (Tamil United Liberation Front). The operation was top secret: Minister Lalith Athulathmudali was only told just before the attack. Poor Lalith, such a good, personal friend and an inspired politician; one of the young generation of Sri Lankan leaders prematurely taken away by an LTTE bomb at a rally in Kirulapone.

The operation was launched on 26 November 1986 and involved over 5,000 troops. The 'Tigers' (LTTE) were reported to be running out of military supplies. They made an announcement that their demand for a separate state was negotiable. General Ranatunga's troops had all the Tiger hierarchy cornered without an escape route. All it would need was a week to ten days of pressure and they would be either dead or captured. Then the phone rang. It was President Jayawardene who stated that the Indian Government was exerting pressure on the Sri Lanka Government to halt the offensive and that relief supplies for the Tamils in the north were being be sent from Tamil Nadu in hired boats. One can imagine the reaction of both the military and the political leadership. Strong protests were lodged with the Indian High Commission regarding unsolicited help and the newspapers, copies of which I have seen, were up in arms.

The next day the President ordered a temporary halt to the operation as the Indian Air Force was bringing in food supplies. Temporary turned out to be for just two hours, as the whole operation was then halted.

The net result was that the one operation that would almost certainly have wiped out the LTTE menace failed because, against all international law, one country – India – chose to interfere with another country. Once again the West did nothing: there were no protests and no understanding of the implications of the interference. Had the operation not been stopped, I for one believe that would have been the end of the Tamil Tigers and the tragedy of the next twenty-one years would have been averted.

Sadly, the LTTE atrocities continued with attacks on both military and civilian targets. In April 1987 these acts of terrorism culminated when the LTTE detonated a powerful bomb at the Pettah bus stop during the rush hour, which killed 106 and injured over 200. Any of us who know the Pettah marvel that even more were not killed. Lessons had been learned and the authorities moved swiftly to prevent any repetition of the July 1983 riots. However, the situation continued to worsen because at almost the same time the LTTE was carrying out regular massacres of Sinhalese villages in what the Tamils claimed was their homeland, even though the Sinhalese had been there for generations.

I met Cyril Ranatunga most recently in February 2015 before I had decided to write this book. We reminisced about what might have been. We wondered, and continue to wonder, why President Jayawardene did not play for time and allow the operation of 1986 to succeed. Similar to the reaction to the 1983 riots, he seemed paralysed. Looking again at all my material it was clearly difficult to keep track of exactly what was happening on the ground, but I have always been clear in my view: India was wrong to interfere and would pay a heavy price.

CHAPTER
Eight

India: Intrusion or Relief of Jaffna?

Between 3.00 pm and 5.00 pm on 4 June 1987, Indian cargo planes, protected by Indian Mirage fighters, carried out a major air-drop which was claimed to be 25 tons of relief food and medical supplies for the people of Jaffna.

In truth, this was no real surprise as the Sri Lanka Navy had blocked the convoy of so-called relief ships coming from India as soon as it had reached Sri Lanka territorial water. President Jayawardene had been told in no uncertain terms by Prime Minister Rajiv Gandhi that under no circumstances would the military action against the Tamils be allowed to succeed.

Even for those of us who were keeping track of what was happening from afar, the issue was plain to see. We all knew Jaffna was surrounded by the Sri Lanka armed forces who were tightening the net on the terrorists who were running out of military supplies. A legitimate knock-on effect meant that civilians too were facing minor shortages but nothing like London in the early 1940s. India realised that she must act quickly or it would be possible that the terrorists would be defeated altogether, resulting in a backlash in Tamil Nadu, accompanied by possible major electoral losses to the Indian Government. It would be a huge dent in Indian prestige in terms of her hegemony control, not least with Pakistan breathing down her neck. The tension between Pakistan and India has always been, and continues to be, simmering just below the surface, primarily over the status of Kashmir which blew up again in early 2019. Additionally, Pakistan has in the past, and probably continues in the present, to supply some arms to Sri Lanka. In addition, there would be the international propaganda furore that India had allowed a 'Sinhalese' army to slaughter the minority Tamils – both freedom fighters and civilians.

I give some praise for the initiative of Rajiv Gandhi who, on 29 July 1987, decided to go to Colombo in person to sign the Indo-Lanka Accord.

The historic fort built by the Dutch surviving through the centuries until destroyed by the LTTE Tamil Tigers- now being faithfully rebuilt.

He arrived, metaphorically speaking, with all guns blazing: that is with an Indian naval flotilla standing by. At the Guard of Honour, a Sri Lanka rating tried to strike the Indian Prime Minister with the butt of his rifle: perhaps it was good thing that the guards only had blanks for a salute. Emotions about India's interventions were running high.

The Sri Lanka military Operation Liberation had already been called off earlier in June before the air-drop. Under the Accord all militant groups would have to surrender their arms within seventy-two hours of the cessation of hostilities. The other key elements of the agreement were:

- The Tamil language was to be given official status (something I had long advocated).
- Some power was to be devolved to the Northern and Eastern Provinces, which could later merge after a referendum (hugely contentious).
- Peace would be established in the Northern and Eastern Provinces and ensured by India sending a peace-keeping force called IPKF (Indian Peace Keeping Force) which duly arrived on 30 July.

There was rumoured to be a darker, murky element to the Accord that the LTTE would be funded by New Delhi so that it would have secure funding rather than having to rely on extortion of its own Tamil people and overseas illegal activities. Why anyone thought this was appropriate or might even work is beyond me (but I will return to the subject of terrorist finance in another chapter).

What was the immediate result? No Sri Lanka person – or, indeed, friend of Sri Lanka like myself – welcomed the Indian intrusion, so there was despondency all around. The Sri Lanka armed forces were totally demoralised but fortunately General Ranatunga was both professional and intelligent, and recognised that the Indians had come to do a job and he needed to co-operate with them. Some of the militants did disarm and the LTTE, in what is often considered the 'usual' way with terrorist groups, handed in its oldest and least useful weapons. Later, we learned that at the same time it was shopping for more modern weaponry in the international market.

Perhaps less predictable was the anti-Indian reaction in the south of the country. This was a violent uprising by the JVP (Janatha Vimukthi Peramuna). I had not expected it at all. I remembered the horror of the JVP rising when Mrs Bandaranaike was President. At that time, it was an all-out challenge to the economic policies of the President, which were undoubtedly causing great hardship to the poor, less well-off and non-hardline Buddhists. However, this was, I thought, different. Yes, hold rallies and hartals demonstrating disgust at the Indian intervention but the JVP had moved away from its Marxist roots and support for the Tamils to become more intolerant with a nationalist, politicised agenda. The Indian behaviour gave it a unique opportunity to ramp up its opposition to what it saw as an increasingly elitist and authoritarian government. I suspect it also realised the government was pretty weak and helpless in the face of the Indian arrival.

The JVP leader, Rohana Wijeweera, was noted for his passion and ruthlessness, so for the next two years the JVP set about a vicious campaign of killing thousands of people and crippling the country's economy by calling general strikes in a country where the unions were strong. The leaders were captured and executed by government forces in November 1989.

There ought to be a comparison between this JVP uprising with the one under Mrs Bandaranaike in May/June 1971. At that time, it was estimated that between 30,000 and 60,000 members of the JVP were killed or reported missing. In the later 1987–9 period the figures talked about were in the region of 60,000. These are huge numbers. Whether or not they are true, nobody knows. There was never any form of enquiry or independent report, neither by the Sri Lanka Government, the UN nor any Human Rights groups. I would like to draw a parallel with the casualty figures quoted at the end of the war in 2009. The UN, based on some statistical calculation, said Tamil civilian casualties were about 40,000. Much more refined analysis, which I shall look at later in the book, came to a consensus of 4,000 to 6,000. That is 10–15 per cent of the initial figure. Indeed, when the work on 'Missing Persons' is further down the track, I would not be surprised to find an even lower figure. Of course, relating these percentage figures back to the two JVP uprisings produce figures of 15,000 for each, which seems to tie up with some other material I have seen. Still, all told, these are ghastly numbers.

Important as the JVP backlash was, it still was not the first issue on every Sri Lankan mind. People were balancing the thought that India, in its Tamil Nadu region, had trained, armed and financed the separatist groups who were wreaking havoc on Sri Lanka, and was now forcing itself into the internal affairs of the country. Was India going to throw its weight around or was it genuinely going to be the catalyst for peace with a united Tamil community playing its true role in a unitary country of Sri Lanka?

For those of us watching from the UK and talking to friends in Sri Lanka from the main three groups – Sinhalese, Tamil and Muslim – no one knew. The Indian spokesman in Sri Lanka was their High Commissioner J.N. Dixit. From London I gained the impression that Mr Dixit was an outspoken man who insisted on being taken seriously. He was emphatic that Tamil civilians had to have full citizenship rights, which might well include a homeland and certainly included considerable devolution. He seemed to leave the impression that if the Sri Lanka Government did not move on devolution then there was a role for the LTTE that India might, indeed, support.

At the same time the IPKF Indian Armed Forces had arrived both in Jaffna and Trincomalee, primarily to disarm the LTTE led by Prabhakaran. This proved to be a challenging assignment as Prabhakaran was clearly outwitting the Indians, allied to the fact that India, in her wisdom, had decided to supply arms to some of the smaller separatist groups, presumably as a counterbalance to the LTTE.

When the news broke, it went down like a lead balloon, particularly with Prime Minister Premadasa who had come to power in December 1988. There is some evidence that the Indians at the highest level were losing faith with Prabhakaran. In the book *Intervention in Sri Lanka* by Harkirat Singh, there is a story that the Indian High Commissioner wanted Prabhakaran arrested or indeed shot when he next attended a meeting.

Who knows?

Although I suspect Prabhakaran knew what was afoot. It appears that the IPKF generals were trying to butter him up, almost treating him as an equal ally but all this did was strengthen the LTTE in its determination to lead the Tamil nation. They, the LTTE, played for time, which thankfully the top military men in India saw through, particularly as the LTTE was behind the anti-IPKF demonstrations. They IPKF then attempted to disarm the LTTE by force but failed miserably with the result of an all-out conflict in October 1987.

However, the well-trained, conventional army of India was no match for the experienced jungle-fighting, ruthless forces of the LTTE who ran rings round it. The frustration for the Indian Army was increasing and it was not long before the ordinary Tamil people complained about the Indians and accused them of Human Rights abuses. One must remember that during this time the Sri Lanka forces who could have helped were confined to barracks. It was not long before politicians in London could sense that the Indians were getting more and more unpopular with everyone, not least the newly elected President Premadasa.

In January 1989 President Premadasa demanded the IPKF's withdrawal. In April he came up with the bizarre policy of ordering the Sri Lanka Army to supply weapons to the LTTE and the TNA (Tamil National Army) in their fight against the Indians. It is true that alongside this the new President decided to open negotiations and to declare a unilateral ceasefire, which the Indians had to accept, thus probably losing them such initiative as they had. In April 1989 a positive response came from the guru of the Tigers in London, Anton Balasingham. Three rounds of talks with Sri Lanka's President followed between May and November, which I tried hard to follow although I did think it strange that Prabhakaran was not involved. However, through Balasingham's negotiations, the LTTE eventually acceded to Premadasa's wish that it form a political party to contest future elections for the North East Provincial Council. It must have seemed to Premadasa that he was making progress.

Indeed, the dice seemed to continue to roll Premadasa's way as Gandhi's Party was defeated in the Indian General Election in December 1989. The new Indian Prime Minister, V.P. Singh, decided to withdraw the IPKF from Sri Lanka and the last troops left on 24 March 1990. The whole sad and cavalier venture involving some 80,000 troops had resulted in over 1,100 soldiers being killed and maybe as many as 5,000 civilians dead, but it still left the threat of the LTTE alive and well. One can but wonder what would have been the effect on the future of Sri Lanka had its army been allowed to wipe out or capture the LTTE in June 1987 before the Indians intervened.

However, the so-called progress was really illusionary because the LTTE was busy eradicating the other rival Tamil groups and it is thought it was also re-arming. There were talks with the Sri Lanka Government headed by the Foreign Minister Hameed. Colombo reported progress but in the end the talks stalled because of the sensitive issue of dissolving the North East Provincial Council and amending the Sixth Amendment to the 1978 Constitution. This had been introduced by Jayawardene in response to the July 1983 riots and reaffirmed the unitary structure of the Sri Lanka state. As if this was not difficult enough, the Sri Lanka Minister of State for Defence demanded that before any elections could take place all LTTE weapons should be decommissioned. This was logical but never likely to be acceptable to the LTTE, not least as it was the President himself who had ordered the rearming of the LTTE against the Indians.

Sadly and ironically it was probably these arms that the LTTE used in the next tragedy in the Eastern Province, which started on 11 June 1990. It began with an argument between a Muslim youth LTTE supporter and a Sinhalese man. The youth was arrested, taken into custody and the police station was quickly surrounded by LTTE cadres. Soon, a dozen other police stations were also being besieged. Colombo, presumably not wanting to ignite a civil war, ordered the police to surrender to the LTTE. I doubt anyone in Colombo could have foreseen the tragedy that at least 600 police officers would be murdered in cold blood.

This was the end of any peace talks.

Moreover, this must be recorded as one of the greatest war crimes in the whole of the conflict between the Government of Sri Lanka and the Tamil Tigers.

No voter apathy in Sri Lanka. A myriad of candidates, names & symbols. Author's agent used to say: 'more colour Michael' – pity he never came to Sri Lanka.

CHAPTER
Nine

Democracy in Reality

I met Ranasinghe Premadasa on a number of occasions during my visits at the time of his presidency of 1989–93, and found him to be quite an astute politician. There was a mutual understanding and respect between us as we had both come into politics at a national level after a decent amount of time working in politics at a local level. He was ambitious and thrilled to have the opportunity to stand for President. He certainly wanted to do the right thing, which is why he invited foreign observers to his presidential election in December 1988 and the subsequent general election in February 1989, which I attended, with a contingent of five UK MPs from all parties.

As a British politician, I was brought up to expect general elections about every five years at the outside, with the actual decision at the behest of the Prime Minister. However, I emphasise 'at the outside' as the UK had two general elections in 1974: in February and in October. There have also been a number of other elections run on a short timeframe. The Coalition Government of 2010, with Mr Cameron as Prime Minister, decided to end all this by passing the Fixed Term Parliament Election Act in 2011, thereby hoping to ensure stability by agreeing a fixed five-year term. There was a get-out mechanism for emergencies and it was not long before such an emergency took place: Mr Cameron's government failed to win the Referendum on Europe in autumn 2016, resulting in a general election being held in June 2017, which was just over two years after the previous one. Yet another example of Cameron's failure to understand political reality.

I recount this as the 'Mother of Parliaments' is supposed to set an example in the pursuit of democracy. Clearly there is still much work to be done in our own system and in a host of different areas: the counting of votes, candidate safety, illegal publicity, voter impersonation or multiple registration, to name a few. I have experienced all of these in the two seats I have fought: Islington North in 1966 unsuccessfully and successfully in my marginal seat of Northampton South in 1974 when I went from a deficit of around 200 on the first count to a majority of 179 on the third count! I went on to hold this seat for just over twenty-three years until taken out by the tidal wave against the Conservative Party in 1997. I might add that little has changed, as it seems clear that in the 2017 General Election voter impersonation reached new heights. Death threats, illegal registration and illegal advertising and, for all I know, questionable reliable counts, were all still very much evident.

If one looks to Sri Lanka, then we see it does have strong democratic traditions. General elections have been held since 1931 based on a universal adult franchise (like the UK, whereby all adults over the age of eighteen have the right to vote without the discrimination of caste, class, colour, religion or gender), and voting is deeply embedded in the electors' psyche. Post-Independence there were regular general elections up until the one scheduled to take place in 1983. Indeed, one should record that Sri Lanka has never been a one-party state, as the opposition or alliance has been able to defeat the party in power.

However, J.R. Jayawardene decided in his wisdom that having triumphed in the provincial elections followed by a referendum in 1982, there was no need to have a general election as the people had already demonstrated their support for his party, the UNP (United National Party). At the same time, he decided that in order to manage the challenges of a deteriorating security situation, executive power was to be given to the President as Head of State, thereby downgrading the role of Prime Minster to, in effect, one of being Chief Operating Officer. The result meant that even if general elections were restored in 1989, Sri Lanka would have been eleven years without one: clearly not good for democracy. Moreover, the domination of an Executive President was always likely to continue unless some form of coalition took power as happened in 2015. But when writing this chapter in the summer of 2018 still nothing concrete has happened although President Sirisena said he would end the Executive Presidency when a new Constitution is agreed.

In fact, democracy did return in 1988. There were two elections: one for the presidency in December 1988 followed by a general election for Parliament on 15 February 1989. It was to the credit of Sri Lanka that international observers were invited to both. The presidential election observer group came from SAARC (South Asia Association of Regional Cooperation) countries, arriving just days before the vote. With the exception of India, these countries had no real experience of free and fair elections. Nevertheless, although the turnout was only 55.3 per cent against a norm of 80 per cent plus, the conclusion was that Premadasa was the winner despite the Opposition SLFP Sri Lanka Freedom Party/ JVP (Janatha Vimukthi Peramuna) and LTTE having fielded a common candidate. There were problems in places like Monaragala where forty-nine of the 215 polling stations did not function. This was due largely to the JVP demonstrations, which certainly would have annoyed voters, but as the JVP had a strong grip in these parts, the ordinary voter would not have been prepared to stick their head above the parapet.

I quote from the observers' report: 'The Group impressed by the strong commitment of the people of Sri Lanka to the electoral process as demonstrated by their participation in an election held in conditions which were far from normal.'

It would be remiss of me to ignore the background to the presidential election, which should go some way to explain the low turnout. Since 1973, the ruling UNP (United National Party) had been trying to find a political solution to meet the aspirations of the representatives of the Tamil people in relation to devolution but to do it within a Unitary State. All the while, the activities of the LTTE were steadily on the increase. The government continued with its objectives and, in October 1986, had held the Political Parties Conference (discussed in Chapter 6) but sadly then and even today no one ever seemed to be able to find a scheme of agreement. The failure of all the discussions in 1986 spilled over into more violence and intimidation, which continued right up to the presidential election in 1988. There is also no doubt that eleven years without any general election allied to 22–25 per cent unemployment and government cutbacks to meet the increased defence expenditure created a heady mix.

I have in my files a paper headed: 'Tentative list of Political Assassination in Southern Sri Lanka from 1 August 1987 to 15 October 1988'. It runs to fourteen pages. These were people (politicians) who were considered to be potential targets and seemed to focus on members of the UNP, the police and local leaders. This leads one to believe much of this horrific picture was due to the DJV (Patriotic People's Front) who had come out against the Indo-Lanka Accord and were not in favour of any devolution. In addition, there clearly was a link with the JVP, which was particularly strong in the south, and possibly the SLFP, as the aims were almost identical.

The result was a formidable alliance of left-wing parties to take on the UNP. I should remind readers that it might have been all so different had Vijaya Kumaratunga, Founder and Leader of the Sri Lanka Mahajana Party (SLMP – Sri Lanka People's Party) not been gunned down by the DJV in February 1988. Sadly, I never met him but I am conscious he was hugely popular.

Against this background one has to ask why Mrs Bandaranaike did not win, as leader of this left-wing alliance. She petitioned the Supreme Court, alleging general intimidation, thereby preventing people from voting; non-compliance with provisions of election law to ensure a free and fair election thus preventing the majority of the electors listed in certain districts from electing the candidate they preferred. The electoral districts referred to covered no less than thirty-four pages of the petition. Reading this submission again as I did in August 2017, it is pretty hair-raising.

The result declared by the Commissioner of Elections was as follows:

Abeygunasekera	235,719	4.63 per cent
Bandaranaika	2,289,860	44.95 per cent
Premadasa	2,569,199	50.43 per cent

A reader might well ask whether Mrs Bandaranaike was not indeed right. However, let me recount what happened to me as an official observer to the second election for the National Parliament a few weeks later on 15 February 1989, with the results by district broadly reflecting the same result as the presidential election.

Observers of the general election were invited with very little notice, much like the observers of the presidential election, which one can assume was a deliberate decision, with the hope of reducing the amount of violence and intimidation of voters, not to mention the threat of murder of candidates. I was invited to lead a delegation of five All-Party MPs from the UK. We were notified on 1 February that a group had to be set up by 3 February (no time at all!), to be briefed by the Sri Lanka High Commissioner in London on 8 February and to fly out on 10 February for the election taking place on 15 February.

Luckily for me two factors assisted my task and helped overcome the extreme shortage of time to understand what had gone on in the campaign leading to Election Day.

First, I had received a letter from a close Sri Lankan friend living in London expressing his concern around both elections, particularly regarding intimidation. He felt strongly and I quote: 'The State's Forces are using ordinary policing controls to hamstring the SLFP's election campaign.' He went on to say that Premadasa was banking on the SLFP being terrorised out of voting, that UNP followers and others would settle for that as the price of being left free to advance their material welfare. Strong stuff, indeed. He finished his letter with the following message that has been a guiding light for me in my many years of trying to help Sri Lanka. He wrote:

Safe journey: enjoy yourself; think back to the Ceylon you once knew, ask how best you could contribute to Ceylon getting back to the values and practices of those times.

Secondly, on arrival we received the most thorough briefing I have ever had and I pay tribute to the initiative of the Commissioner of Elections of Sri Lanka, Mr Chandrananda de Silva, who explained the dizzyingly complicated situation to us, a group of eighteen official observers. We were a mix of experienced politicians, ambassadors, judges, attorney generals and ministers from the UK, USA, India, Pakistan, Bangladesh, Egypt, the Philippines, Nepal, Uruguay, Zambia and Algeria. Mr de Silva went to great trouble to explain the election procedures and ensured we met the leaders of the contesting political parties and alliances. We were briefed on the administrative and security arrangements, including the particular challenges in the north and south. We then had separate sessions with the leaders or representatives of each political party, listening to their concerns. We asked questions, easier for someone like myself as an active UK politician who knew Sri Lanka quite well. There was the added element of this being the first election in Sri Lanka to use the proportional representation system: Our group noted in our report:

All the parties commented on the fact that for most of the voters this would be the first time they would be voting in a national election under a proportional representation system. They would have to mark on the ballot paper not only a vote for the party of choice, but also indicate preferences for three out of a panel of candidates. This was likely to result in a number of votes being spoiled.

Between us, we were to cover 229 polling stations in twenty of the twenty-two electoral districts. I was allocated Kegalle and Ratnapura, both of which I knew quite well from previous visits. We had a Press Conference on the 13th and set off early on the 14th, meeting up at Kegalle Rest House where I was to stay with returning officers, security personnel and members of the political parties.

The next morning I was up at 6.00 am and after a wonderful breakfast of fried eggs, was ready for the road and a very long day ahead. I had decided to split the day and to spend the morning and early afternoon in Kegalle District followed by Ratnapura District for the rest of afternoon and 'the Count'. There was a schedule of visits to polling stations but in each district I changed two so they could not all be fixed! In reality, it was an unnecessary precaution, but you never know.

Thirty years later, what do I remember? Two things stand out.

First, the incredible enthusiasm of people to vote: often walking miles and standing in line quietly until it was their turn. I spoke to many of them, as their English was quite good.

Secondly, each candidate had been issued with five repeater shotguns for their own protection. On my travels I met several candidates. They were usually in one of a convoy of two vehicles, each bedecked with banners and loud speakers and guys really riding shotgun. Totally bizarre. I suppose it was necessary given the number of killings that had taken place.

I found the whole experience fascinating: ranging from voters having to put their finger into a pot of purple indelible ink to prevent multiple voting (quite a thought for the UK) to political processions taking place before my very eyes (supposedly illegal), complete with a hub-bub and noise which was deafening. Despite all this, on the whole the election seemed to go smoothly with just a few minor hiccups. In Ratnapura I witnessed one of the parties seeking to escort the ballot box but the police saw them off. I was fascinated to see they count in fifties and bundles of ten, making 500 in each bundle, unlike the UK where we count in twenty-fives with four bundles making a bundle of one hundred.

I stayed to watch the boxes arrive safely, viewed the counting and the cross-checking, and spoke to the party members who were watching the count and seemed in good heart. I decided not to wait until the early hours for the declaration of the result. Even so, it was past midnight when I returned to the rest house. Remarkably, I still have my notes of the day.

Next day, 16 February, a more leisurely breakfast was followed by an hour of going through my notes and drafting my report, then back to Colombo for a lunch meeting with my old friend Robin Talwatte, Chairman of the Bank of Ceylon, who was really despondent about the economic situation facing the country but pleased that President Premadasa had returned the country to democracy.

During the afternoon the British MPs had a meeting with the UK High Commissioner, David Gladstone, where we recounted our experiences and gave him a copy of our report. To our amazement he stated that he had been into a couple of polling stations where he had seen a huge amount of abuse, not least with the use of party tellers on the premises. He indicated he would be sending a report to Her Majesty's Government in UK stating the election was really no more than a put-up farce discriminating against the Opposition. We were amazed, tried to explain the legitimacy of tellers and stated we disagreed.

At 5.00 pm all the members of the Observer Group met in the Conference Room of the Renaissance Hotel. Each of us had submitted our report within a framework provided by the Election Commissioner. Each of us gave an oral summary. I found the most fascinating to be that of my colleague Dr Michael Clarke, MP who had been to the deep south around Hambantota, the stronghold of the JVP. Here democracy sadly had not prevailed. Voters had been prevented from reaching polling stations by tyres set on fire and wooden strips with nails blocking roads.

There was also clear evidence of ballot box stuffing, with more voting slips than electors and all for one candidate. All much more interesting than my experience! The north and east were not perfect either but even there a reasonable turnout had been achieved. After our reports we had dinner whilst a draft report was prepared.

The concluding observations were ready by 8.30 pm, which we went through carefully. The overall turnout was 63.96 per cent, lower than the historical 77–87 per cent, but better than the presidential election. Bearing in mind the very low turnout in the south of no more than 20 per cent and the atmosphere of violence, threats and intimidation in certain areas, the Observers thought the turnout a significant achievement.

I still have a copy of our final report, which was later published by the Elections Commissioner. Our concluding paragraph read:

> Despite the qualifications mentioned above, it is the opinion of the Observers that by and large the Parliamentary Election was free and fair in most areas. However, the Group is concerned at the malpractices reported in some areas and the widespread climate of violence and intimidation both of which need to be eliminated. It is the Group's firm belief that the people and authorities of Sri Lanka share this concern, given their own strong commitment to maintaining the highest traditions of democracy.

Even now I take a deep breath to think I arrived in Colombo at 7.35 am on Monday 13 February and was back in London at 10.15 on Sunday 19 February and the events we had witnessed. I produced my own Press Release on 17 February, which was issued in Colombo and London. My conclusion:

> Sri Lanka now has a new Parliament of 225 MPs of whom 125 are UNP, the present Government and 100 in opposition, a healthy mix. Democracy has survived; now the challenge is to tackle terrorism in the South and thereby begin to return this beautiful country to normalcy.

Once I was back in Parliament in the UK I asked to see the Foreign

Secretary, the Rt Hon. Douglas Hurd, MP. I gave him a copy of our report and expressed my consternation that our High Commissioner had chosen to interfere in a General Election in a friendly country. Furthermore, I felt sure the Sri Lanka Government would be lodging a protest, which it subsequently did. I made it clear that in my opinion that Mr Gladstone should be recalled. Mr Hurd listened carefully but stated firmly there could be no immediate recall. However, some months later he was recalled and appears to have retired.

Looking back now, I still maintain my views from the time: that credit should be given to President Premadasa for having the guts to hold the elections despite all the difficulties. And there were legitimate difficulties as I have explained. However, these elections were a major stepping-stone to normalcy being restored, not least due to the hundreds of government workers, such as Mr de Silva, who were deeply committed to restoring democracy to Sri Lanka.

This bridge was 257.4ft long and was destroyed by the LTTE. After Operation Kiniheera VIII which began on 29 December 2000, the 5 Field Engineer Regiment of the Sri Lanka Army reconstructed it and was opened on 10 January 2001.

CHAPTER
Ten

Despondency All Round

Reflecting on the decade from 1990 through to 2000 and the following couple of years, my overriding memory is one of deep sorrow, not only at what was happening to the country I loved but also at the lack of understanding for Sri Lanka's plight shown by the West.

The decade started with high hopes, with the election of a new president, President Premadasa, and a newly elected Parliament. The IPKF (Indian Peace Keeping Force), which had originally arrived to rehabilitate the LTTE by undertaking the disarmament and demobilisation of all the Tamil dissidents had been called home. Sri Lanka was finally free from foreign intervention.

However, the IPKF had totally failed: indeed, if anything it had strengthened the LTTE. India had not only lost significant numbers of security personnel but also its standing in the international community. In addition, India was now hated by just about every faction of Sri Lanka society. Another significant blow came at 10.20 pm on 21 May 1991 when Rajiv Gandhi was out campaigning in Tamil Nadu where he had been instrumental in encouraging the training of the various Tamil dissident groups from Sri Lanka. We politicians all categorise the places we canvass in terms of potential support, as: safe, borderline, unknown or really difficult. I had a death threat from the IRA in the second election of 1974 which I was advised to take seriously, so my agent and I revised our canvassing schedule, leaving out a part of Northampton known for its Irish sympathisers. I suppose Gandhi felt the opposite, being with friends and allies whom he had supported and helped. He was in Sriperumbudur meeting the party faithful. Somehow a young woman avoided being screened by metal detectors. She went up to Gandhi to place a sandalwood garland around his neck and then, as is the tradition, bent before him to touch his feet. As she did so she detonated the bomb killing Rajiv and sixteen others, as well as herself. The assassin was a Tamil Tiger named Dhanu.

Revulsion was felt worldwide, including in the UK, where at last the government began to understand the true threat of the Tamil Tigers (however, it took another ten years before the UK Government actually took the step of proscribing the LTTE in 2001 – surprisingly four years after the USA proscribed them).

The hope in Sri Lanka was that the LTTE would work with the Premadasa Government but as has already been illustrated in the previous chapter, that hope was soon dashed by the cold-blooded murder of over 600 policemen who had surrendered in the Eastern Province on 11 June 1990.

Worse was to follow with what was termed Eelam War II.

It began with the Tamil Tigers systematically eliminating government military outposts in the north through a viscous campaign of murders. Then, in August 1990 they butchered more than 300 Muslims, 120 of whom were at prayer in a mosque. Then, in October, Tiger forces 'ethnically cleansed' the whole of Jaffna Town of its 72,000 Muslim community. They were given less than a day's notice – for some it was as little as three hours. The women were forced to give up their jewellery and money. Every Muslim was removed with no thought for the elderly, sick, pregnant or dying.

This was true ethnic cleansing.

Slowly but surely the Tigers were defeating garrison after garrison and by April 1991 they were besieging the Elephant Pass base: the narrow strip of land controlling entry to the Jaffna Peninsula. I knew the area a little from my work days in 1963. I visited it again on my 2017 trip where there is now a small museum with a book of remembrance for all government forces killed in the battles that followed over Elephant Pass. I signed the book and as I did so I reflected on the hundreds of young Sri Lanka army personnel killed by the Tigers, which they claimed was in their bid for devolution but of course that really was not it at all. It was their pure neo-socialist revolutionary ethnic ideology to create a separate state. They had no interest in a democratic way of life. Much of the Tigers' ideology was aided and abetted by British citizen and Tamil, Anton Balasingham, together with his Australian wife who later was the mastermind, recruiter, trainer and leader of the Tamil Tiger child soldiers, 40 per cent of whom were girls.

The killings did not just affect the army and police. On 1 May 1993 President Premadasa was addressing a May Day Rally when a suicide bomber approached and blew both of them up. He was succeeded for a brief period by D.B. Wijetunga on an interim basis. I had actually met him on my holiday visit in January, little thinking he would have to take over the reins. He seemed to me a thoughtful man who could give good support to probably my closest Sri Lankan friend at the time, Gamini Dissanayake, the chosen UNP candidate for the forthcoming presidential election in November 1994. Gamini had stayed at my house in Sandy, Bedfordshire in 1980 at the time we were putting together our plan of campaign to get Sri Lanka cricket elected to the ICC: a campaign that was successful in 1981.

1994 proved to be similar to 1988/9, with two elections held within just a few months, namely a general election in the August followed by a presidential election in the November. The UNP (United National Party) had been in power for decades and in my view there was a certain amount of disillusion around. Chandrika Kumaratunga led the SLFP (Sri Lanka Freedom Party), campaigning on a peace platform at the general election. She did not win an overall majority but persuaded some left-wing parties to join a coalition with her as Prime Minister. True to her word she initiated an approach to LTTE leader Prabhakaran with a view to opening talks.

A first round of talks was held in Jaffna (controlled by the LTTE) on 13 and 14 October 1994. Just ten days later, on 23 October, a bomb at a UNP rally killed the entire leadership of the UNP, including the presidential candidate Gamini Dissanayake. Sri Lanka could ill afford the killing of dynamic young men like Gamini and Lalith Athulathmudali. These were the future leaders of the UNP and probably of Sri Lanka; certainly no one else in the UNP has since then had the charisma or stature to really give the country suitable leadership.

The presidential election duly went ahead and Kumaratunga won a massive 62 per cent of the vote, taking over the presidency on 12 November 1994. Following an intensive effort, a Declaration of Cessation of Hostilities, with a structure to monitor its implementation, was signed on 2 January 1995.

I had made a private visit to Sri Lanka in September 1994. I say private as by then I was Chairman of Ways and Means and First Deputy Speaker with the result that I was not able to take part in frontline politics for the years 1992–7. This did not help Sri Lanka's cause. Nevertheless, during this visit, I did meet the leadership of both the UNP and the SLFP, thereby maintaining political balance if challenged in either Colombo or London. Whilst I thought Gamini would make an excellent President, I was also impressed by Kumaratunga, who clearly had that gift of appealing to ordinary people despite coming from the upper classes.

The position of Chairman of Ways and Means goes back to the Restoration of the Monarchy in 1688 and I would like to take a moment to explain its origins. The Speaker at the time had been closely involved in the negotiations to bring William and Mary to the UK from Holland. Even in those days MPs were wary about giving the Speaker control over the 'Money' (i.e. Ways and Means), so they elected a senior MP to be responsible for the budget and all matters financial. It has remained so until today despite the Rt Hon. Betty Boothroyd, MP suggesting to me when she was Speaker that it was anachronistic. My response was that I was not prepared to be the one to change this important tradition: she backed off and I was privileged to be the 58th Chairman of Ways and Means.

Although James Hill, MP who had taken over the Chairmanship of the All-Party Group in late 1992 was an assiduous MP, he did not have the depth of understanding about Sri Lanka to enable him to put pressure on the UK Government to help the country, particularly over stopping the illegal financing of the LTTE.

Despite the hope that came with the New Year agreement, it soon became clear that Prabhakaran wanted much more than a declaration. He wanted real devolution in both the north and the east, in effect Eelam. He was not interested in Kumaratunga's proposals to restore the infrastructure of the north, stating he would do that once Eelam was granted, which was an impossible demand for Kumaratunga. The talks broke down and the ceasefire would end on 19 April 1995.

Sadly, I found I was not in a position to persuade the weak UK Government to call in Balasingham and put real pressure on him. Actually, Mr Major's Government itself looked under threat. The Labour Party sensed an election was not far off and decided to do all they could to support the Tamils as they were concentrated in key marginals.

Kumaratunga could be a fiery lady who would not sit back bemoaning failure. So it was to be with her handling of Prabhakaran. With the ceasefire gone she decided to take the fight to him with a policy called 'War for Peace'. Her armed forces set about re-taking Jaffna, which they did in July 1995: freedom after ten years of LTTE rule. However, the LTTE forced over 350,000 people to evacuate the city and march to the Vanni. Jaffna was left a ghost city.

The LTTE was not going to take this sitting down. It retaliated in July 1996 with what it termed its 'unceasing waves', overwhelming the Mullaittivu base. It also extended its activities to the more heavily populated urban areas, setting off a bomb at the Central Bank in Colombo, which killed eighty and injured over a thousand. This was followed with an attack on the Colombo World Trade Centre in 1997 and then a truck bomb which damaged the Temple of the Tooth in Kandy, the most sacred of Buddhist shrines. This was the final straw.

The Sri Lanka Government moved to outlaw the LTTE and brand it a terrorist organisation, which, in my view, it always had been. An appeal was made to get the LTTE proscribed around the world. The USA, under Bill Clinton's presidency, had already responded in 1997 but the UK government under Tony Blair refused.

1998 should have been a year of celebration for Sri Lanka, celebrating fifty years since Independence. Everyone tried hard to make it so and a lavish brochure, Sri Lanka Today, was produced, of which I have a copy. It includes a sombre message from President Kumaratunga, although she concludes with the words: 'Independence is much more than throwing off the shackles of foreign rule ... as committed democrats we must face the challenges placing our trust in the wisdom and strength of the people.' It is also interesting to read Prime Minister Blair's message, which focuses almost exclusively on trade opportunities in South Asia [his words]. Not a single word of praise or congratulation to Sri Lanka on its milestone. Indeed, the two words 'Sri Lanka' do not even appear.

The severity of the challenges faced by Sri Lanka from the now terrorist organisation LTTE was underlined in a powerful speech given by Lakshman Kadirgamar, Minister of Foreign Affairs of Sri Lanka on 15 April 1998 at the Royal Institute of International Affairs, Chatham House in London. I was given a copy of the speech. Over the years I have been to a number of important and moving speeches there, but this one held nothing back in highlighting the development of the threat of terrorism to the whole world. I sat transfixed by this long and detailed exposition and have no hesitation in reproducing the key paragraph. It read as follows [copied directly from the speech]:

> The struggle for Independence was bloodless. We have remained friends, staunch friends, close friends for fifty years. That is why the question of the role of the LTTE, unarguably the most effective, ruthless terrorist organisation that we have seen this century. Its role in the United Kingdom in relation to Sri Lanka, is one that gives my people, our people very great, pain of mind. I cannot tell you how deeply grieved and sad the Sri Lankan people have been in recent years when they have seen bomb after bomb has gone off in our cities killing, maiming, hundreds, thousands of people; a response from the United Kingdom that has been far less positive than we would expect from a close and valued friend. How galling it is to our people, I must tell you, to see, the day after a bomb goes off, a flurry of communication supporting the brave LTTE issued from 211 Catherine Road in London (Balasingham's Office). I do not say for one moment that what happens there at 211 Catherine Road or elsewhere is something which the Government of the United Kingdom, past or present, connives at or condones. But I do say that there is a degree of passivity in its reaction to the role that this terrorist organisation plays in this country that causes very great distress to the Sri Lanka people. I hope in the very near future, the Government of the United Kingdom will adopt such legislative measures as are necessary to honour the international treaty obligations that it has undertaken by virtue of the newly adopted United Nations Convention on the Suppression of Terrorist Bombings.

Sadly, Kadirgamar's wishes, himself a Tamil, fell on very stony ground; all the more surprising as the Good Friday Agreement which, it was hoped, would bring an end to IRA terrorism had only been signed a few months earlier. We are led to reflect that the governing Labour Party only won certain London seats on the Tamil vote. Indeed, one of the junior ministers in the Foreign Office sat for one of the seats where the Tamil vote was dominant.

Later that year I was invited to join a Commonwealth Parliamentary Association team to Sri Lanka, although not as its leader. On my return in early December, I wrote to the UK Foreign Secretary, Robin Cook, MP who had been my pair in the House of Commons for many years. I stated: 'It does occur to me that at some point we in the UK may be asked to help find a solution to the Tamil Tiger problem. Maybe we could be asked to provide a member for a Peace and Reconciliation Commission?' I then went on to say that all I wanted to place on record was that I would be more than happy to help in any way possible, not least as I now had the time, the commitment and knowledge of Sri Lanka and – having been Deputy Speaker – the patience.

A reply came in early January and the key sentence stated: 'We stand ready to provide further help if asked. If we are asked to play a role, we shall certainly bear in mind your valuable offer.'

I still have three pages with my thoughts of how to explore different forms of devolution and weave them into a Peace and Reconciliation Commission. I also see a note that time was not on our side as the LTTE was already very active in no less than fifteen countries.

I also wrote to the President of Sri Lanka, Chandrika, and received a charming letter back on 7 January 1999:

> I deeply appreciate your concern about Sri Lanka and your efforts to restrain LTTE's fundraising activities. I also thank you for the kind thoughts expressed about me and the Government. Such kind words are a great source of encouragement to me.

However, the attacks by the LTTE continued and were unrelenting. Even in the short few weeks between my return to the UK and receiving responses to my letters, more attacks were carried out in Sri Lanka. On 18 December there was an assassination attempt on the President. She survived, but lost an eye, and another twenty-one people were killed and 113 were left severely injured. This was followed by another bomb on 5 January outside the office of the Prime Minister. I could fully understand

Chandrika's sense of nervousness about what the year 2000 might bring and I wondered how I could help. I decided to speak in the House of Lords debate on 'The International Situation' on 12 January. I spoke for ten minutes, describing in graphic detail the attempted assassination of the President and recalled the successful assassinations on her husband and father. It was quite a long speech but it was delivered from my heart. The main message was to urge the International community to put pressure on the LTTE supremo Velupillai Prabhakaran to renounce violence and hold talks with the Sri Lanka Government. I pointed out the varying attempts to persuade Prabhakaran through, amongst others, The Secretary General of the Commonwealth, but he never actually met him face to face which, in my judgement, was no way to negotiate. I pointed out the huge geographical spread of the LTTE and the atrocities its followers undertook around the world. I finished with an appeal for international action to put pressure on Prabhakaran to hold talks and to be personally involved. Finally, I could not resist challenging the UK Government to close down the LTTE office in Camden. The full text of my speech is in the Appendix (Appendix II).

There is a saying in London that whilst you are waiting for a bus suddenly two or more appear together. It is a bit like this with speeches. No sooner had I spoken in the House of Lords than I received an invitation for my wife and I to go to Colombo as guests of The Sri Lanka-United Kingdom Society and for me to make the keynote speech at the Colombo Hilton on 18 February.

The full text is in the Appendix (Appendix III) but I quote from the last page: 'It is my earnest wish that these few but deeply thought about views might ignite a helpful move to peace. Peace is like deep sleep after many months of interrupted nights. Peace is the culture of the Buddha and Hinduism and Christianity and Allah.' I then listed the challenges, drew some analogy with the Maastricht debate that took twenty-five days and then said that as Chairman all I could do was to keep calm, be patient but make some progress. I recommended to my listeners that they too would need to keep calm, be patient and try to make progress by finding the art of judicious compromise. I finished: 'How joyful it would be if what is said to be the true Millennium, that is 1 January 2001, were the announcement of peace in Sri Lanka.'

On the flight back to the UK I thought it was about time I confronted Mr Balasingham in person. I also thought I ought to try to keep my government on side. I approached the office of Peter Hain, the minister responsible for Sri Lanka. A meeting was set up for 7 March at the Foreign & Commonwealth Office. At the meeting, I gave him a brief history of my involvement with Sri Lanka, including my latest visit and told him what I thought the options were that he faced with the LTTE and raised the prospect of my having a role to play in any future involvement to work towards peace. At the end of the meeting I mentioned I would try to see Balasingham. Peter responded that I should let Mr Balasingham know that we had met and re-emphasise the importance of timing and that now was the time to negotiate. Peter saw no point in coming to Sri Lanka unless he could meet Prabhakaran himself. His background and involvement in the freedom struggle for South Africa should be viewed positively by Prabhakaran, and lessons could be learnt from that experience. Peter also indicated that my speech on devolution had, in his view, the kernel of a solution.

We then discussed the LTTE and I painted the picture as I saw it of its near-worldwide coverage, its illegal methods of fundraising and its success at infiltration through bogus asylum seekers. Our strategy would be to encourage the leaders of the LTTE to act on their own account to stop these illegal activities and if they did, we the UK would put real pressure on Sri Lanka to negotiate properly.

I duly wrote to Mr Balasingham. I then met him and he was cordial, deeply non-committal but thanked me and indirectly the minister, Peter Hain. He said he would talk to his colleagues. Sadly, that was the first and last time I met and talked to him: it was as if my initiative had vanished into thin air.

On the military front matters were also not good. In April 2000, Elephant Pass fell; then Jaffna looked as if it might fall but somehow the army held on. Worse was to come and by mid-2000 the Tigers claimed control of 70 per cent of the Northern and Eastern Provinces. In July the following year there were more audacious attacks, including one on Colombo International Airport where just twenty LTTE cadres destroyed no less than eight frontline attack aircraft and also blew up three SriLankan Airlines jets and badly damaged a further two. This really hit the headlines in the UK media particularly on television.

On the political front matters were not easy with a general election scheduled to take place on 10 October 2000. The PA (People's Alliance) coalition of Chandrika won but it was still six seats short of an overall majority.

I had been approached in September to lead a small UK delegation of All-Party, electorally experienced MPs to witness the general election. Alongside us was a team from other Commonwealth countries including Canada, Cameroon and Trinidad. Although we had hoped for a party of four, in the event we were just three: Tom Cox, MP, Andy Love, MP (both Labour) and myself, Conservative. We were all active members of the All-Party Group for Sri Lanka. Tom Cox and I had been observers at the Parliamentary Election in February 1989 and both knew Sri Lanka well. We arrived on 4/5 October, were briefed on the morning of the 6th, set off for our respective Districts and returned late on 10 October. I chose exactly the same Districts as 1989, which were Kegalle and Ratnapura. We had a checklist of the problems encountered in 1989. It would be tedious to go through our report in detail but the main points we noted were:

1. No election was possible in Jaffna, Vanni, Trincomalee and Batticaloa due to terrorist activity. This removed approximately 11 per cent of the electorate; just over 1.3 million potential voters.
2. There were no complaints about gangs intimidating voters and no weapons in sight at the polling stations.
3. There was evidence of violence affecting actual voter turnout in the run-up to Election Day.
4. We were entirely satisfied with the polling stations, voter security and better security over the ballot boxes and ballot papers.
5. The count went well with strict verification of votes cast.
6. There was abuse of banners, posters, etc, and some People's Alliance candidates appear to have used government transport.

Our conclusions were, and I quote: 'On the question of voting procedure we were deeply impressed by the improvement. The administration of the democratic process was sound. We were deeply impressed at the commitment of the ordinary person to vote.'

Clearly Chandrika and her People's Alliance party coalition were less impressed at their loss of a majority.

On our travels we had picked up rumours of the probable contact between the Norwegians, the government and the LTTE, with Balasingham as its political guru. I delved a little deeper and was told the Norwegians had opened an official embassy in late 1996. As major aid donors, they saw their role as a conduit for a negotiated settlement but it was not until January 1998 that the project had achieved a degree of lift-off under the new interlocutor, Erik Solheim.

It was in late 1998 that Solheim had his first contact with the LTTE and that was in Paris. He had been told by the LTTE that the reason he was chosen was because he had shown interest in Sri Lanka's problems and was considered a reliable conduit to Norway's Foreign Minister. It was made clear to him that the chief negotiator for the LTTE would be Anton Balasingham, based in London. All this seemed reasonable but then a problem was disclosed; namely that Balasingham was ill and hiding in the Vanni. Solheim realised that it would be nigh on impossible to get Balasingham out of the country without at least tacit acceptance by the government.

The delicacy of the project meant that President Chandrika and Foreign Minister Kadirgamar had to handle it themselves. Understandably they decided Balasingham could only leave for medical treatment if there were reciprocal, helpful actions by the LTTE. I do not know what demands were offered but they were rejected by the LTTE. Whether they were appropriate in a humanitarian issue is now history but the word 'humanitarian' for a man like Balasingham seems a bit rich to me.

Anyway, by November matters had reached an impasse. The LTTE made its own arrangements and Balasingham was smuggled out of Sri Lanka on 23 January 1999 to Bangkok, and after a couple of months he turned up in London. It then transpired that despite the medical attention in Bangkok, he was now in need of a kidney transplant. The Norwegians obliged again with an offer of an operation in Oslo. A donor was found in Sri Lanka and airlifted to Norway via Amsterdam. Apparently, after the operation in February 2000 the young donor was, by arrangement with the British authorities, transferred to the UK where I believe he probably still resides. Solheim, in his notes, says: 'The British were helpful as always'! [my exclamation mark].

The peace initiative from the Sri Lanka government's point of view went all the way back to 1995 when G.L. Peiris, a former Foreign Minister, produced a reform package which included wide-ranging suggestions on self rule. I certainly was aware of this document and its broad outlines, although they were rejected by the LTTE as they had been produced by just one side; nevertheless, the feeling in Colombo was that progress was being made and this was the view of the Norwegians.

Every time I went to Colombo I met the Norwegians but never came away with a clear picture of their role or their intentions. The 1999 Presidential Election called a halt to operations, not least the attempt by the LTTE on Chandrika's life. What amazed the world, myself included, was that the day before the election Chandrika announced on the BBC that Norway was the preferred peace negotiator. Her message was clear that she wanted peace straight away. Whether this was a tactical move to scupper Ranil Wickremesinghe's chances is open to debate but it worked. Immediately after the election the Norwegians were asked to facilitate, which they tried to do up until the presidential election when Ranil Wickremesinghe was elected Prime Minister on 9 December 2001.

Meanwhile, throughout 2000 and 2001 I continued with my own strategies at home in the UK. First, I wanted to keep up pressure to get the LTTE proscribed. On 19 February 2001 I tabled a written question asking: 'Whether it is the intention to proscribe the Liberation Tigers of Tamil Eelam under the terrorism act 2000?' The answer stated that the Terrorism Act would be brought into force on 19 February but by way of a draft order listing which organisations should be added to Schedule 2. It went on to state that it would only come into force following debate and approval in both Houses. Rumour had reached me that it did not include the LTTE so I contacted the minister responsible just to ensure it did. I was told I would not be disappointed. The list was published on 28 February and number 11 was: 'Liberation Tigers of Tamil Eelam: terror group fighting for a separate state in Sri Lanka'. Success at last, but it had taken three years of hard lobbying.

I also raised another issue on 20 February about the question of illegal economic migrants. I asked:

My Lords, is the Minister aware that it is no exaggeration to say thousands come here from Sri Lanka? Among those thousands are probably several hundred who are supporters of the LTTE, the terrorist group which imposes extortionate demands on legitimate Sri Lankans living in this country. Will the Minister encourage his Department (The Home Office) to redouble its efforts to ensure that those Sri Lankans staying here illegally are returned to Sri Lanka, not least because welcome progress is now being made towards peace in that Country?

The answer referred to the new terrorism legislation, stating that officials always acted firmly but due regard must be given to asylum. Sadly, even in 2019 the procedures are still not executed, as they should be due to skilled immigration lawyers using every device available to string out any hearing. There are still instances and evidence of certain LTTE supporters being granted asylum.

I must now return to what the Norwegians were doing following the 2001 General Election. On 1 November, Solheim and his team left Colombo in an air force helicopter, flying to Vavuniya and then travelled on by road to a meeting place with the LTTE cadres before continuing on to a place along the coast where they waited for Prabhakaran. The following morning he appeared in person. Solheim reported that the meeting was practical but Prabhakaran challenged why the world would not recognise the Tamils' right to self-determination. Solheim explained that nobody wanted it to happen and particularly not India. They then discussed confidence-building measures. Balasingham had already determined that before any peace talks could take place there had to be a process of de-escalation: the total cessation of armed hostilities, the removal of the economic blockade, the restoration of normalcy in the Tamil homeland (conveniently overlooking the fact that the government agents were still in post and operating as best they could). These demands were relayed to the Sri Lankan Government but did not create much traction. The government wanted to discuss core issues, whereas the LTTE wanted to see evidence that its demands would be considered and all the time, hidden in the wings, was the issue of de-proscription. The Norwegians decided to move forward by producing a Memorandum of Understanding – basically about easing the restrictions on everyday items for those living in the east and particularly the north but not much stirred in Colombo not least as only Chandrika and Kadirgamar knew what was happening.

Then in his Heroes Day speech of 27 November, Prabhakaran implied the LTTE would respond positively if the government took the initiative. A month later Prabhakaran declared a one-month ceasefire effective from 21 December. There was considerable surprise and suspicion in Colombo about the real motives behinds these two LTTE initiatives. (Personally, I suspect Balasingham. He knew that the 9/11 terrorist attack on the USA on 11 September 2001 meant the LTTE had better move fast to be seen as a reasonable organisation.) One always had to keep at the back of one's mind the stark difference between the two parties. The Tigers' preconditions of a ceasefire namely: the LTTE's de-proscription and lifting of economic sanctions prior to any talks whereas the government asserted that the implementation of these measures were dependent on talks towards a political settlement. The net result was the ceasefires offered were rejected. It was exceedingly difficult in London to keep track of the to-ing and fro-ing of the two sides as the months passed but I was acutely aware following talks over the phone with friends in Sri Lanka that there was considerable disillusion with Chandrika's Government: basically, people were war-weary.

The UNP (United National Party) was flexing its muscles and contemplating a vote of no confidence, not least as the five Muslim MPs appeared to be prepared to cross the floor to the UNP. Then, out of the blue came the al-Qaeda attack on the US on 11 September 2001. I still remember being called in by Ann to see the television – I imagine every one of us will always remember where we were and what we were doing when the news came through. I do remember thinking that this must change the world's attitude to all major terrorist groups. Then it happened just as I had witnessed with the end of the Callaghan Government. A motion of no confidence was tabled, debated, as it had to be, and a vote was taken which the UNP won under the leadership of Ranil Wickremesinghe in October 2001. This changed the whole political spectrum as Sri Lanka now had an Executive President from one party and a Prime Minister from another, with a clear mandate of 'peace and a negotiated settlement'.

On the surface the mood was helped by the intelligence of Balasingham who must have realised after the 9/11 atrocity that the LTTE had to be perceived as a responsible party just seeking a Tamil homeland.

Wickremesinghe is an interesting man whom I have known almost from the time I started the All-Party Group for Sri Lanka in 1975. He is still centre-stage in 2019, although he was unable to find time to see me when I travelled 5,400 miles in both 2015 and again 2017. I suppose I am not alone in finding his laidback attitude strange. Erik Solheim reported: 'It felt as if Ranil was not really interested in boring Norwegians, who in any case didn't understand anything. With us it was like this was one of the meetings he had to attend.' Maybe it is something to do with being asked questions by foreigners; foreigners who he knows only want to help but he seems reluctant to accept our help. Anyway, he was centre-stage, and continues to be, and as the saying goes: 'The buck stops with him.'

Back to reality in Sri Lanka: the LTTE responded to the UNP win by announcing a ceasefire. The government reciprocated and agreed to lift the long-running embargo on non-military goods going into the LTTE areas. The Sri Lanka military was totally against the decision, not least as there was a group of Special Forces who had now found where Prabhakaran was hiding and that he had planned to carry out an attack on Christmas Eve – just fifteen days after the result of the election. Quite a dilemma for the new Prime Minister. However, knowing most Sri Lanka ministers, they were bound to fear the collapse of the ceasefire negotiations. One can only wonder if this was missed opportunity number two to eradicate Prabhakaran: the first being when General Cyril Ranatunga had Jaffna surrounded but his final push was vetoed by President J.R. Jayawardene in deference to, and fear of, India.

By February 2002 the Norwegians were back in harness to produce the Sri Lanka Monitoring Mission to oversee the permanent ceasefire agreement. True roads were re-opened, including the vital A9 to the north which I have driven along many times. Traffic was moving again, albeit still having to pay a tax to the LTTE. Foreign Aid perked up and swarms of NGOs flowed in.

NGOs can and do provide wonderful support to disadvantaged citizens with medicines and healthcare in times of conflict, and they carry out many other extremely worthwhile projects. However, they have become such big businesses in their own right that there is a real danger of insensitivity to the culture of a foreign country and almost a political desire to manage situations with a Western political agenda. There is certainly little or no understanding of the private sector in these areas, or of international finance. This critical feeling was never far below the surface in Sri Lanka; indeed, some in Colombo have referred to it as NGO colonialism. Just as an aside, when I visited Jaffna in 2015 and 2017 it seemed to me there were more NGOs operating than genuine traders.

Once the ceasefire was formalised it meant that the LTTE was recognised on an equal basis to the Sri Lanka Government. The inevitable knock-on effect of this was that the views of all other Tamils, themselves in a majority, were to be ignored. Furthermore, the LTTE Tamil Tigers became the leaders/spokesmen of all Sri Lankans in their zones of control; in effect the Northern, much of North Central and the Eastern Provinces. When one remembers that all Sri Lankans are highly legalistic, particularly so the Tamils, one has to assume that Ranil Wickremesinghe really knew what he was letting himself and his country into. De facto the Colombo Government had ceded territory and sovereignty of at least a third of the country. What did it get in return? It seemed to me more hope than substance. I was not the least surprised to see the UK newspapers calling it 'The greatest give away in history.' I just wonder if the quid pro quo flowing from the Confidence Motion Ranil won in parliament in the early part of 2018 does not in effect mirror the situation in 2002. We will see.

From London it was not really possible to keep track of the meetings orchestrated by the Norwegians. There were six direct talks in Thailand, Norway, Germany and Switzerland. It appeared to the outside world, or so we were led to believe, that there was some progress towards a federal system. Additionally, the Norwegians, with the help of Denmark, Sweden, Finland and Iceland, set up a monitoring mission called SLMM (Sri Lanka Monitoring Mission). At the same time Colombo set up a Peace Secretariat.

The biggest challenge was to enforce the decisions and to decide who would be responsible for maintaining this. If left to goodwill, it would never work with the Tamil Tigers. Each time I visited Colombo in 2002 and 2003, I made a point to visit the SLMM. And on each visit I raised the question of the heavy bias of infringements in terms of the ceasefire by the LTTE. The only response I received was that was to be expected, as the Tamil Tigers were far harder to control than government employees in either civilian or public service or the armed forces.

Maybe Balasingham and the government were making progress but all the reports I received were that the LTTE was extending its reach around Trincomalee; that LTTE recruiting continued and even more worryingly, the recruitment of child soldiers had started up again – not too difficult for Adele Balasingham. Worst of all there was clear evidence that, during the lull of terrorist activities in Sri Lanka, the LTTE international networks could be, and were being, expanded. In London I was acutely aware of credit card crime, extortion of the professional class Tamils, blatant protection racquets and bogus charities, like the White Pigeon being set up. Every time either the High Commissioner or I raised the issue it was met with a retort from the authorities that they needed hard evidence. And it was not just happening in London: a man called Kumaran Pathmanathan had set up offices in Bangkok, Kuala Lumpur, Johannesburg and even Paris with the view of laundering dirty goods behind some respectable front. The LTTE's reach was global: even in Canada, where the Tamils had amassed huge influence, plus the never-to-be-forgotten USA, particularly Wall Street.

The government seemed to have no answer. Indeed, in London I felt that the reluctance to investigate was tantamount to being complicit to the crimes. I know that some members of the Sri Lanka military, who I knew reasonably well, were incensed about what they saw as appeasement. It all came to a head in April 2003 when the LTTE, through Balasingham, overplayed its card by stating it was not getting proper economic dividends from the ceasefire. The government was dumbfounded but appeared to do little to pin down Balasingham about what was really happening all over the world, none of which was in the spirit of the Ceasefire Agreement. No wonder hardliners in Colombo stated the LTTE was just going through the peace motions to allow time for the war to start again. All this clearly weakened the UNP Government, who appeared to be unable take new initiatives, rather like rabbits frozen in the glare of headlights.

Of course, sometimes in life problems are really opportunities and so it was when, in March 2004, Colonel Karuna, the Number 2 in the

LTTE, decided to swap sides, together with his key lieutenants. He had got wind that Prabhakaran felt he had become too powerful and might challenge him and therefore he needed to be eliminated. As far as the Sri Lanka military was concerned, the defection was 'pure gold'. No one in power seemed to know how to handle him and so, to the amazement of those of us following the saga, he was sent abroad. The government seemed to see him as a mixed blessing. One wonders why there was not an immediate call to Balasingham to say the game was up in the East and to put pressure on him to agree a settlement.

Reflecting on Balasingham's strategy, it was probably flawed from the start. Neighbouring India would never countenance partition with two states, so the pure homeland idea was impossible to achieve. Maybe he could have achieved a Northern Ireland or even a Quebec solution but he never once, as far as I can see, came up with any such creative solution. I met him in his office on one occasion and left with the impression that he was a wonderful creator of theoretical possibilities, but he never had the skill to go for the structure that could have preserved in legislation matters such as the Tamil language, customs and even law. I write this on the day that partition took place in India exactly seventy years previously at midnight 1947. The two hotspots were the Punjab centred on Lahore in the west, and Calcutta in the east. I visited my father in Lahore in 1955 and worked in Calcutta in 1962/3: terrible scenes took place in both places with thousands butchered. It is easy to blame the Attlee Government for what happened and certainly the British, in allowing this horror to take place, did not cover themselves in much glory.

Who could have achieved a peace in Sri Lanka? I have to believe firstly it could have been the Norwegians but they too were found wanting. There is however a wonderfully detailed book called *To End a Civil War* by Mark Salter, which charts in great detail (over 549 pages) Norway's peace engagement. It saddens me to think so much effort was put in for so little result.

What was the UN doing? It is an organisation that seems always to want to prosecute for alleged war crimes after the event rather than concentrate of preventing them taking place in the first instance. What happened to British diplomacy and action? After all, Balasingham and his wife were British citizens. My assessment is that the British Government turned a blind eye, frightened that the Tamil diaspora vote would be decisive in any general election. The Commonwealth? Well, without any UK lead it appeared powerless. To think if any of these organisations had acted there would have been no war, thus preventing the killing fields of several thousand civilians (but not the 40,000 claimed by the UN or the even more exaggerated claims from some of the LTTE diaspora and published by friendly media of over 100,000).

However, this is reflective hypothesis. Reality on the ground dictated that another general election was due on 6 April 2004. It took place and the winner was the United People's Freedom Alliance, consisting of almost all parties except the tainted UNP. The leader was Mahindra Rajapaksa, elected on the ticket of a tougher policy towards the Tamil Tigers.

What still mystifies me is why Balasingham, as the so-called sure-footed guru of the LTTE, could not foresee that allowing a hardline Sinhalese based government into power would be the end of its aspirational homeland which I believe it might have got out of Ranil Wickremesinghe.

The new government had hardly got going when a tragedy of nature struck on Boxing Day 2004: the tsunami. I sat in my TV room at home in Sandy, Bedfordshire and watched the terrifying images of the two-phase massive waves crashing on to the southern and eastern shores of my beloved Sri Lanka. I said to my wife, a retired GP: 'It is no use my being Chairman of the All-Party British Sri Lanka Parliamentary Group and just staying here. We need to get out there to help as soon as possible.' Which is exactly what we did.

It was as a result of my work to help handle the tragedy of the Tsunami that I was later awarded the highest Honour for non-nationals i.e. 'Sri Lanka Ratna (Titular) – 14 November 2005

CHAPTER
Eleven

Tsunami: Time and Tide Wait For No Man

It is one of the ironies of life that just as I started writing this chapter, on 6 September 2017, it was overshadowed by reports of Hurricane Irma smashing into the British Virgin Islands before moving on to the Turks & Caicos, then Cuba and Florida, causing total devastation. The loss of life from Hurricane Irma is low at under fifty, but the economic consequences throughout the northern part of the Caribbean and the state of Florida will last a decade.

On Friday 8 September 2017, I asked an Emergency Question of the UK Government about its response to Irma. It was last business but I questioned the Duty Minister hard on the delayed meeting of COBRA, the seemingly late take-off from RAF Brize Norton of transport aircraft which was ready to fly with much-needed equipment and personnel, and I also asked the location of HMS Ocean with its heavy lift equipment. I was asked by Sky Television to do a lunchtime broadcast, at which I jumped. I received a ministerial briefing, which did not assuage my concern. Finally, I put down an Oral Question for answer a month ahead. All in all, not Her Majesty's Government's finest hour in terms of speed of response.

Ghastly as this worst-ever-recorded hurricane was, it pales into insignificance at the impact of the 2004 tsunami on Sri Lanka, the Maldives, Western Indonesia, Thailand and Malaysia. The total death toll was a staggering 226,500, of which no less than 35,262 were killed or missing in Sri Lanka; add to this 519,063 made homeless.

The tsunami struck on Boxing Day. The next day I telephoned both the Sri Lanka High Commission and the Maldives High Commission in London with an offer that Ann and I would be very willing to go out to help just as soon as permission could be obtained. In the meantime, I met with the Disaster Emergency Committee (DEC) who had masterminded the Disaster Appeal. I was amazed and thrilled at the hugely generous response by the British people as money flooded in. At the end of the appeal a massive sum of over £400m had been donated.

My offer of help was welcomed by both countries: the Maldives responded first with President Gayoom stating he needed real help from the UK, as between a third and a half of the atolls covering tens of islands had been hit hard by the double-wave action of the tsunami. Red tape was cut and my wife and I took off on 8 January, arriving in Male on the 9th. Bearing in mind my first call out of the blue was made on 27 December, arrival on station in just twelve days by a backbench peer, albeit Chairman of both the All-Party Groups, was not bad.

Actually, I had been planning a more leisurely winter break to assess the coming general election in the Maldives and to check on the peace negotiations in Sri Lanka. As a result, a relaxing holiday was transposed into energetic practical help on the ground, culminating in an assessment of what the UK had been able to do, where we had failed and what we might do in the future. This resulted in a full report sent to the then Secretary of State for the Foreign & Commonwealth Office, Jack Straw, MP, who went out of his way to thank me.

What did we find in the Maldives? First, it must be said that they were neither sitting on their hands, 'Eastern style' nor rushing around with no plan. The President himself quickly gave me an audience and summarised the situation. All of the 197 inhabited islands were flooded to a depth of between 4 and 40 feet. All communications had been lost for twenty-four hours as the radio masts had been smashed by the waves. None of the islands had any power, as the generators had been swamped by sea water. To get them going would require each generator to be stripped down and cleaned.

I met our First Secretary Development Adviser, Steve Ainsworth, who, although stationed in Colombo, had responsibility for the Maldives as well. He had done a thoroughly professional assessment of what help was needed. Top of the list was electricians. As the Maldives had very few capable of striping down a generator, we jointly telephoned our High Commissioner in Colombo, Stephen Evans CMG OBE, who had responsibility for the Maldives. I asked how many electricians were available on the two Royal Navy ships moored off Batticaloa, which had been sent to help with the relief work. Soon after we got a reply saying eight could be spared and would be flown to Male the next day. The High Commissioner also said he was trying hard to locate a landing craft, as otherwise it would be very difficult to transport heavy equipment on to the islands. I suddenly remembered that many of the islands were 'dry' in terms of alcohol. I said to the President that he would have to give a temporary dispensation to the naval electricians. He looked at me and said: 'Are you sure, Michael?' I replied I was never more certain and the dispensation had to start the minute they arrived. It worked. I made a number of other calls to Stephen Evans.

Having sorted out the vital electricians I thought it important to visit some of the islands affected, including one of the resort islands and three of the inhabited but decimated islands. The resort island was already making strides to repair the damage it had sustained but the other three local islands were a tangled mess of uprooted palms, rubble, sand, etc. We listened to tales of people climbing up palm trees just in time to escape the huge waves and I have a photograph of a large fishing boat stranded inland next to a school. I shall never forget that in the midst of all this disaster I was taken to a new pond which had been created entirely by nature, located in the middle of the island, in which there were a number of fish still swimming. Apparently once the waves had stopped passing through, the villagers discovered that this pond was full of fish.

Ann and I even experienced mini challenges of our own. Our Otter flying boat did not have enough fuel to get safely back to Male so we had to reverse thrust the engine, beach the plane and walk off the aircraft using the floats: all good stuff for a former RAF pilot. There was no electricity on the island so fuel had to be pumped by hand from the 25-gallon fuel drums into a fuel line and then attached to the moored aircraft. All this did not happen in a few minutes. Indeed, it took a couple of hours. However, we were not idle and took the time to tour the island, seeing the tented village and a highly original mobile desalination plant producing fresh water which had been provided by Germany. Just as we returned to the aircraft the wind got up and the water became increasingly choppy. The pilot called us over to say it looked pretty unlikely we would be able to leave that evening. We stayed overnight in the well-built bungalow used by travelling civil servants.

We woke next morning to clear skies and sea like a mill pond, so after a quick breakfast, we waved goodbye to a hundred or so local Maldivians who had gathered on the beach, boarded by way of the floats and took off. As we did so, the aircraft banked so we could see the devastation of the island below.

On our return to Male, Steve Ainsworth told me Oxfam had chartered a plane with bottled drinking water. Additionally, the Red Cross was sending seventeen generators. Indeed, a huge number of countries reacted positively – particularly Saudi Arabia, whose tents seemed to be everywhere. I was also pleased to hear that Kofi Annan had arrived, which lifted everyone's spirits, particularly in a small country like the Maldives. Finally, bearing in mind that sixty out of eighty-seven resort islands were fully open, I suggested to our High Commissioner that the Foreign & Commonwealth Office put out on their travel advice the fact that the majority were open for business, with a list of those which were not.

So, after an exhausting but really worthwhile week we set off for Sri Lanka, our seventeenth visit to this beautiful country and by far our most important.

The capital city Colombo was unaffected. Indeed, the main economy of the island was only marginally affected but there was a belt of total devastation about 400 yards deep from about 25 miles south of Colombo all along the south coast up the eastern side and finishing in Jaffna in the north. By the time we arrived on 16 January the disaster relief was in full swing with 500,000 displaced persons in relief camps with emergency food and shelter seemingly flowing in. The US Marines were doing a superb job; in terms of disaster relief, what a lesson it was to see their heavy equipment at work.

I digress for a moment to point out that, we, the UK, after nearly 15 years, still have not learned the lesson that it is absolutely key to any successful disaster response to get heavy lifting gear in place within a few days. HMS Ocean, kitted out with the UK's heavy lifting gear, did not arrive in the Caribbean in response to Hurricane Irma until seventeen days after the storm had hit. For me this is far too long and unacceptable. Back in Sri Lanka in 2004/05 our Royal Navy was on the east coast at Batticaloa and doing wonderful work.

Before we set off to help, we had a briefing meeting with President Chandrika Bandaranaike Kumaratunga, along with the Foreign Minister and a senior officer from the Foreign Office, Kshenuka Seneviratne, later to be appointed High Commissioner in London – probably the most effective High Commissioner I ever worked with. The welcome was extremely warm, not least as I had worked with the President on a number of earlier projects. They were so pleased that we had moved so quickly to help, the briefing was efficiently done and a clear message was conveyed for our High Commissioner to thank him and his staff. I was asked to give a verbal report before I returned, with the words: 'We know you understand our country, we trust you and will listen to what you have to say.' As soon as the meeting was over I met with our High Commissioner, relayed the government's thanks and reported on the Maldives experience, mentioning in particular the good work of Steve Ainsworth. That evening we set off for the Taj Hotel at Bentota and although it was dusk the scene we saw was horrific.

Ann and I had decided that I would do the official work of liaison with the authorities and meet up with the UK officer who turned out to be the same Steve Ainsworth I had already met in the Maldives, whilst Ann would link up with the UK volunteers who appeared to be based at the Bentota Beach Hotel which was well-known to us. Most surprising of all were the British volunteers, not waiting to be asked but just setting up ad hoc units to help Sri Lanka. They were either ex-patriots or people on holiday when the tsunami struck and who had decided to stay on. They set up supplementary help, micro workshops, helped in schools, etc, and did a magnificent job.

There were dozens of such groups but typical was a group called 'Rebuilding Sri Lanka', a group of individuals and families who had been staying in Bentota at the time of the tsunami. They were united by their love of Sri Lanka, its people and a desire to help the rebuilding of a part of the country. They focused on enabling the people living in the area to re-establish the means to earn their own livelihoods again. The catalyst that seemed to make it all happen was a journalist/tourist, Alison Noble, who co-ordinated much of the work, helped by volunteers locally in Bentota and in the UK. I believe she created a charity and a website: www.rebuildingsrilanka.org.uk

A little further down the coast in Galle I came across volunteers who had set up 'Project Galle'. Their first objective was to provide primary aid to displaced persons and at the peak they were providing for between 17,000 and 20,000 people. Much of the food – about 80 per cent of it – came via the IMPACT Foundation and the remainder from private donors. IMPACT anticipated that this kind of work might be required for another six months but with each day it noted the numbers in the camps were falling. The budget anticipated to fulfil this commitment was in the region of £190,000. At the time I noted that the contact point was Edmund Hempel. I was told that Oxfam would probably take over these tasks fairly soon. Appendix IV shows a breakdown of costs to run Project Galle for six months.

Steve Ainsworth's operation was based next to Project Galle inside the old Dutch Fort. He recounted to me the whole operation of dealing with the challenge of the repatriation of those UK citizens affected, both the injured and the dead. I sat and listened in admiration at the sheer drive, dedication and efficiency of the man. Why this was never recognised with an honour is beyond me. He also recounted the horror of the tsunami sweeping through the Test Match cricket pitch just outside the Fort. In 2012, it all came back to me when I went to the Test Match between England and Sri Lanka and sat in the commentary box with 'Aggers' during the lunch interval commentary.

In the meantime, Ann had joined a lorry involved in giving relief and aid to babies in a camp, a medical centre and hospital still standing situated away from the coast but with no doctor. The local people were reticent to use the hospital, as it had been used as a mortuary.

I was given a government vehicle and an official, tasked with checking on those projects that had hit difficulties. I visited some schools that were not damaged but which had to be used for housing displaced persons as well as running normal school lessons. Additionally, some of the damaged schools were being patched up enough to hold temporary classes. Suddenly an 'Adopt a School' campaign was created in embryonic form involving schools in Sri Lanka outside the stricken area. Some of the UK volunteers managed to get UK schools involved as well. Later this mushroomed into a real involvement for some UK schools. My official was able to give the go-ahead for a tailor to restart his workshop on the basis he would provide school uniforms. There were initiatives such as this all over the place. A number of women had lost their husbands in the tsunami and thus their means of support. The area is known for its lace-making and one lady was supported to restart her business, which became a local tourist attraction.

I also visited Weligama further down the coast from Galle. Here 'Adopt Sri Lanka' had been set up by a group of local Sri Lanka and expatriate business people immediately after the tsunami. The website www. adoptsrilanka.com explained in detail which projects were underway and how donations could be made. Since there was no time to set up a registered charity they had organised to piggyback on to 'Children in Crisis'.

A completely different initiative had been started by a British chap renting the island of Taprobane. I had already met Geoffrey Dobbs but I went to see the two workshops he had set up to enable the fisherman to repair their outboard motors. It required someone with his leadership qualities to make it happen and it did, at no cost to the public purse, just his generosity. Geoffrey also recounted the lucky escape of his sister-in-law who was swimming at the time the tsunami hit. She was taken in by the first wave, managed to catch hold of a palm tree, looked up and saw a snake directly above her, decided that a snake was not good news, fell back into the water which took her out again and was then washed further inland and hung on to a vacant tree.

I must mention 'Fish and Ships', a wonderful project which was launched by a very good friend of mine, Anthony Steen, MP, at a lunch in England on 12 January 2005 to help rebuild the fishing fleet. It was estimated that about 50 per cent of the 29,694 fishing vessels had been destroyed by the tsunami. The result of 'Fish & Ships' was hugely successful.

By any yardstick the combination of Britons and Sri Lankans with a 'can do' attitude did produce some highly creative and pertinent solutions. On my last day out and about I wanted to see what was happening about housing. Many of the bigger charities were already beginning to build, guided by the relevant Sri Lanka ministry. At least one large NGO commented adversely on the small size of the houses but having been Chairman of the Housing Committee in the London Borough of Islington I disagreed with their assessment. The most impressive project to be underway was a village of potentially forty-one houses, a little shop and a small community centre with money donated by Marks & Spencer, built by their local supplier MAS and overseen by CARE. I went back a year later and was hugely impressed.

As an aside, I must just mention that I think I inspected all the dozens of different types of tents sent by the overseas donor countries. My 5-star award went to Italy whose tents were quite outstanding, so much so that they were the last to go and the most treasured possession of people able to acquire one. I would also highly commend the tents of Saudi Arabia.

On Saturday 22 January I had a debrief with officials before flying home. I recounted what I had seen, shared notes on what I would be saying to the Ministers in DFID (the Department for International Development) and the Foreign & Commonwealth Office. I was surprised to hear that well over 300 charities worldwide had responded to the call for help – quite wonderful.

However, it did create a huge challenge of co-ordination. It was not so wonderful to be told that shipping containers sent from the UK, alleged to contain aid, actually had hidden in them arms, light aircraft parts and war material for the LTTE – quite shameful. We talked about the train tragedy where over 1,000 people died: thirty seconds longer on the red signal in the station would in all probability have saved most of them. I had found it harrowing to walk along the railway track, see the upturned coaches and the abandoned clothing and footwear – another direct result of the tsunami.

On a lighter note there was the seemingly true story of the elephants in Yala sanctuary thumping the ground with their feet to warn the other animals of the approaching tsunami before retreating inland. The result of which was that every creature that could walk, slither or fly retreated inland, except for the poor stranded fish. Whoever said animals are not as intelligent as humans?

However, it does not end there, as there was the issue of the fish caught after the tsunami and whether they were safe for human consumption or not. The UK Foreign & Commonwealth Office in their 'Advice to Travellers' notice clearly stated that tourists or British Nationals in Sri Lanka should avoid eating fish: really great news for the local fishermen trying to recover their living and an economy heavily skewed to fish. I discussed with my doctor wife who could not see how this advice could possibly be true, as fish do not eat human corpses. I contacted my doctor son in the UK who checked with the World Health Organisation, which stated categorically there was no problem and declared this publicly. I then telephoned our High Commissioner, Stephen Evans, in Colombo who said he would pass it on immediately to the Foreign Office, which he did. I checked again the next day by telephoning my youngest son in his law practice in London. No change and still the warning. More complaints from me and at last after a further two days the negative advice was withdrawn. How good it was to have two medics and one lawyer in the family liaising over the miles to get incorrect advice changed.

As we flew out I reflected on what had been the most demanding, exciting and worthwhile overseas visit I had ever made. I knew Ann and I had done a lot of good. Much would have to be followed up in Parliament on my return but that was not as important as the hope we had given to both the government and the ordinary people of Sri Lanka. I also reflected on the way the Government of Sri Lanka handled the massive challenge of the tsunami. I have only the most genuine praise for the way the Prime Minister Mahinda Rajapaksa took command, as President Chandrika was abroad. This was my first insight of him: dynamic, efficient, suffering no nonsense, communicating to his own people with a passion, understanding and confidence I had never seen before in a senior politician in Sri Lanka.

We promised we would return in a year to see what had happened. It was a promise we kept, returning in January 2006 followed by my initiating a debate in the House of Lords on 10 February 2006 to report my findings.

However, much had changed on the political landscape in the intervening twelve months. There was a new President because the Supreme Court of Sri Lanka had decreed that there had to be a presidential election in November 2005 despite Chandrika's plea that it should not be for another year. There was clearly, too, no love lost between Chandrika and Mahinda, largely due, I would imagine, to the fact that she had demoted him on her return from abroad despite his excellent work on the tsunami recovery, or, knowing Sri Lanka as I do, because of it!

The fascinating part of the election build-up was that Mahinda understood the mood of much of the country and particularly the

Sinhalese vote. He stuck his neck out by allying his campaign with the hard-line Buddhist Nationalist JHU Party (Jathika Hela Urumaya, known as the National Heritage Party) and the left-wing Marxist JVP (Janatha Vimukthi Peramuna) both of whom were passionate about a unitary state. In contrast, Chandrika's campaign for the nomination emphasised the federal solution but few apart from the international community favoured this solution, which had been so long in gestation. Of course, had not Kadirgamar been assassinated by the LTTE in August 2005, she might well have succeeded but the LTTE hated Kadirgamar, seeing him as a Tamil traitor, but from her point of view he probably would have openly campaigned for Chandrika and so persuaded the key members of the SLFP (Sri Lanka Freedom Party). It was not to be and Mahinda got the nomination as the SLFP candidate.

I have now known Mahinda for well over a decade. My reading is that his number one priority was to build his power base in the core Sinhalese vote. Having done this, and he was good at it, with ordinary rank and file members, my guess is he was open to any proposal that would promise a swift end to the violence within the context of a single unitary state.

The election was basically between Mahinda Rajapaksa for the SLFP and the UNP candidate Ranil Wickremesinghe who appeared to be offering the prospect of some sort of peace settlement. The voting was tight but Rajapaksa won. It does not bear thinking what the outcome would have been if Wickremesinghe had won. My own opinion is that it would have resulted in the merger of the North and East Provinces with such extensive devolved powers that the nearest analogy I can think of would be Northern Cyprus, in effect a subservient part of Turkey, which in this case would have been India in general and Tamil Nadu in particular. The question that remains unanswered is why did the leadership of the LTTE tell their followers not to vote. Had they voted then Wickremesinghe would have almost certainly have won.

Mahinda fought his campaign with the platform including the ultra nationalist JVP and the new JHU National Heritage Party, which was a quasi-Buddhist party.

His basic tenet, which he often espoused, was that he did not want to pass on to the next generation the problem of Eelam and the Tamil Tigers. Either there had to be real peace in a unitary country or if the

130

LTTE refused peace then there would have to be a military solution at a time when the government was really ready and equipped. He may well have been emboldened by the defection of Karuna and the increasing military successes in the Eastern Region. Nevertheless, he knew peace was better than a campaign to defeat the Tigers in the north. It seemed to me he was sceptical about the LTTE's commitment to peace. He was half encouraged, though, by his meetings with Tony Blair and the huge progress of the Belfast Agreement. This gave him some encouragement to go the extra mile. However, before doing anything else he recruited his two brothers: Gotabaya to be Secretary of Defence and Basil to be in charge of all civilian implementation. I got to know both of them quite well. Frankly, all three were leaders and I sensed for the first time ever that Sri Lanka's leadership was in the hands of people who would act decisively and would be prepared to follow through.

Before I went out again in 2006 the Rajapaksa team had done two things that impressed me and augured well for the future. Gotabaya had been a successful officer in the army and recognised that morale in the armed forces was low. He set about changing this by dealing with pay and conditions, and tried to attract young recruits of a better quality. I used to be in advertising. It was always in the blood to keep a weather eye open for developments in the communications world. I heard that Gotabaya had commissioned a company called Tri Ads to prepare a new, in-depth PR campaign to boost military morale. Gotabaya was also able to use his US experience and set up www.defence.lk to rival and undermine TamilNet, taking the communications war online.

Whilst this was being planned his brother Mahinda was quite clear that his first priority was to make tracks to India to secure her support. Before the year was out arrangements were made for him to go to India and meet with the Indian Prime Minister Manmohan Singh. Manmohan Singh was not a Hindu but a British-trained economist, principally at Cambridge, where I too read Economics. He was a practical man with no airs or graces but anxious to move India forward. Thus, he welcomed the new President, his neighbour, and by all reports they got on very well. The result was to agree to share intelligence on the LTTE's advances, particularly on its equipment and its plans to attack certain key installations. This was gold dust for the Sri Lanka brothers.

Although I had already planned to return to Sri Lanka in January 2006, I received an invitation from the former President Chandrika to come to Colombo in November 2005 with my wife to be given the award of the Sri Lanka Ratna – the highest award that can be given to a foreigner. To put it mildly, I was astounded. We went to Sri Lanka for a few days in November so I could receive the award personally, whilst Chandrika was still President. She was two hours late for the ceremony, which covered other award winners as well, but it was very special, even if it was totally unexpected and came out of the blue. Nevertheless, I did feel very proud and indeed vindicated. The full regalia has been worn to a number of Livery and Lord Mayor occasions and is a treasured gift. Indeed, at one it was recognised by the host, which amazed me.

The citation for the 'Sri Lanka Ratna (Titular)' reads as follows:

This is the highest honour of the country conferred on non-nationals, and is awarded for exceptionally outstanding and most distinguished service to Sri Lanka in particular and/or humanity in general. The award will be a citation and a gold medal studded with Navaratne Nine Sri Lanka gems with a Manel symbol.

I have known all the Presidents from Mrs Bandaranaike onwards, however Chandrika is someone for whom I have a soft spot. I got the impression that she did not really choose politics but in a sense politics chose her. She responded, as she clearly has a keen sense of what was right and wrong; she knew the peace process was vital to her country but sadly she was undermined by the Tamil Tigers whose only policy was to achieve Eelam, something quite alien to her and totally unacceptable to the vast majority of Sri Lanka citizens. I still look upon her as a true personal friend.

Ann and I did return again in January 2006, as promised. The President asked to see me the day after my arrival. He said my award of the Sri Lanka Ratna by the former President for services to the country was totally in keeping with his own feelings. He thanked both my wife and me profusely and recounted the 'no eating of fish story'. I, in turn, thanked him and said I was going to see for myself the developments since my last visit, would write a report and then hold a debate in the

House of Lords as soon as I could, which I did on Friday 12 February 2006.

We finished the meeting on the subject of cricket, which we both enjoy and follow. I said I was authorised by the MCC to offer him, Mr President, £50,000 for the restoration of the Galle Cricket Ground outside the Fort but it was only for the original site and not for the suggestion of moving inland. He was genuinely thrilled and stated that that settled it, no new ground and would I please thank the MCC for its generosity. He confirmed the Galle ground would now be restored. It has been sensitively restored, as I saw with my own eyes when I went to the Sri Lanka v England test on 26 March 2012.

The next day Ann and I set off for the Taj Hotel, Bentota to see what progress had been made in the south; we could not go east because of the security situation. The basic statistics are etched into my memory: 35,262 killed or missing, 40,000 widows and over 500,000 made homeless. No less than 900 camps in tented accommodation had been set up originally which had provided clean water, food, shelter and, miraculously, there had been no reports of disease. By the time I left, over 53,000 transitional homes had been built and fewer than 150 families remained in tents. On top of this a home ownership project had been launched, allowing people to rebuild their original home and thus rebuild their lives and their livelihood. The only real problem was the government had introduced a 100/200-metre blanket buffer zone so that homes would not be so susceptible to violent storms again. This was understandable but officials seemed to have forgotten about the fishermen and indeed all those who provided back-up to the vital fishing sector. I must record my thanks to DFID (the Department for International Development) who helped persuade the Sri Lanka Government to think again, based on its experience globally.

The mention of fishing brings to mind what a joy it was to see all the newly brightly painted and repaired fishing boats: 9,000 had been repaired and more than 1,200 replaced. I noticed some English names on the sides, reflecting the excellent work of my colleague Anthony Steen, MP with his 'Fish & Ships' appeal. There remained on the 'To do' list the replacement of the trawlers lost but this would take longer – and it did happen. I also noticed that Trinity House (a charity dedicated to safeguarding shipping and seafarers) was generously gifting a supply of buoys to replace those lost.

Cottage industries play an important part in the Sri Lankan economy, so I visited the Oxfam micro-industry project which was fascinating and involved a considerable number of widows. The new charity, Adopt Sri Lanka, was continuing with its good work in lace-making and tailoring. Since we come from Bedfordshire, one of England's most famous lace-making counties, my wife was thrilled to see the beautiful lace.

I also visited Colombo Port to check on alleged delays and supposed shortage of warehousing, which had been true in January and February 2005 but were all resolved now. Some sceptics in the outside world might suggest that things were bound to look much better as the government officials only took visitors to the best. I am sorry to disillusion these people, but I always made a point to organise my own car and only told my driver and guide where we were going on the day. The one area I regret I was not allowed to visit was the east coast: even the Sri Lanka NGOs had trouble getting there due to terrorist activity by the LTTE. This brought home to me the gulf between ordinary Sri Lankans from across all the ethnic groups finding that in their hour of need the Tamil Tigers were not really interested in their plight, but preferred to keep fighting. Having worked in India for a couple of years myself, I know that this is not part of the Hindu faith.

How was it all funded? An amazing £400m was donated by the UK public to the charities in the Disaster Emergency Committee. Added to this, the UK Government donated £290m from the aid budget. Additionally, there were a great number of hefty donations from many, many countries, not forgetting the Sri Lanka diaspora.

During the debate of 12 February, for which I was thanked profusely by colleagues, questions were raised about where the United Nations had really fitted in and who should do an evaluation of what was successful and what was less so. The minister replying to the debate said the evaluation had already been started by a body called the Tsunami Evaluation Coalition (TEC) – a group of NGOs and UN agencies with a budget of £100,000 from DFID. The interim findings highlighted the huge number of NGOs on the ground, leading to some confusion which I, too, had experienced. For me the other key finding concerned the broader capacity of the international humanitarian system. It concluded that the appeals-based system for funding humanitarian emergencies leads to inconsistencies in funding with many emergencies left short of resources.

Thankfully, out of this disaster came an initiative from the UK Government for a global humanitarian fund through expansion of the Central Emergency Response Fund. This was agreed in December 2005. The primary use of the fund was for urgent crises in order to ensure that funding was immediately available. As I sit tapping my keyboard, it makes me think: has this been used in relation to Hurricane Irma or not? I also re-read the National Audit Office Report on 'Department for International Development Tsunami: Provision of financial support for Humanitarian Assistance'. In part 2 it lists the DFID's immediate response to the Indian Ocean Tsunami. It is so heartening to read that just one day after the Tsunami hit, the DFID despatched an aircraft with plastic sheeting and tents to Sri Lanka. Further despatches of vital supplies went on 29 December and again on 4, 5 and 8 January. All credit to the DFID.

The other outcome of my own review concerned the Tamil Tigers. It was not just their callous decision to make it virtually impossible for outside help to reach the poor souls in the eastern region with its tri-part population of Muslim, Tamil and Sinhalese, but even worse was the sending of arms through the worldwide charitable response. No one knows how much actually came in but it must have been substantial, as the containers holding the ball bearings and aircraft parts were only discovered by chance.

I decided to have a closer look at home in the UK to see what the LTTE diaspora were really up to. After much lobbying from Sri Lanka's representative in the USA, the LTTE had been made a proscribed organisation in the USA in 2000 but it took an amazing four years more to get it proscribed in the UK. During this interim period the LTTE openly undertook extortion, illegal financing, money laundering, credit card fraud and phantom charities were set up. Why was it able to get away with it? The answer quite simply was that it had infiltrated the Labour Party at grass roots level and its Tamil sympathisers had congregated in marginal seats.

Of course, I raised it on the floor of the House of Lords in the debate on

10 February 2006 but I received the courteous answer from the minister, Baroness Royall of Blaisdon, and I quote:

> With regard to the LTTE and its proscription in the UK, no organisation which is proscribed in the UK may raise funds in the UK. That would be an offence under the Terrorism Act 2000. It is for the police in conjunction with the Crown Prosecution Service to take action where there is evidence of an offence being committed. If Lord Naseby has any information indicating that the law is being flouted naturally he should contact the police.

Knowing something illegal is happening and collecting hard evidence to prove so are totally different, particularly with a foreign community which is afraid of retribution either here in the UK or even in Sri Lanka. From that point onwards I decided to work closely with the Sri Lanka High Commission to see if we could crack this cancer together.

I met the High Commissioner Mrs Kshenuka Seneviratne. We set about trying to collect evidence jointly and we kept the Charity Commission informed with a degree of success. It was still a long struggle and the police did not seem keen to get involved. As so often happens with crooks, they become over-confident and take risks that expose them. So it was on 25 July 2006 when a rally was called in the name of The Tamil Youth Organisation, a well-known front organisation for the LTTE. They named it the Black July Remembrance Rally at Speakers' Corner Hyde Park, London. We had it watched and saw it was attended by over 3,000 people, collections were made, LTTE banners flown in LTTE colours, placards displayed of the Tiger leader Prabhakaran and an 18-foot stand-up portrait of him was positioned at the side of the stage. The entire proceedings were broadcast worldwide on TTN (Tamil Television Network).

I discussed the challenge we faced with some of the finest anti-terrorism lawyers who suggested I should not rush in but wait to see if any proscriptions were forthcoming or not. As I am not a lawyer, I thought we had an open and shut case but I can be a patient man, as I had proved when I took the Maastricht debates, so we waited, giving the authorities six months to act. Then on 6 February 2007, I pounced with a tough letter to Andy Hayman, Assistant Commissioner of Metropolitan

Police, New Scotland Yard, which is reproduced in Appendix V. I claimed that the LTTE was flouting the Terrorism Acts, particularly Section 12v & 13 of the 2000 Act and Article 2 of the 2006 Act. I finished the letter:

> There is little point in Parliament passing Terrorism Legislation when it can be so openly flouted. The Police have hard concrete evidence. May I on behalf of my colleagues ask what exactly is preventing the four persons mentioned from being prosecuted?

I also reflect that right up to 2017 there were still flag-waving LTTE supporters demonstrating at Sri Lanka events, be it a cricket match or any number of national occasions, all with banners showing Tigers. But apparently not the Tiger pictures listed in the proscription order. Is it any wonder that Sri Lanka lawyers are deeply respected?

Whilst all this was going on, unbeknownst to me or any of the other twenty-five or so members of the All-Party Sri Lanka Parliamentary Group, someone in the LTTE or a well-placed sympathiser decided the one Sri Lanka group was far too balanced and even-handed, so work had been put in hand to set up a rival group. It is open to any group of colleagues across the two Houses to set up a new group of some particular interest if they so wish, providing they can find three members from Government, two from the Opposition and one other. They simply need to place a notice on the All-Party Whip and hold an inaugural meeting. Etiquette is that if it is a new group, it is publicised in the preceding week's Notices under the subject 'Future AGM/ Inaugural Meetings'. There also had been an unwritten rule that there should be no ethnic-orientated groups, particularly where there was an existing country group as there was for Sri Lanka. I study each week's Notice. To my amazement, scheduled for Monday 30 April 2007 at 1600 hrs in Room 21 was 'Tamils Group-Inaugural Election of Officers'. Afterwards I checked back and found there never was any prior notice. The notice goes out with Whip, which in those days arrived on a Friday. Of course, holding it on a Monday meant few, other than those in the know, would notice it. I certainly missed it. No one had informed any of the Sri Lanka Group, although at least one of the officers of the new group was a member, namely Simon Hughes, MP, Liberal Democrat. The driving force for the new group was one Keith Vaz, MP. I need hardly say more: a man of varied interests as reported in the press. I complained to the House authorities who agreed convention had been flouted but they were within the rules. One might reflect – clever lawyers again!

This new group soon became a thorn in the side of Sri Lanka, as was almost immediately evidenced by an adjournment debate just two days later on 2 May 2007 in the House of Commons. So, one notes a brand new Parliamentary Group set up without any prior notice to anyone on Monday 30 April 2007 followed by adjournment debate on 2 May just two days later: a coincidence or was it just engineered by the then Labour Government? This was no usual thirty-minute debate initiated by a single MP. This was a fully fledged debate lasting more than four hours involving twenty-three MPs from Labour, Liberal and Conservative members, almost all of whom had LTTE activists in their constituencies. The majority of the twenty-three members who spoke were really all petitioning for the LTTE to be de-proscribed. In fact, Keith Vaz, Jeremy Corbyn, John McDonnell, Chris Mullins and Ed Davey specifically said so. Mentioning the first three makes one think hard about these three leaders of today in 2018 being the heart of the Labour Party.

With the debate in the Commons over I asked the authorities in Sri Lanka if they could provide a list of those civilians assassinated by the LTTE from the beginning of the troubles in July 1975 when the Mayor of Jaffna, Alfred Duraiappah, was killed. The horrific figures up to 11 February 2007 were 2,706 civilians murdered, of which 1,598 were Sinhalese, 1,024 were Muslim and 84 Tamil. These terrible figures were overshadowed by the June 1990 horror of the cold-blooded murder of about 600 policemen in the Batticaloa area police stations who, finding their police stations surrounded, surrendered in good faith only to be slaughtered.

Although I used to try to visit Sri Lanka once a year to keep up with events and to draw my own conclusions, I chose not to go in 2007, not least as an election was expected in the UK, as well as the continuing saga of peace one minute and warfare the next would have meant considerable restrictions on where I might go. What did interest me was the strategy that the new President Mahinda Rajapaksa would deploy to deal with the LTTE.

Over the years I had met him a number of times, the most recent during his handling of the tsunami challenge. I thought to myself that here at last was someone who knew what needed to be done and got on with it – not the norm for Sri Lanka politicians. I was not the least bit surprised to be told by friends that the new President appeared to have a two-pronged approach to the LTTE. He clearly did, ideally, wish to find a way to achieve lasting peace but all his experience with Prabhakaran and the other senior LTTE leaders, along with their philosophical theoretician Balasingham, had led him to believe there would only be an outside chance of success. Moreover, he seemed to have sharpened up the country's intelligence gathering. This in itself helped him to understand the sheer depth of support the Tigers had achieved across the Western World, despite being a proscribed organisation.

I was not surprised to learn that alongside a genuine attempt to move peace forward through the good offices of the Norwegians and the four sponsoring nations he decided to have a plan 'B' which was simply to build up the armed forces of Sri Lanka into a force capable to take on the Tamil Tigers if it came to real war. Mahinda Rajapaksa had appointed his two brothers to positions of authority and Gotabaya, the new Head of the Armed Forces, had set to work to bolster Sri Lanka's army. He decided that nine divisions were totally inadequate so they were increased to twenty. At the time that his brother was elected, the army numbered 120,000 and by the end of the war the figure had risen to approximately 230,000. The same sort of increases were needed for the navy to 74,000 and even the air force reached 40,000. Additionally, there was the police, including the special task force which reached over 80,000 and civil defence around 40,000. Back in 1983 the total number of armed forces personnel was around 20,000. The army's sheer scale of increase meant that when ground was taken it could be held, and it also enabled advances to be made on several fronts at a time.

On the question of effective armaments the Rajapaksa brothers remembered that in the early days of the insurrection the UK Government had reneged on spares and ammunition, so they were not going to make the same mistake. They knew, and rightly so, that the West was not to be trusted, so the new modern armaments came from Pakistan, Israel and China.

There were two other dimensions that fascinated me. Professionally, I am a successful advertising man who understands the need to communicate clearly to a target audience with a weight and scale that enables domination. In essence, the propaganda war had to be won at all costs. Churchill knew this, which is why Beaverbrook was in charge. In the case of Sri Lanka, Gotabaya ensured that both television and radio transmissions were made in three languages. The product was the individual soldier portrayed not as an outsider but as one who was saving the country. The team dominated all the news channels but the spokesmen were officers in uniform not politicians. Did it work? As far as I could see it did for over 80 per cent of the population but not for the Tamil community. It also worked for the soldiers themselves and their families, alongside better pay and care for the wounded. Indeed, as the army moved forward the media relayed the success, thereby keeping up morale. Of course, it did not really improve relations with the West but it probably never could have with the level of propaganda coming from the Tamil diaspora.

The reader may wonder why I do not recount the varying peace initiatives. Truth to tell, at the time, I found it very difficult to keep track of them. Moreover, I was acutely aware that every time there was a ceasefire for a peace conference, two things happened. First, there were immediate breaches, almost always by the LTTE. Secondly, there was clear published evidence in some of the Western media that the LTTE was continuing to buy arms, some of a very sophisticated nature. To me as a keen observer this did not augur well for a successful peace.

The deciding event for me was the illness and then death of Anton Balasingham in December 2006. It was he who had provided the acceptable face of Eelam to the West and indeed to India. As far as the UK was concerned he had considerable influence with the incumbent Labour Government. They also had influence on him, having granted him UK citizenship. Once he was out of the scene I suspect Prabhakaran had to decide either to sue for peace or go all out to defeat the Sri Lanka military, which he must have thought was possible. To me he seemed a hardened, ruthless, successful military leader with a well-trained and effective force. Besides which, the perceived wisdom of all the experts in the West was that the Sri Lanka army would fail and as they did the world would step in to announce that Eelam was de facto and should be accepted.

When I think back to the period of the Norwegian initiative I wonder whether I should have tried to play a more pro-active role but I reflect that the leadership of the LTTE was only ever interested in Eelam either by force or by dint of international pressure on the government of the day in Colombo. I knew it would never happen, as it was based on the false premise of unity through language. This was the only common factor between the Northern Province and the Eastern Province. Whichever way it was looked at, the Tamil community in the Eastern Province was a minority and a decreasing one at that. Had the LTTE leadership ever seriously considered something akin to the Northern Ireland Good Friday Agreement solely for the Northern Province, they might well have succeeded. Indeed, it might well still happen in the future.

Returning to the context of the Rajapaksa presidency period of 2005 through to January 2009, the so-called peace conferences were in effect nothing more than an opportunity for the LTTE to rearm.

In late January 2008 I touched base with the President and key ministers by visiting Colombo for a short but comprehensive four-day visit after a major visit to the Maldives. I was briefed on the All-Party Reconstruction Committee as the Interim Report had just been presented. I must confess I had a certain scepticism, as the key element was an amendment to the Constitution called Amendment 13. In simple terms it would allow provincial councils to be set up without concurrent powers from central government; in effect a form of devolution. The problem was, and still is, that the powers have been there for years but not acted upon by the UNP. At the time of writing in January 2018, the amendment has still not been sorted out, so my scepticism in 2008 was fully justified.

In the report I submitted to the UK Foreign Secretary, David Miliband, following that 2008 visit, I suggested the UK should use aid money to help with the rehabilitation of the young rebel soldiers from the Karuna faction, help with the cost of training Tamil policemen and generally see how we could assist the ambitious programme to ensure all middle-ranking civil servants could converse in both Tamil and Sinhala. Sadly, my suggestions fell on stony ground as apparently Sri Lanka was a medium wealthy country and therefore not considered to be eligible.

I also raised the issue of Human Rights with the President, explaining that the lack of progress was jeopardising the way the world saw Sri Lanka. Both the minister in charge and the President made a plea for some understanding and no outside interference. Certainly the rumours that the EU was contemplating removing Sri Lanka's involvement with the Generalised System of Preferences because of slow progress on the Human Rights front would be disastrous for the garment industry and if implemented would adversely affect 350,000 workers, many of whom were Tamils. I urged the UK Government to intervene but as I found out later it chose not to do so. I should just highlight my comment on the UK High Commission in my report: 'We are no longer regarded as helpful and have lost influence. We have now had two High Commissioners who appear to have overstepped the diplomatic mark: Gladstone and Chilcott.'

Finally, I met the Hon. Douglas Devananda, Minister of Social Services and Social Welfare and leader of the EPDP (Eelam People's Democratic Party) in his office. He showed me a film recording of the female suicide bomber who had tried to blow him up. The hugely dangerous task of being a government minister in Sri Lanka hit home: something not really appreciated in the West and particularly not in the UK.

I left Colombo with the clear impression that the Rajapaksa Government was well organised. It had made real progress in winning back the Eastern Province, hugely helped by the defection of the Karuna faction. This had forced the LTTE to change tack. It had returned to its campaign of suicide bombings in the urban areas of the south, which only served to stiffen the determination of the Rajapaksa brothers and the Sri Lanka government to deal with the problem once and for all: the die was cast for an all-out war to win back the north. I decided that I should come back in another twelve months, which I did, arriving on 4 January 2009.

British Army Cemetery in Kandy

A reminder of war – the author was partially responsible for the restoration of this British Army Cemetery in Kandy

CHAPTER
Twelve

The War

My flight to Colombo arrived at 2.25 am on 4 January 2009. I started my official engagements the next day. The visit was longer than usual, lasting nineteen days, which enabled my wife and I to catch up with old friends like the Talwattes, Nathan Sivaganathan and family, Drs Gunawardena, Geoffrey Dobbs and Royston Ellis. The official part of the visit was from 4 to 9 January, followed by a private visit touring the country from 10 to 20 January and a final day of briefings with the Foreign Minister and the UK High Commissioner on 21 January.

In my report I stated the following:

> I last visited Sri Lanka a year ago when to the surprise of many commentators I stated that there was a chink of light both in resolving the Tamil Tiger issue and for progress on the political front. My overall impression is that the Tigers will now be defeated and Eelam is dead after 25 years. I expect this defeat to be followed by a General Election in May/June and I anticipate the Government coalition may well get its ⅔rds majority enabling it to change the Constitution. If the Tigers are removed, I expect the Tamils in the North to quickly return and by a combination of their own energy, the huge number of Tamils in the South, the diaspora around the World and hopefully real and significant help from the International Community normality will return & Democratic Elections will be held in a united Sri Lanka.

Sadly, this prognostication proved far too optimistic.

However, the President had a clear strategy to initially seek a negotiated peace and to follow this up with a measured military campaign. The Tigers rejected the peace initiative offered in Geneva and had refused to lay down their arms and negotiate, particularly over the previous six months. Government forces had methodically moved forward up both the western and eastern sides of the country. The Tigers had fought hard but lost every battle and, in doing so, forced the civilian population of over 300,000 to withdraw with them, causing considerable hardship (a war crime in itself). They refused every appeal from a number of quarters, including the UN, to release civilians. Remarkably, since the Government forces had taken Kilinochchi and reopened the A9 road, there was not a single civilian death reported at the time of my visit.

The success of the military campaign was due to the battle-hardened Sri Lanka forces which came from all ethnic groups, helped enormously by India and the USA who pinpointed the location of ten supply ships belonging to the Tigers. The ships were sunk and thus the normal supply lines to the Tigers were cut off. I wrote in my report of this visit that I expected the Tigers to be defeated as a fighting force and their leader Prabhakaran would try to flee. I anticipated there might be some suicide bombings in Colombo but as there would be very few safe houses for the Tiger, I felt a guerrilla war was unlikely. I talked to a large number of ordinary civilian Tamils all over the island. Four years previously there had been considerable sympathy for the Tiger cause but by this visit, in 2009, that feeling had totally evaporated.

A key issue facing everyone was the number and fate of Internally Displaced Persons (IDPs).

The UN estimated that there were at least 250,000 civilians being used by the Tamil Tigers as a human shield; in reality it appeared to be nearer 300,000. In addition to this number, were the 100,000 other IDPs arising from the war in the Eastern Province and the LTTE's forcible move of Muslims out of Jaffna. The picture remained clouded and fluid as hundreds tried to escape through the lines in response to the army's leaflet drops, which promised safe passage to any who did escape the clutches of the LTTE. Nevertheless, thousands still remained trapped and were being used as a human shield for whom food and medicines had to be delivered by the government, the UN and the government agents on the ground. Doctors who had checked the several thousand who had escaped reported no malnutrition.

The Sri Lanka Government was clearly taking very seriously the need for a 'Hearts and Minds' campaign in the Northern Province. The army organised an industrial exhibition in Jaffna in December 2009, which was hugely well attended. Government plans were announced to give priority to the Northern Province for infrastructure replacement. There were many Tamil businessmen working in the private sector who were keen to help, together with many promises from the outside international community to assist with financing and the rebuilding of Sri Lanka's infrastructure and economy. This included offers from the UK Government. I raised this whole issue with Prime Minister Blair who promised real and significant financial help. I recommended that the UK took the lead on a specific project, such as the repair and modernisation of Kilinochchi Hospital. There would be little point in the UK wringing its hands over Human Rights if we refused to help the Tamil and Muslim communities in the near future. Sadly, no real help was forthcoming, except for assistance with de-mining.

It is important to take stock of what had happened in the Eastern Province, which the Tigers controlled until April 2008. By the time of my visit in January 2009, all reports showed that there were still tensions between the three ethnic groups but that they were reducing. Elections were held and the former Tiger breakaway group was becoming active in democratic politics. I was saddened, however, that the proposal I had made in my report of the previous year that the UK should fund 'a project to rehabilitate the young rebel soldiers' had not been acted upon. This continued to be an issue, albeit one that was diminishing. However, I was particularly impressed by my meeting with the Ceylon Chamber of Commerce whose members reported that food production and fishing had revived much quicker than forecast. All in all, the experience in the Eastern Province gave great hope for the revival of the Northern Province.

Perhaps somewhat inevitably, whilst the war had been raging there had been much slower progress on constitutional matters with the APRC (All-Party Reconciliation Commission) not having yet resolved the thorny issue of the 14th Amendment. The thorny part being the proposed 10 per cent of concurrent powers and which should be kept by central government and which should be devolved to the provinces. The Chairman assured me that real progress was being made. I wondered about that, especially as the UNP was so weakly led by Ranil Wickremasinghe and I questioned his ability to deliver any tentative agreement before a general election likely to have been held in May or June 2009. This forecast was too optimistic and the election did not take place until April 2010.

One of the biggest worries for me was the ever-growing presence of the media and its freedom of expression. Whilst there was no formal censorship, the media was not expected to criticise the war against the Tamil Tiger terrorists. This, of course, was far less draconian than the measures the UK had in place during World War II but people forget. There were two significant events whilst I was in Sri Lanka: the smashing up of a TV studio and the murder of the popular editor of the *Sunday Leader*, Lasantha Wickrematunga. He had been extremely critical of the government but he had been tolerated for three years. He was also in regular and friendly meetings over a meal with the President. We do not know who did the killing but it made no sense for the government to create a *cause célèbre* just at a time when the war was moving in its favour.

At the time, the global economy faced a huge liquidity crisis and I reported that it was inevitable that it should hit Sri Lanka soon after. There was not only the huge cost of the war but also a heavy budget deficit and the downgrading of government loans to below junk status. On the brighter side, I noted, there would be a peace bonus and, thanks to the peace, rice production in the east was already now in surplus. Peace would also help tourism. However, the challenges continued to be very real as the garment industry reported companies such as Marks & Spencer reducing their orders by up to 25 per cent.

I also reported that our new High Commissioner, Peter Hayes, had made a very positive impact on all in government, including those in opposition. However, he certainly had his work cut out to try and explain the UK Government's mystifying statements, such as the Prime Minister's response to Keith Vaz, MP, a well-known supporter of the Tamil Tigers, on 14 January during Prime Minister's Questions. Mr Blair stated that Sri Lanka should negotiate a ceasefire with the terrorist group and that he would discuss this with France and Germany (who had no real locus at all). This was followed by the Foreign Secretary's visit to India and the unfortunate linking of Kashmir to the Mumbai Terrorist bombings and finally the issue of a statement on Sri Lanka which, in effect, contradicted the Prime Minister but raised the issue of the thousands killed in the civil war but failed to mention the remarkable fact that there had been no civilian casualties in the war in the prior twelve months. I recognise that certain marginally held government seats have large Tamil diaspora but UK policy must not be made to just suit these electorates.

I concluded my report by reiterating my plea that the UK Government should make a significant and focused contribution to the rebuilding of the Northern Province which would help to restore Sri Lanka's faith in us.

Sadly, faith never was restored and when Prime Minister Cameron visited Jaffna at the CHOGM (Commonwealth Heads of Government Meeting) in January 2013, he visited an IDP camp and complained that it was terrible to see it with his own eyes. He then failed to offer any form of practical or financial help to alleviate the suffering he had seen.

These were broadly my thoughts at the time, submitted in my report to the UK Government. However, I did not report probably the most fascinating meeting of all which was with the UK Defence attaché, Lt Col Anton Gash. I had met him on my visit in January 2008 and had taken an immediate liking to him both for his professionalism and his ability to realistically assess the military situation. Of course, it helped having been an RAF pilot myself, one of an increasingly rare breed in Parliament. Anyway, on this 2009 visit I asked if we could meet, which he readily accepted. I booked a room at the Hilton where I was staying. Then, just before he arrived, I changed the room in case the original room was bugged. Lt Col Gash was quite open in saying that in his opinion the Sri Lanka armed forces were carrying out a very careful and measured campaign. Every effort was being made not to kill civilians, even to the extent of slowing down their advance in places. Moreover, he was amazed at the number of civilians who were managing to escape the clutches of the LTTE in response to the leaflet drops which promised safe passage and that they would be looked after by their Tamil brethren. He made it clear that he was free to go wherever he wished, in principle, accompanied by the relevant staff officer. I cannot remember precisely what he said about the timing of the end of the war but he was confident the Sri Lanka Army would prevail. He also drew my attention to an article written by General Fonseka (I think it appeared in the local *Sunday Times*) which was critical of the Rajapaksa brothers. I read the article and was struck by the thought that this could never happen in the

UK, as army commanders were there to fight a campaign and not to dip into politics. However, when General Fonseka stood for the presidency after the war, all became clear. At the time I had absolutely no idea that some five years later I would have the inspiration to try for a Freedom of Information request to get the despatches sent back to the UK and published. I now know just how vital this inspiration turned out to be. I have not spoken or contacted Lt Col Gash but I hereby apologise to him if I have caused him a mountain of aggravation, which is quite possible!

The second half of my visit was as a tourist but one who avidly read the daily papers and watched the television to keep abreast of what was happening on the ground. By the time I boarded my plane for London, Kilinochchi, the LTTE's administrative capital, had fallen after weeks of constant pressure which included the deployment of Special Forces who had crossed a lagoon to enable them to attack the LTTE from behind. This was quickly followed by the reopening of Elephant Pass, the gateway to Jaffna, its naval headquarters at Mullaittivu. The LTTE was now confined to a small area in Mullaittivu District on the north-east coast.

Once back in the UK it was relatively easy to keep track of progress in the war. Soon after this advance the government designated a 2-km safe 'No Fire Zone' to the north of the A35 highway between the townships of Visuamadu and Puthukkudiyiruppu, together with two other smaller NFZs on 19 January 2009. At the same time thousands of leaflets were dropped advising the perhaps near 250,000 civilians trapped in the remnants of rebel-held territory that they would not be fired upon if they moved to this area. In theory, this was a bold humanitarian strategy but to work, both sides had to respect the No Fire Zone. The LTTE had no intention of losing its human shield, so it placed considerable fire power in the No Fire Zone and started shelling the advancing Sri Lanka Army which understandably had to return fire to try and knock out the guns. Returning fire by a well-equipped, trained artillery unit is precision shelling and not just random fire, as described by many, indeed too many, Tamil-inspired sources.

It was these same sources who totally ignored the fact that if the LTTE had not placed its artillery next to the hospitals or elsewhere in the No Fire Zone and then opened fire, there would have been no shelling from the advancing Sri Lanka Army. Even more sinister were reports stating that the LTTE was shelling the hospitals themselves to ensure the media was kept awake.

On 12 February 2009 the Sri Lanka Army re-designated a new No Fire Zone near Velanayanmadam, north of Mullaittivu, forcing the displaced civilians and the LTTE hiding in their midst to relocate. In effect the LTTE could not retreat much further as it faced the sea on the east side and advancing Sri Lanka units from the north, west and south. However, this was difficult terrain: mainly jungle. On the seashore and the lagoons the LTTE had constructed a series of heavily fortified bunds, or perhaps I should say forced the civilian Tamils to do all this hard work. The net result was the war was to last another three months: partly because of topography and partly because the Sri Lanka Army chose not to press really hard as casualties – both civilian and military – would have risen appreciably. I have in my possession a despatch from Anton Gash indicating what was happening in the NFZ in mid-March, and I quote:

Reports via the UN are that LTTE cadres visited a dwelling in the NFZ to recruit family members. The IDPs resisted and a large crowd gathered. Scuffles broke out and two children were shot. The brawl expanded and then spread to the area where ICRC (International Committee of the Red Cross) food distribution was taking place. IDPs appealed to ICRC members to help them and to allow them to leave on the ship or to open up road egress. The LTTE became heavy-handed and it is rumoured that one international staff member was detained by the LTTE. Subsequently it was learned that a 16 year-old girl had been forcibly recruited.

One might note the reference to the ICRC distributing food brought in by ship.

A final NFZ (number 5) was designated on 9 May 2009. It is important to note that the Sri Lanka Army followed international Rules of Engagement ensuring that all parties, both LTTE and themselves, were fully briefed on these.

It was dring this period that the West decided it must act. It had been heavily pressured by the LTTE/ Tamil diaspora which included a tornado of publicity alleging atrocities by the Sri Lanka Army: the shelling of hospitals, killing Tamils trying to escape and even surrendering, and allegations of huge medicine and food shortages, which in the latter resulted in starvation. It started with the UN High Commissioner for Human Rights, Navi Pillay, accusing both sides of war crimes. On April 16 2009 (with just about a month until the end of the war on 18 May), Ban Ki-moon, the UN Secretary General, sent Vijay Nambiar, Chef de Cabinet, to broker a ceasefire. This was rejected. Then the US State Department called on the LTTE to release its civilian hostages and surrender to a third party. There were even rumours that Western warships would help to evacuate the trapped civilians as well as the surviving LTTE leadership. This, too, was rejected, not least as Colombo knew full well that the LTTE was about to be smashed forever.

The UK did not wish to be thought or seen to be idle, so on 29 April Foreign Secretary David Miliband and his French counterpart, Bernard Kouchner, arrived in Colombo to try to stop the bloodshed. The truth, as far as I could see, was that the Labour Party was putting huge pressure on him to do something otherwise the Tamil voters, particularly in the marginal seats, would not vote Labour in the next general election. What really stuck in my gullet was Mr Miliband's allegation of starvation as so little food was getting through. It is true that after the fall of Kilinochchi less was getting through but this was largely due to the fact that the UN had pulled its aid workers out of Kilinochchi, against the recommendation of the local UN officials on the ground. It was really the UN's disgrace. I went through all the tonnages that had been sent and they totalled considerably more than Mr Miliband's figures.

However, the key failure was that no one in the West understood the importance of the Government Agents. All the way through the war, be it in the Eastern or Northern Provinces, these wonderful people kept local government and its services operational – particularly hospitals, schools and, above all, strategic stock levels of key commodities like rice, fuel and medicines. Moreover, the rice harvest in the north-east had been good and it was in the government warehouse. I do not know whether Mr Miliband deliberately distorted the picture to please the UK audience or he did not know about the key function of a government agent. Subsequently, when I met the President he commented on how rude and arrogant Miliband had been, adopting an embarrassing colonial master demeanour when addressing the President who was made to feel like the servant. I was not surprised to hear this, as I had seen Miliband's lack of understanding of Indian etiquette when he visited Mumbai.

The other extraordinary UK dimension was the role of Des Browne, MP who Mr Blair had designated as his Special Envoy to Sri Lanka. Indeed, so special that our own High Commissioner in Colombo was unaware of his visit, along with a small party of Cross-Party MPs, until his arrival on 4 May! Following this brief visit a statement was made by officials in London, stating: 'Britain would continue with its concerted drive to achieve a fully inclusive political settlement.' What a wonderful thought when they had done virtually nothing before or during the war. Actually, I have my personal suspicion that Prime Minister Blair recognised that Miliband's visit had been a disaster and he wanted an appraisal from one of his closest colleagues.

The one country which did have some clout and influence was India. Tamil Nadu, with a population of 70 million Tamils, had been the safe-haven and training ground for many of the Eelam leaders and its treasury. However, the murder of Rajiv Gandhi had put a halt to most of this closeness. Nevertheless, the ruling party in Tamil Nadu, the DMK, was crucial to the Indian Government Coalition. So it was on 23 April that India's Foreign Secretary telephoned Gotabaya. After talking to his brother, the President, the Sri Lanka Government agreed to invite the Indians to attend talks over breakfast the following day, which they did. The Indians recounted that the people of Tamil Nadu had been told their kith and kin were being slaughtered. The President made it clear that, having come so far, the war could not be stopped now. I understand it was the Indians who asked that in the final stages there should be no use of air power or heavy guns. This was not an easy request to handle, as the Tigers were still a force to be reckoned with. Then there was another twist in that the Chief Minister of Tamil Nadu, Muthuvel Karunanidhi, decided to go on a fast, to death, unless the big guns were silenced. It says much for the tenacity of these Eastern negotiators that the following communiqué was thrashed out and posted on 27 April:

The government of Sri Lanka has announced that combat

operations had reached their conclusion and that the Sri Lankan security forces have been instructed to end the use of heavy calibre guns, combat aircraft and aerial weapons which could cause civilians casualties. Sri Lankan forces will now confine their attempts to rescue the civilians who remain and give topmost priority to saving them.

The wording and timing of this carefully crafted statement still enabled the army to finish the job of defeating the Tigers who never chose to surrender and finish the war. Readers may wonder how I know about this episode. I had picked up rumours from Indian and Sri Lankan friends but the detail comes from the excellent book by Paul Moorcraft, entitled *Total Destruction of the Tamil Tigers*.

The Sri Lanka Army had entered the last NFZ (number 5) on 18 April with the key engagement on 20 April when it breached the huge Puthamathalan bund, releasing to safety the vast bulk of the thousands who had been held hostage (maybe as many as 200,000). Nevertheless, up to 20,000 civilians were still hemmed in. Slowly but surely the Sri Lanka Army squeezed the LTTE from the north and the south, releasing trapped civilians as they went until 16 May when the two arms of the army met. The west was covered by the army on the edge of the Nandikadal Lagoon and the east by the sea. Even as this was happening the international community was still putting pressure on Sri Lanka for a ceasefire; a total misreading of the situation on the ground and the implications for the future of Sri Lanka. I write this on the eve of the centenary of Remembrance Sunday, so it is appropriate to reflect that the Sri Lanka Army casualties for the Eelam War IV, which lasted two years and ten months, were 5,800 killed and 29,000 injured.

On 19 May 2009 at 9.30 am President Rajapaksa addressed the nation and an expectant world media to announce that the LTTE had been defeated. This was 4.00 am UK time so I did not pick it up at home until breakfast. As it happens, my wife and I were going to Ascot that day so we had much to celebrate. I could not help but wonder what had happened to Prabhakaran. Later there were to be all sorts of rumours but it is now clear that he and his key lieutenants were hiding in a thick mangrove swamp. The army, seeing heads bobbing up and down, sprayed shots into the mangrove swamp. They killed Prabhakaran with three shots to the ribs and took out some of his key lieutenants as well.

So ended the life of possibly one of the most ruthless, demonic terrorist leaders of all time. He had killed all his Tamil rivals with ruthless precision, murdered in cold-blood two presidents and tens of political leaders. He had forcibly recruited thousands of young boys and girls to man the front lines and to be the first to be killed. He had been responsible for the loss of thousands of the ordinary citizens of Sri Lanka during his twenty-five-year reign of terror, all in the cause of so-called Eelam. There can be few men as terrible as him to live on this earth.

The war was over but certain parties in the West, egged on by the Tamil diaspora and the Human Rights NGOs were quick to make claims against the Sri Lanka Army about extensive war crimes committed particularly in the final few days of the war, like the 'White Flag incident'. It was said there were incidents on both sides but the LTTE was all now gone or killed whereas the Sri Lanka Army was still in place, and therefore, in the eyes of some, accountable.

There is proof, primarily from Lt Col Gash's despatches which I have supplied to the UN, that there was no evidence of any form of genocide by the Sri Lanka armed forces. Indeed, it should be noted that they went to great lengths to avoid killing Tamil civilians. It is my belief that the UN must have seen these despatches at the time; the UK Government certainly had access to them all along. If I am correct, then this totally undermines the integrity of both the UN and the UK Government in the period between 1 January and 16 May 2009. My personal view is that there should be a total amnesty across all sides and all sides should take part in a Truth and Reconciliation Commission similar to those employed in Columbia or South Africa. The key point is that this would not only put the minds of all Sri Lankans at rest (those living in the country) but equally important it should reassure the diaspora and all the Human Rights organisations. Surely it is time to draw a line in the sand? This is not the first time I have made this proposal in public.

Peace in Sri Lanka brought the enormous challenge of looking after its own people, particularly the 300,000 (mainly) Tamils spread across a number of refugee camps, together with a further 100,000 (mainly) Muslims who had been evicted from their homes in Jaffna by the

LTTE. There were also those left homeless in the Eastern Province. The Government of Sri Lanka had wisely set up a small number of reception camps, the largest of which was Manik Farm, which my wife and I visited, albeit towards its end of its life. No one could have foreseen the scale of need that descended on the camps in the last few days of the war. Three hundred thousand people forcibly taken from their homes in Jaffna, used as human shields, rescued by the government after five months of hell. These people were so thankful to have a roof over their heads, free food, medical checks and safety. However, it was not a straightforward process as hidden in this huge number were over 11,000 LTTE cadres who had thrown away their uniforms in the hope of being classed as civilians. Clearly the policy of interviewing everyone would take time, so no one could be let out until the process was completed. This was the reason for no freedom of movement. It is easy to see that this was desperately depressing for all those poor people after what they had gone through and understandably, as Tamils, they were worried about recriminations. However, I cannot help but feel the situation was not helped by the bleating of the NGOs, particularly the Human Rights specialists, who saw it as their task to undermine the government at every juncture. Had I been in the camp I would have been reassured by the presence of the ICRC (International Committee for the Red Cross) who were there from day one. Later, when I met the Head of Mission from the ICRC I was told they were full of praise at the way such a huge challenge had been handled. It was not helped by some journalists calling the camps 'Concentration Camps' with all the memories of what that meant from World War II alongside the UN's own unhelpful comments. I was pleased that a group of MPs from Tamil Nadu came and issued a statement thanking the Sri Lanka Government and expressing satisfaction for all that had been done and would be done. I reflect that these were Tamils from India who would have been the first to complain if matters were wrong.

Few outsiders seemed to understand the dreadful state of northern Sri Lanka as a result of the war: little power, homes ruined and millions of landmines littered the landscape. So I was surprised and delighted when Foreign Minister Bogollagama announced to Parliament at the end of September 2009, just four months after the end of the war, that 59,600 people had been resettled, 8,000 released, 7,000 returned to Jaffna and

3,400 to their own districts. Slowly but surely the people were resettled principally in the de-mined areas. I have visited these operations at least three times in recent years. I am full of admiration for the way this painstaking work is done. I pay tribute to the Sri Lanka Army, India, US, Canada, Japan and Britain's own Halo Trust who have all contributed to this vital work (and anyone else I have overlooked). This successful work really is painstaking: a highly skilled operator can clear about 1 metre a day. This surely should be one of the world's real achievements that deserves recognition. At the time of writing in January 2018 progress is still good but the work may not be finally finished to 2020. I hope I can go to see the work finished. I am also delighted that in December 2017 the Sri Lanka Government signed the Ottawa Convention, the anti-personnel Mine Ban Treaty (MBT). Sadly, and somewhat typically, there was little or no coverage in the Western media or words of praise from Western leaders.

In addition to having to wrestle with this massive resettlement programme, Sir Lanka faced huge financial challenges and the need for an IMF loan. At last, in July 2009 funds were released: US$2.5 billion. The US, the UK and France abstained: really helpful. Indeed, but for their indifference it would have been released earlier. Furthermore, appearing on the horizon were rumours of the EU withdrawing GSP (Generalised Scheme of Preferences) which 'allows vulnerable developing countries to pay few or no duties on exports to the EU, giving them vital access to the EU market and contributing to their growth' (http://ec.europa. eu website) which was of huge importance to Sri Lanka's wonderful garment industry. The grounds for this rumoured withdrawal was that Sri Lanka had not made sufficient progress in meeting certain Human Rights targets. This clearly demonstrated absolutely no understanding or appreciation for a government that had been focused in winning a deadly war. How anyone in Europe could think that throwing out of work 200,000 directly and a million indirectly, mainly Tamil women, would aid reconciliation is beyond me. Nobody listened. Sadly, it did happen, it did hurt and no one benefited other than the diaspora who claimed another victory on hard-pressed Sri Lanka whilst they enjoyed the luxury of the Western life.

There were other examples of a complete lack of understanding for

Sri Lanka's plight but the one that stuck in my throat was the call on 2 October 2009 from a British Labour MP, Siobhain McDonagh, for a boycott of Sri Lankan goods and tourist visits. I noted an editorial in the *Financial Times* of 21 October stating that 'Sri Lanka should keep its special access to EU markets'. I quote just one sentence 'Using trade as a strategic tool makes the global trading system hostage to endless political posturing and negotiating games.' I wrote a letter to the Editor, which finished with the phrase 'Why cannot the UK Foreign Office and the EU understand that all Sri Lankans need is a breathing space to return to normal in a united island?'

Despite all the brickbats from the West, I noted in an update sent to me that as of 4 November 2009 no less than 99,001 IDPs had been resettled. Indeed, the progress continued apace. The President stated that by 1 December there would be total freedom of movement for all in the camps; somewhat to the surprise of all the Western sceptics this actually happened. It was duly implemented and the camps became open camps.

I myself took the opportunity of the 2009 Queen's Speech at the opening of Parliament on 19 November to focus on Sri Lanka. The full text is in Appendix VI, but in brief: 'I wish to make an appeal for a new start and a completely new look at the relationship between our two countries.' I highlighted that Ceylon had the eighth highest losses in World War II and Sri Lanka was just one of eight to support us over the Falklands. I called for a better understanding of the results of twenty-five years of terrorism and its effect on the economy. I highlighted that 284,000 people who went voluntarily into the refugee camps. I quoted the results of a visit of MPs from Tamil Nadu who were comfortable with what was being done and hugely encouraged by the rate of resettlement. I covered de-mining, GSP+ but the most telling was the memorandum left with the British Government in early November by the Catholic Archbishop of Colombo along with Buddhist, Hindu and Muslim faith leaders. This read:

As responsible religious leaders we are saddened by the fact that our European friends with whom Sri Lanka has always cherished such excellent and cordial bilateral relations, have given a larger than necessary sense of attention to certain groups with vested interests who are intent on destroying this country and pushing it once again into the abyss of political and economic confusion and chaos. Therefore, we appeal to our friends to stand by us at this hour and to help us guide our leaders and people towards a greater sense of spiritual and material progress. We appeal to you to help us in this matter and thank you for any consideration given to this very deserving request.

I concluded my speech by saying 'I appeal to Her Majesty's Government to open a new chapter and to help Sri Lanka in its hour of need rather than kicking the people when they are down.'

I followed this up with a letter dated 22 November 2009 to David Miliband, the Foreign Secretary, highlighting my speech and adding there was still time for the UK to intervene about GSP+. The response came dated 30 November, claiming the UK had long been at the forefront of international efforts, as well as giving £12.5m since 2008 to support humanitarian organisations and NGOs in Sri Lanka. This hardly seemed an earth-shattering sum. On GSP+ his response was that the EU had commissioned a Report in October 2009 and found that Sri Lanka had not done enough. Of course, this showed a total disregard to the fact that the country had been wholly focused throughout 2009 on its civil war.

Good, succinct oral questions are a vital part of a politician's armoury and so it has proved for me over the years in relation to Sri Lanka. One of the best I asked was on the day after the end of the war. It read:

My Lords, have Her Majesty's Government congratulated the Sri Lankan Government on defeating the Tamil Tigers and bringing peace to the country? On the international front is it Her Majesty's Government's policy primarily to tackle the resettlement of the 250,000 Tamils and the 100,000 Muslims who were ethnically cleansed from Jaffna, or is it to continue to lecture that there should be a constitutional settlement which really rests with the Parliament of Sri Lanka?

Lord Malloch-Brown, the Labour Minister and formerly a senior official at the UN responded:

My Lords, we certainly respect the noble Lord's final point – that the political solution to this must come from inside Sri Lanka from a process set up and led by President Rajapaksa. Indeed in our initial contacts with the President, we congratulated him on the finishing off a brutal twenty-six year civil war, which was instigated by the Tamil Tigers – a terrorist group. But we also made it extremely clear to him that, whether or not that victory would be seen as the opening of a new and happier chapter in Sri Lanka depended on whether he could now go that next step and show the statesmanship to find a political as well as humanitarian solution to this community's issues.

I followed this up with a series of oral and written questions, all aimed at trying to get the British Government to help with de-mining and resettlement, particularly in the Jaffna area. I succeeded on de-mining but failed to get any real help for the Tamils in Jaffna. Indeed, I never did succeed even on later appeals to help with modernising Jaffna Hospital. It was almost as if the dead hand of the Tamil diaspora in the UK did not want to see any real help going into rebuilding Jaffna.

One or other of my questions must have struck a raw nerve with the Eelam-orientated part of the UK Tamil diaspora, for on 17 June 2009 I received no less than eighty-two telephone messages between the hours of 8.20 am and 2.07 pm all asking me to call. The House of Lords authorities have stated this is by far the largest number of calls ever made to any one Lord in a single day.

The increasing normality of life with more and more IDPs being resettled, in a manner seemingly accepted by all interested parties, alongside the huge government effort to restore the infrastructure, particularly power to Jaffna and road links, were punctured by the excitement of the forthcoming presidential election set for 26 January 2010. I say punctured because of the sudden appearance of the retired General Fonseka as the Opposition Candidate not standing as an Independent but as the flag carrier for the UNP, the JVP and the SLFP (Mahanga wing).

There was a penetrating editorial in the Hindu of 1 December. It highlighted the fact that this was the first time in sixty-one year history of independent Sri Lanka that a mainstream effort was being made to politicise the military. It noted that Army Chief Fonseka commanded the respect of his men as long as he stayed a soldier. The problem was he crossed the lines and betrayed quirkiness, triumphalism and chauvinism. At the height of the Eelam War IV he went on record with assertions such as, 'I strongly believe that this country belongs to the Sinhalese.' The editorial lists a number of other provocative statements. They finish with the observation 'for the combined forces of the Opposition to be essaying into political adventurism, with a maverick and unpredictable General at their head is to court humiliation and possibly trouble'. They might well have asked or was their leadership so weak that they dare not stand? What on earth was the once proud UNP doing?

The result was a triumph for Mahinda Rajapaksa with 57.88 per cent of the vote: the Opposition candidate could only muster 40.15 per cent. Rajapaksa's share was a near record although perhaps understandably not with Tamils. This was slightly surprising and disappointing, given he said his main priority would be the rehabilitation of the displaced Tamils and reconstruction of the Northern and Eastern Regions. One might have thought that would strike a chord. Indeed, the *Hindu*, in its editorial of 28 January 2010 declared: 'The 17.73 percentage point margin is a reaffirmation of the maturity and good sense of ordinary voters who, given the choice chose an experienced political leader.'

In electoral terms this was half the battle, as a general election was to be called on 8 April 2010, something the Tamil Leaders had been pressing for. President Rajapaksa's coalition won 139 seats against the official opposition UNP tally of 60 – their lowest ever total. It was my privilege on 31 January to send to the President a handwritten letter as Chairman of the All-Party British Sri Lanka Parliamentary Group. I have a copy. My second paragraph is worth recording:

Unlike the British media our group recognises the challenge Sri Lanka has faced over the last 25 years and most of our members supported your campaign to see the Tamil Tigers defeated.

For once it looked as if things were looking up, particularly with the continuing resettlement of the IDPs, the massive effort to get the Jaffna

Peninsula back on the National Grid, as well as road and rail services being restored to normal. However, there were straws in the wind suggesting some future buffeting. The former LTTE activists overseas had set up the Tamil Global Forum threatening war crimes action and there were some rumours of incriminating photographs. It also transpired that the former Prime Minister Ranil Wickremesinghe had recruited to the Fonseka campaign team a Tory activist who had worked for both David Cameron and Boris Johnson – one James McGrath.

The general election in the UK scheduled to take place in May 2010 soon caused problems for Sri Lanka. The biggest problem was the tacit support of the Global Tamil Forum by the Conservative leadership of Cameron, Hague and Simpson. Naturally, I recognise that with significant numbers of Tamils in key seats there had to be some rapport between the Tamil diaspora and the Conservative Party hoping to win the election. William Hague as Shadow Foreign Secretary addressed the Global Tamil Forum on 24 February. I do not know who briefed Mr Hague but he should have known that the two key aims of the Tamil Global Forum were to use all resources to establish Tamil people's right to self-determination and nationhood, and furthermore to help empower the Tamil people in their pursuit of a self-governing Tamil Eelam.

I remain amazed that in his first paragraph he said: 'We all congratulate you on the Establishment of the Global Tamil Forum which unites your diaspora around the world.' There were also phrases such as: 'We urged the Sri Lankan Government to allow a humanitarian ceasefire to grant innocent civilians safe departure.' To an innocent bystander this might have seemed reasonable but not for a Shadow Foreign Secretary who knew how the civilians had been herded in by the Tamil Tigers as a human shield and would not be released. Then there were references to war crimes. He should have known from Lt Col Gash's despatches just how hard the Sri Lanka Government was working to minimise civilian casualties.

I also had cause to complain about a meeting of the Tamil Eelam referendum when Eelam was specifically supported by our prospective Conservative candidate for Harrow West, Dr Rachel Joyce. I wrote and complained to William Hague, whose response came via the Junior Shadow Foreign Minister, Keith Simpson. Frankly, if they had handled the issue as I had handled the IRA in Northampton South there would have been no problem – and I was defending a majority of 179. I met the Irish but refused to attend any meeting. Certainly, Dr Joyce's involvement supported by the Conservative leadership deeply upset the Sinhalese diaspora; made worse by Mr Cameron congratulating the Tamils on their New Year but choosing not to do the same for the Sinhalese.

I still find it incredible that the leadership of the Conservative Party should take the line they did, of virtually bending over backwards for the Tamil vote when they knew full well what Sri Lanka had been through in facing up to the Tamil Tigers for over twenty-five years. One asks the question: Where was the leadership to set themselves apart from the Labour Party? I helped in my home territory of Northampton and Bedford but one sensed there was no dynamic leadership to take us on to a clear-cut victory; indeed I bet on a hung Parliament and won. I thought to myself: We shall have to do what Harold Wilson did in February 1974 at my first successful election. Namely, as the largest party we should decide to govern until defeated and hold another election in the firm knowledge that the electorate would back us the second time. Wilson was an astute politician; sadly Cameron was not. The temptation to be Prime Minister in a coalition and live at Number 10 Downing Street was just too great. However, in that fateful decision was to lie the seed of failure. Cameron decided to agree to give the people a referendum over leaving the EU without stating whether it was binding or advisory, then losing it by pure ineptness and landing the UK with Brexit. To cap it all he then walked away by resigning his seat. Poor Sri Lanka was caught up in the slipstream as the President found to his cost in the visit in December 2010 which saw the UK Government cow-tow to the demands of LTTE groups and activists.

Continuing with reflections, I have to say the UN badly let down the people of Sri Lanka in this terrible near thirty-year experience. There is no doubt in my mind it should not have pulled out its help at the time of the fall of Kilinochchi; the UN should not have listened to the propaganda of the diaspora and the Human Rights organisations. The evidence seems to show that UN headquarters ignored the advice of their local officials. The UN showed so little leadership at a hugely difficult time for Sri Lanka. I suppose, too, that had Prabhakaran actually attended the Norwegian organised peace talks then it is just possible the war could have been averted.

Even today the massive funds – probably in billions – raised by fair and foul means by the LTTE from the Tamil diaspora in the USA, Canada, all over Europe as well as in Tamil Nadu and even amongst some Tamils in Sri Lanka, is used to pay for propaganda across the world. Propaganda to achieve two ends: the prosecution of war crimes on false evidence and the perpetual criticism of any Sri Lanka government until they achieve their goal of a separate state based on the Northern and Eastern Provinces. How sad that these people have not the vision to think a little more creatively about the future of their fellow Tamil brothers. Just think what a wonderful force for good it would be to see these funds focused on education, health, training the Tamil youth and the Tamil community in all its aspects. That would be a true act of reconciliation. All it needs is the Tamil fraternity to show some vision and leadership.

I must digress no further but just as the wounds were beginning to heal Sri Lanka was hit by a terrible piece of powerful TV propaganda heavily skewed and for all I know underwritten by a section of the diaspora who having lost the war were out to undermine Sri Lanka. I refer to the Channel 4 TV film *Sri Lanka's Killing Fields*, broadcast on 14 June 2011, followed with another hammer blow with a second Channel 4 TV film *Sri Lanka's Killing Fields – War Crimes Unpunished* on 14 March 2012.

Lover's Leap division was the only estate which was owned by Mr. James Taylor the pioneer tea planter who started the tea planting enterprise in Sri Lanka when he planted 17 acres of tea in 1886 in Loolecondera Estate Hewaheta. 200 Tea Plants were planted in Naseby Division of Pedro Estate in 1867. This is the earliest recorded planting tea in Sri Lanka.

Tea remains one of the symbols of Sri Lanka. The Naseby tea estate was the first to be planted by the British in Sri Lanka. Why would a Scot name it Naseby?

CHAPTER
Thirteen

Post-war: The View in Sri Lanka

There were two aspects to my reflections and subsequent reports on post-war Sri Lanka, during the period between 2011 and 2014. There was my assessment formulated by contact with Sri Lankan friends and my own nearly three-week visit in March–April 2012 when I covered a great deal of the country geographically and met with a number of those who were involved and mattered in rebuilding a country ravaged by war, from President Rajapaksa down. I tried to assess what I found on the ground against the charge that the Government of Sri Lanka had done too little in the years since the end of the war to achieve reconciliation with Tamils in the north. It must be noted that this does not apply to the Tamils in the south who are in a majority and have never felt alienated. I have used much of my report to the UK Secretary of State for Foreign & Commonwealth Affairs, submitted in April 2012 to illustrate, in my opinion, the remarkable efforts Sri Lanka had made to rehabilitate itself – its infrastructure and its people.

By way of background: I was a boy during World War II in England, sent to the depths of the countryside with my mother and baby brother. My father, an architect and surveyor, was a divisional manager at the government's Ministry of Works and stayed in London throughout the Blitz. His specific responsibility was to decide which buildings to demolish and which to shore up after a German bombing raid. We returned to London in 1943 once the heavy bombing had virtually ceased. From 1943 to 1955 I often accompanied my father to view rebuilding work. I clearly remember him saying to me, a teenager, how difficult it was to establish original ownership when all the records had been destroyed. It took London ten years to recover and land title challenges lasted almost twenty years. Northern Sri Lanka has gone through a very similar experience, especially in terms of smashed infrastructure, lost records and competing ownership claims.

Achievements:

As I reflect on the early post war period the huge prize is peace in every part of the island; something not experienced for nearly thirty years.

'PEACE' was achieved on 18 May 2009 when the Tamil Tigers were finally defeated and nearly 300,000 human shield hostages were rescued into government hands and looked after. Peace is the overwhelming need of the country and is the first priority mentioned in a recent poll. There have been no bombings since May 2010 (still the position at the time of writing in 2018). People of all ethnic groups travel the length and breadth of the country by day or night without fear.

In just three years the whole infrastructure of Jaffna had been restored and modernised, including links to the south. As far as the ordinary Tamil is concerned, life is back to normal. There is twenty-four-hour electricity with no power cuts, thanks to linkage to the National Grid. The railway reopened to Mannar and Jaffna after the railway lines were melted down by the LTTE for armaments, and excellent roads have been reopened, particularly the A9. The construction of a new water grid provided Jaffna District with clean, safe water. All this was geared to ensuring Jaffna and the rest of the Northern Province, the heartland of the Tamils, was restored and open for business. Add to this in the south-east the Hambantota Port complex, along with a new airport and the creation/building of a new town. Even Colombo had been cleaned up. These were huge achievements that we in the West would be pushed to match but were almost ignored by the USA and the UK governments, as well as by the UN.

The biggest handicap to the re-settlement of the Tamils in Manik Farm and the other smaller re-settlement camps was the challenge of de-mining. The LTTE had scattered thousands upon thousands of landmines as it retreated, without keeping any records, all over the land it once dominated. I have visited the mine fields twice to watch clearance in action; the sheer dedication of the mainly Sri Lanka personnel covering just a square metre a day has to be applauded, as does the enormous support from India and the UK's Halo Trust, as well as other countries such as the US and Canada and of course the Sri Lanka Army. I have never heard the complaining diaspora ever give a word of recognition to this massive achievement as the clearance enters its final stages. I say a particular thank you to the UK Halo Trust financed by the UK aid budget, which was there on Day One of freedom and are still there in 2019, hopeful of finishing its task somewhere between 2020 and 2022. Once it has finished, all the IDPs can return home.

The resettlement of the IDPs has clearly been of the highest priority. What a challenge: nearly 300,000 people. Ann, my doctor wife, and I visited the camp Manik Farm where we met officials and the people living in the camp. On our visit in early April 2012 there were the last 6,202 IDPs. (The camp closed in September 2012.) One of the most depressing features was the biased attitude of some of the Western media and leaders to the really well meant and sensitive attempt by the Government of Sri Lanka to look after its own people, be they Tamil, Muslim or Sinhalese. Phrases peppered the media, such as 'being sent to a concentration camp' or 'to a high security camp surrounded by barbed wire with no one allowed in or out'. There was absolutely no understanding that within these 300,000 were no less than over 11,000 LTTE cadres, most of whom were wearing civilian clothes at the time they escaped to the government side. I discussed this with the Head of Mission of the ICRC who confirmed to me that it, the Red Cross, had access to the camp from Day One and was full of praise at the way the way such a huge challenge had been handled. However, the closing of the IDP camps still left some of the 100,000 Muslim and Sinhalese IDPs who had been ethnically cleansed from Jaffna with just twenty-four hours' notice by the Tamil Tigers in 1990. I discussed the issue with Minister Richard Badurdeen, MP (himself an original IDP). Even today there are still about 13,500 families awaiting resettlement.

One of the other key issues that had now been resolved was language. At the time of Independence, Tamil was not an official language. Indeed,

I clearly remember when I worked in Ceylon in 1963 that Tamils had to write to government departments in Sinhala or to senior levels in English. President Rajapaksa's Government had the vision to make Tamil one of the official languages. He went further by requiring middle-level government officials, including the police, to learn and speak Tamil. The issue is no longer as the government had not only made Tamil an official language but all school children across the country now learn Sinhala, Tamil and English. One could even see for oneself the change, as road signs and government notices are now in three languages. This achievement had done more than anything to make ordinary Tamils feel included and an equal part of Sri Lanka society. However, who outside Sri Lanka recognises it? The remaining challenge, which continues to this day, is to find more teachers of English both to teach directly or, perhaps more importantly, to teach other teachers who are not proficient in English. Surely this is a tailor-made opportunity for the British Council to help?

Property and land remained emotive issues, as they are in any society. Military requisition was undertaken during the war both by the LTTE and the Sri Lanka armed forces, as is normal in times of war. Certainly it happened in the UK during World War II. The army had already returned over half the acreages to their previous owners. They expected to continue this process further. However, there remained a key strategic need for a substantial defence force in Jaffna because of its proximity to Tamil Nadu where there were still significant numbers of LTTE supporters, as well certain key naval establishments. The army presence had reduced considerably to what it had been during the war and numbers continued to fall. During my 2012 visit I met the Commanding Officer at Palaly Camp, Major General Hathurusinghe, a Tamil. He and his team had just been awarded the Gucci Award against nineteen other nations for his 'Hearts and Minds' programme. I wonder why the varying UN rapporteurs or visiting politicians or, indeed, any of Sri Lanka's persistent critics always choose to ignore this type of initiative which by any yardstick is a success story. One final observation: not a single person I met on my visit wanted the army to leave.

Civilian land title claims are extremely difficult to resolve. Firstly, the LTTE had ethnically cleansed 100,000 Muslims at twenty-four hours' notice and about 20,000 Sinhalese fled, as did thousands of moderate Tamils. The land was not left empty but filled with other Tamils either as followers of the LTTE or because they saw an opportunity. Indeed, some of the claims will go back as long as thirty years when the army defences of the Jaffna Peninsula had to be strengthened. Just as in the UK after World War II, settlement of competing claims will take time and must be the responsibility of the courts. It is too easy and, in my view, irresponsible for the West led by NGOs and certain diaspora to state all land must be handed back, not least when there is a question of the rightful owner.

On my visit I went to two housing schemes in Jaffna District with the government agent (civil servant). Both schemes were on land that had to be de-mined. The houses were being built by India, Switzerland and the army; such a pity the UK was not helping with the housing. I spoke to a number of occupants who were thrilled to be back in their original area. I reflect how much better it would have been if Prime Minister Cameron, in addition to visiting one of the few remaining IDP camps, had also taken the opportunity to view this sort of success. Even more, how much better for all if he had offered help to finance some housing to allow the IDP camp to close.

Personally, I look back with sadness at the wonderful work and understanding shown by Mrs Thatcher, and before her the Labour Government of Mr Callaghan, in helping Sri Lanka. What a contrast to Messrs Blair, Brown and Cameron: all talk, usually criticism, no understanding and certainly little or no help to anyone.

Democracy remains a key feature for the people of Sri Lanka regardless of their own political persuasion. In September 2013 a full democratic election for the Provincial Council was held as the government had promised. The Northern Provincial Council was then in exactly the same position as every other Provincial Council in the rest of Sri Lanka. There was much talk and pressure from the TNA (Tamil National Alliance) to combine the Northern Province with the Eastern Province on grounds going back centuries to when the Tamils invaded Sri Lanka. This was unacceptable in principle, as it would be totally contrary to the Unitary Constitution. It is true that the everyday language in the east is Tamil but the Tamils are in a minority and their population share is falling. It is also totally unacceptable in historical terms, as the Sinhalese arrived on the island from North India at least a century or more prior to the Tamils. There were calls from some of the local Tamil politicians and the diaspora for a referendum of independence from Sri Lanka for the two regions, reflecting Prabhakaran's vision of Eelam. This idea falls foul of the Constitution of the Unitary State, exactly as what happened in Spain with the Catalan referendum in 2017.

I strongly recommended that the all the organs of the United Nations and the West stayed out of these local constitutional wrangles. They were, and continue to be, purely internal rather than international.

There are a great many NGOs at work in Sri Lanka but for me the most outstanding is the ICRC. I have made it a point since the end of the war to always make time to visit the head of the ICRC on every official visit. In my judgement it knows far better than any other NGO what is actually happening on the ground in terms of practical Human Rights issues, particularly in relation to alleged torture. Unlike the Middle East, torture is not endemic in Sri Lanka or South Asia. In a war it is always possible there may be isolated cases but the Sri Lanka Army is well trained. The first reports of alleged civilian torture appeared in the diaspora media. I made a visit to Sri Lanka in January 2012 and made a specific request to see the head of the ICRC, which I did in Boosa Prison. I asked him specifically if the ICRC had seen or had received any reports of torture. His answer was an emphatic 'no'. However, there had been allegations of heavy-handling. I can think of no more reliable source than the ICRC, which is totally independent, objective and unbiased. On my official visits in 2015 and 2017 I raised exactly the same issue and the answer was exactly the same, although the person in charge had changed.

However, in contrast there have been two published reports, firstly, from the Freedom from Torture group entitled, *Out of Silence: New Evidence of Ongoing Torture in Sri Lanka, 2009–2011*. A second report, called the Sooka Report was titled, *An Unfinished War: Torture and Sexual Violence in Sri Lanka 2009–14*. Both reports covered the bulk of the period before I met the ICRC and were totally in contrast to my own findings. I contacted and wrote to the Chief Executive of Freedom from Torture on 12 January 2014 after I had looked in depth at its report and

171

consulted knowledgeable, independent Tamils. My conclusion was the claims were highly questionable and there were no independent witnesses to corroborate anything, nor any complaints from the mainstream of Tamils. I also read the Sooka Report, which was surprisingly similar on the allegations of torture but again with no hard, independent evidence. I even wondered if it was not just a mirror report.

I concluded that whilst there may be just a few cases of torture, there is no independent evidence at all. Of course, there was questioning of former LTTE cadres, officers and known sympathisers but that is no different to the UK where there are occasionally allegations of heavy-handedness. However, I repeat that if the ICRC has never seen or had direct reports of torture and it is everywhere on the ground in Sri Lanka, then I believe it rather than those producing anti-Sri Lanka allegations from abroad. Even the UK government which is noted for its leniency to Tamils seeking asylum has, after extensive enquiries, rejected the majority of asylum claims. At the time of writing this report in 2018, well over a thousand Tamils who had sought asylum in the UK, Australia and Germany have returned to Sri Lanka with no reports of harassment. I think the UK authorities need to better understand the psyche and religious practices of self-chastisement and sacrifice of aspects of the Hindu faith which encompass the tolerance of extreme self-inflicted pain or that inflicted by those seeking to help a person achieve their goal. Recently, in 2017 the UK authorities refused an asylum request when it was clear that the seeming torture of extensive burns had been self-inflicted. Against all this evidence I suggest it is time Freedom from Torture focused its time, energy and funding on those countries that clearly do allow torture, which must include Guantanamo Bay.

Numbers killed are understandably an emotive issue, although there are those in officialdom who feel numbers are not the issue, rather the fact that any were killed. I totally disagree with this viewpoint. Suffice to record, I stated in my 2012 Report: 'Numbers killed is a key issue since the original claim of the external UN that 40,000 civilians may well have been killed; Mrs Sooka claims 70,000 in the last stages of the War and that 147,000 remain unaccounted for. All these are absolutely absurd suggesting as they do genocide. I do cover the numbers issue in depth in the chapter on war crimes.'

There are a host of NGOs in Sri Lanka. Many of them do wonderful work. However, there are a few who venture outside their field of activity and start to take sides in internal and external issues.

This first example came to life during the tsunami relief. As mentioned earlier, Ann and I went out to help a few days after the disaster struck. It was not long before I noted a couple of charities challenging the agreed relief programme and, indeed, interfering in government policy. This was capped by finding in at least one container arms for the LTTE sent from the UK. Charities in the main have done and are doing wonderful work but then there are the three Human Rights groups – Amnesty International, Human Rights Watch and Crisis International – who appear to see their role to never applaud but to continue a barrage of criticism with no allowance for verifiable independent verification let alone availability of resources or time.

If I move forward to my visit in 2017, I noted in Jaffna that there seemed to be more NGO establishments and teams seemingly duplicating what the government was doing, or more worryingly interfering, or even more worrying latently supporting extensive devolution and the amalgamation of the Northern and Eastern Provinces. Society in general in 2018 has been shocked at the terrible stories about the Haiti earthquake and what the leading relief charities got up to. Additionally, it is quite clear that many of our UK leading charities, such as Oxfam and Save the Children, have depressingly weak governance, which I noticed in Sri Lanka at the time of tsunami in 2005.

The conclusion I wrote in my 2012 Report was: 'My final observation on Sri Lanka is that today any person can go anywhere, day or night, without papers, without check points, without fear of bombings. Tamils I have met travel regularly by bus, day or night, with total confidence. Surely this is solid proof of reconciliation for ordinary Tamils but maybe not for those politically motivated who are still trying to achieve Eelam.'

What was true in 2012 remains as true as ever in 2019.

The Galle ground.

CHAPTER
Fourteen

Post-war: The View From Overseas

Post-war governments succeed not by slavishly following the policies they had put to the electorate in the first election after a war but how they deal with the issues that subsequently arise. For it is issues that inevitably come thick and fast. In a sense, that is why Churchill failed in the 1945 election; he did not communicate enough hope to the electorate.

President Rajapaksa was either astute or lucky: I tend to think astute. He knew full well that the Tamils who had fled the Tigers had to be rehoused as quickly as possible. Furthermore, he knew that the infrastructure in the north had to be restored and so his government set to, restoring and opening the A9, main road link. He also recognised that the railway had to rebuilt, as the Tigers had melted down all the rail track for weaponry and, above all, ensure that Jaffna was put on the National Grid for power. While all this was going on he knew he needed to make an official visit to the country's nearest neighbour, India, the power player in South Asia.

The visit took place in June 2010. From President Rajapaksa's point of view, it was vital to reaffirm the close ties there used to be between India and Sri Lanka. Prime Minister Manmohan Singh recognised that the twin triumphs of the Presidential and Parliamentary Elections had raised Rajapaksa's stock to a level unmatched in South and Southeast Asia. The meeting went well, providing a signal to all that the bilateral relationship could build to a new level.

Rajapaksa, now with the defeat of the Tigers accomplished, took the initiative and offered India the opportunity to open an Indian Consulate in the southern city of Hambantota, as well as the already-agreed diplomatic outpost in Jaffna. The challenge remained of how to meet the long-standing political grievances of the Tamil people in a way that did not undermine the unitary nature of the State, presumably by building upon the 13th Amendment. Both leaders recognised it would be a challenging task but at least, for the first time in thirty years, there was a platform of peace, from which negotiations could begin.

Following the President's successful visit to Delhi and Professor Peiris's successful visits to New York and London (Peiris was Foreign Minister and the President's right-hand man), it was time for the President to visit London, not least to underpin the progress and stature of the Lessons Learnt and Reconciliation Commission.

However, hanging in the air were the dreadful pictures and video taken by an unidentified source and originally circulated in January 2010, which would later feature again in the Channel 4 film *Sri Lanka's Killing Fields* in June 2011. The pictures were originally stated to be genuine by an UN official, but had then been analysed and found to be fake. However, they still provided wonderful propaganda for the LTTE group in London. In addition, the images had been promoted by both Crisis International and Amnesty International; indeed, they were believed to be genuine by virtually every NGO working in Sri Lanka. I will comment later in detail about this film and its sister film of March 2012, *Sri Lanka's Killing Fields – War Crimes Unpunished*, but the large LTTE cells in London, New York, Canada and Germany now had a weapon with which to beat the President of Sri Lanka.

President Rajapaksa arrived in London on Monday 29 November 2010. There was an immediate reaction from the LTTE Tamil diaspora who organised a major demonstration at London Heathrow Airport and a sit-in outside Parliament's 'Carriage Gates', which are supposed to be kept clear regardless of any demonstration in Parliament Square. However, the LTTE had cleverly provided female demonstrators with small children, which made it doubly difficult for the police to move them on. I immediately submitted an urgent question to the Lord Speaker seeking the removal of the demonstrators.

Further problems suddenly developed. One of the President's key engagements was to address the Oxford University Union on Thursday 2 December. The original invitation had come in September and was very special to him, as he had addressed the Union once before in 2008. He intended to use the address as an opportunity to call for reconciliation of Sri Lankans in all parts of the world and invite all Sri Lankans in the UK to join in the new task of rebuilding a nation. The address was aimed to heal old wounds and look to the future as a nation where all communities could live together in peace and amity.

However, this was not a story that any of the several thousand LTTE activists wanted to hear, not least after being shown the bogus but horrific pictures and film. They were determined to demonstrate en mass. The police in Oxford were prepared to handle a major demonstration but the President of the Oxford Union clearly took fright and, at the last minute, cancelled the invitation. This did not deter the demonstrators who just moved to take up position outside the President's hotel in Park Lane. As many commented at the time, so much for freedom of speech in the UK.

Sadly, things went from bad to worse as later in the week the President was due to give a presentation in the City of London about investment opportunities in Sri Lanka as well highlighting the delightful tourist resorts. Once again a huge demonstration took place: the City Police caved in, forcing the event's cancellation. Then, when the High Commissioner for Sri Lanka, Dr Chris Nonis, suggested key guests went to the Presidents' hotel, this was again refused. Finally, there was an even more insidious rumour/attempt to indict the President for war crimes; for once the UK Government moved swiftly to ensure this could not happen. I think the only successful part of the visit was the lunch with the All-Party Sri Lanka Group led by me, which involved five Lords, three MPs and two MEPs.

I cannot but wonder what the President thought about the UK. Her Majesty the Queen had sent a message to him ahead of his visit on 19 November, which read: 'I send my congratulations on your re-election as President of Sri Lanka. I wish you and the people of Sri Lanka peace and prosperity in the years to come. Elizabeth R.' To arrive with such hope but only to be met with such hostilities a few weeks later; virtually chased out by demonstrators belonging to a proscribed organisation since 2001 but still able to cause mayhem. Even in 2018, at the time of writing, there was yet another demonstration on Independence Day outside the High Commission. In addition, to cap this whole sad episode I never managed to find out exactly why a visa was refused for Minister Hon. Douglas Devananda, a very brave Tamil Minister who survived a suicide bomber attack. I wonder who got at the Home Office to deny him a visa. Actually, I have unearthed a letter from the then Minister of Immigration who stated, and I quote: 'When assessing a case where there is evidence that the individual has been involved in war crimes, UK Border Agency use reliable sources of information such as Human Rights Watch, Amnesty International, the UN and BBC.' That says it all. Not least as Mrs Balasingham, the leader of the Tamil Tiger child soldiers, continues to live in the UK. Even worse, Douglas Devananda was the only Tamil leader who had stood up to Prabhakaran and had suffered a suicide bomber in his office.

Some may wonder from where the LTTE Eelam supporters in the UK and elsewhere got their money. In the UK there was evidence of credit card scams, particularly at garages, and there were illegal charities such as the White Pigeon, along with allegations of extortion and threats to professional Sri Lankans, not least if they had family still in Sri Lanka. Unfortunately, the UK police, allied to the Crown Prosecution Office, never investigated in depth.

However, in Canada in January 2011 the police were more active in prosecuting the World Tamil Movement (WTM) of Ontario and the World Tamil Movement of Quebec. The WTM was taking in US$763,000 a year and the police traced US$3m to an account in Malaysia. Then in May 2011 there was the trial of Raj Rajaratnam, whiz trader and prominent philanthropist, alleged to have made some US$45m trading on illegal tips about firms. He was also alleged to have given millions of dollars to a Maryland-based charity that the US Government accused of being a front for the Tamil Tigers.

All this was continuing after the defeat of the Tigers, after the peace and real attempts at reconciliation. It seems to me that as long as funds on this scale – in fact on any scale – are available then there really is an uphill struggle for any Sri Lanka Government. How can any real headway be made to combat all the fake propaganda which sadly officials the world over do not seem to challenge? At some point, perhaps the Sri Lanka authorities themselves will put time and resources into tracking down and exposing all these millions – probably billions – of funds, raised to support the notion of Eelam, so detrimental to every law-abiding Sri Lanka citizen.

The other element of funding concerns the aid programmes from friendly countries. I know India has done a huge amount but I am less enthusiastic at the British Government's response and even at the actions of the European Union. No one in the EU seemed to appreciate that an exhausting war against the Tamil Tigers had been waged for nearly thirty years. Against this background and faced with having to concentrate all resources on rebuilding the nation immediately after the war finished, it can hardly be surprising that past Sri Lanka governments had not made as much progress on Human Rights issues as Europe had wanted. On 15 February 2010 the European Council had decided to withdraw GSP+ preferences from Sri Lanka textile exports to Europe, oblivious of the impact it would have on the very economy that was trying to recover. Seemingly oblivious, too, that it would hit the employment of about 200,000 female breadwinners in the textile factories, nearly all Tamil, let alone the knock-on effect to about a million others.

Human Rights obligations are important but to insist they are given top priority just nine months after a debilitating war is, in my view, a nonsense. Sadly, the Minister of State, Gareth Thomas MP, wrote to me on 18 February 2010 confirming that 'the UK was fully supportive of Europe's action'. Looking back at the fifteen conditions, did no one in authority in the West have a look at the implications so soon after peace? I could go through all fifteen but I highlight point two, which relates to the 17th Amendment to the Constitution. In effect it leaves no discretion to the government or the people of Sri Lanka to decide on this issue of vital national importance. It is in effect, colonialism at its worst.

The UK did give some aid in the form of funding to NGOs to support returning IDPs (Internally Displaced Persons) to rebuild their lives. I have correspondence covering the period January to April 2010. The UK gave £13.5m in this period – hardly a huge sum given the enormity of the task of re-settling about 300,000 people. It certainly did not match up to the promises of Prime Ministers Major and Blair. Furthermore, the money went direct to the NGOs who decided themselves how it should be spent. At the time of the tsunami I made it abundantly clear to the UK authorities that our NGOs must be co-ordinated by the host government, otherwise the funds are likely to be ineffective. The one charity I have commended over the years is Halo's contribution to the de-mining effort: quite brilliant.

I cannot resist quoting from a letter I wrote on 6 April 2010 to Michael Foster, MP, Parliamentary Under-Secretary for International Development:

Of course the Government of Sri Lanka would listen to the UK more if your Government wasn't so obstructive and unhelpful. You opposed the IMF loan, lead the campaign to remove the EU tariff concession and seek a war crimes investigation against a democratically-elected Government fighting against one of the most ruthless terrorist organisations the world has known. Meanwhile we give sanctuary to Mrs Balasingham the former LTTE Tiger leader seemingly responsible for the recruitment of child soldiers.

Sadly, this negative attitude never changed. On every visit I have made I have put forward suggestions of projects that were desperately in need of help, such as the Jaffna Hospital, but all to no avail.

I must now turn to the media. Any politician worth his salt learns to try to work with the media. Certainly I have, through all my political career, not least when my first majority in the February 1974 General Election for Northampton South was 179 after three counts. There was another election in the October where my majority fell to 142 on the same Register but I consoled myself that the missing fifty-seven between the two elections were people who had supported me but sadly died.

I have kept three articles from the latter part of 2010. The first was in the *Telegraph* on Tuesday 19 October 2010, headlined: 'Pictures show massacre of Tamils'. I responded later in the week on the 22nd, with a letter to Mr Gallagher, the newspaper's editor:

Last Tuesday you ran an article from your South Asia Editor to coincide with the first visit of the new Sri Lanka Foreign Minister here to talk with our Government about progress in resettling the refugees now down to about 30,000, a success by any yardstick and a host of important matters on the reconciliation commission etc. It is so sad that the thrust of your article revived old material and repeated old allegations totally unproven but believed by many to be the work of the Tigers. Why on earth run this old story and make no comment on the good work done by so many parties in Sri Lanka led by the Government? All it does is drive hatred with some of the UK/Sri Lanka diaspora.

The editor replied on 5 November, in essence, 'hiding' behind the government official line that there needed to be a credible and independent investigation.

The next 'helpful 'article was from David Piling in the *Financial Times* on Thursday 26 November, headlined, 'Sri Lanka's victors must be magnanimous' referring specifically to the Tamils. I wrote a letter stating that even before the victory President Rajapaksa had started to recruit Tamil policemen, insisted that all civil servants above a certain grade had to learn Tamil, Sinhalese and English, and that all children now had to learn all three languages. I went on to commend the resettlement of refugees, almost all Tamil, and wondered how the removal of GSP+ would help build community relations and reconciliation as those adversely affected were almost all Tamils.

Finally, I noted a leading article in *The Times* of Thursday 2 December, headlined 'Keeping the Peace'. I will not comment on the biased copy but just note one phrase: 'The investigation by *The Times* revealed a civilian death toll of 20,000 in the closing stages of the war, a majority of whom were killed by artillery.'

Suffice to say we now know that the so-called civilian casualties in the period 1 January to 18 May 2009 were about 7,000, of which as many as between 20 and 25 per cent are likely to have been Tamil Tiger cadres who had thrown away their uniforms so as to be counted as civilians, making a net civilian death toll of about 5,500. So much for the forensic analysis by *The Times*. Even these figures may well turn out to be too high in the light of research I have done on the census and alleged missing persons turning up in another country. However, note the timing: these articles appeared during the President's visit. I repeat: what must he have thought of our country?

This all paled into insignificance when Channel 4 released their two films on UK television which got worldwide coverage, namely, on 14 June 2011, *Sri Lanka's Killing Fields* and on 14 March 2012, *Sri Lanka's Killing Field's – War Crimes Unpunished*. The highly emotive phrase 'Killing Fields' came from the 1984 Oscar-winning film on Vietnam. It would be another year before almost all the allegations in the two films were publicly debunked.

There were in essence three levels of complaint about both films.

First, as Chairman of the All-Party Sri Lanka Group I complained to Ofcom, innocently thinking I would receive an objective and detailed assessment, particularly as Channel 4 was a publicly owned broadcaster rather than a commercial one. My first detailed letter of complaint reminded Ofcom that the LTTE was a proscribed organisation in over thirty countries, including the UK, and emphasised the lack of 'Due impartiality and Due accuracy and Undue Prominence of views and opinions (Section 5)'. I sent it on 19 June 2011, just five days after the showing of the film. This was followed by two more letters sent on 12 July and 16 September. It took until 24 October for a substantive reply to be received, by which time a huge amount of damage had been done to Sri Lanka due to the unfettered showing of this film. The response which covered three pages made no reference to the LTTE being a proscribed organisation nor did it really address the heart of the matter, namely due balance, and finally Ofcom said it had no control of the website which continued to display the film.

I quote from the letter with the paragraph headed:

Channel 4 website

You refer in your letter of 16 September to the website set up by Channel 4 to show the film and publish allegations against the Sri Lanka Government. Ofcom has no power or duty to regulate this website under the Communications Act 2003 or other broadcasting legislation. Therefore, the availability of 'Sri Lanka's Killing Fields' film and the content of that website has, and could not be considered as part of our investigation.

The net result was that Channel 4, through its website, had complete freedom to publicise the film and show it worldwide: an opportunity it took to with commitment and enthusiasm causing massive anguish and anger in all the Tamil diaspora throughout the world, let alone the NGOs, Human Rights organisations and probably all the member governments of the United Nations.

I felt badly let down. Ofcom appeared to have checked in with Channel 4, a respected TV channel who in turn assured it that it had met all the requirements of due impartiality. This, to my mind, is a whitewash, as frankly Ofcom did not have the competence or knowledge to do a thorough assessment. The opening statement in the film was that war crimes on a terrible scale had been committed by the Sri Lanka armed forces and that those responsible were at the very top. Furthermore, phrases like 'no one knows how many civilians have been killed: it could be 40,000, possibly based on more recent information 70,000 or more'. And to cap it all the commentary states that the 100,000 who were rescued in the final stage by the army were now in government custody, and thus implied that this was a bad thing and that they may not even get out alive.

I still have my notes on this. However, help was at hand from an organisation called Sri Lanka Media Watch, which, a month after Ofcom's report, issued a publication called, *Appalling Journalism – Jon Snow and Channel 4 News on Sri Lanka*. This twenty-six-page report of forensic analysis really began to put Sri Lanka on the front foot, or so I thought.

- It challenged the two independent female witnesses who turned out to be active members of the LTTE.
- It exposed that the demonstration outside the UN office was organised by the LTTE.
- It pointed out that even Human Rights Watch stated the 300,000 civilians had been forcibly taken by the LTTE.
- It pointed out shelling of the No Fire Zones started with LTTE artillery being placed in the Zone.
- It pointed out there was evidence that the LTTE had actually fired on the hospitals itself.
- It pointed out the Tamil government doctors were coerced into saying medicines supplies were short.
- It pointed out that the mobile telephone footage left no idea who was shooting whom.

At the end of this exhaustive and fascinating report, the authors asked eleven penetrating questions of Jon Snow and Channel 4. I reproduce just one:

Does Channel 4 not accept that a statutory requirement for 'balance' in a programme dealing with human rights abuse is not achieved by the cursory inclusion of 49 seconds out of 50 minutes dealing with LTTE human rights abuse when UTHR (University Teachers for Human Rights) reports that the LTTE may have deliberately killed one quarter of those said to have died in the Vanni just for trying to escape from its illegal detention, ignoring for the moment how many more may have been killed by deliberate shelling?

Channel 4 makes much of its claim to be broadcasters of the highest integrity. I think I need to do no more than quote the view of A.A. Gill, the late well-known and respected British journalist. His view on the film, documented in his book of 2013, entitled *Corrupted Journalism – Channel 4 and Sri Lanka – Engage Sri Lanka*, was this:

> The channel has accumulated a large collection of samizdat amateur footage from mobile phones and video cameras – mostly unattributed and uncorroborated. It mixes this footage with comment from unnamed sources with distorted voices and shadowed faces. And human rights lawyers. It was brutal, it was shocking, but it wasn't journalism. Not a second of this has been shot by Channel 4; none of the eye-witnesses accounts comes from journalists.

He went on to say: 'Channel 4 News has drifted from providing news broadcasts into being an outlet for nodding spokespeople and assorted NGOs and environmental pressure groups, or anyone who can provide interesting or sensational film. It follows the old American news adage, "If it bleeds, it leads".'

Personally, I concur with the authors of the report who wrote: 'He [Jon Snow] claimed that the government had been responsible for a number of war crimes and the programme presented "evidence required to convict". There is a name for those courts in which one person is the accuser, judge and jury: a kangaroo court'.

I doubt if Channel 4 ever bothered to read the report or even deigned to reply to the questions asked by its authors, not least as its back had been covered by Ofcom. Of course, neither the authors nor I were aware that a second film was being prepared, focusing on alleged Human Rights abuses: timed to have maximum international impact. This second film,

Sri Lanka's Killing Fields – War Crimes Unpunished, would be broadcast nine months after the massive challenge to the first film. This time the topic was war crimes – with supposed evidence. However, this time those of us who knew the truth were better prepared to respond.

The terrorist Ditch Cum Bund (DCB) in Puthumathalan was constructed by the terrorists to protect themselves with innocent civilians as a human shield in the final stage against the humanitarian operations to justify their action of terror. At the time of breaching by security forces, they held a land stretch of approximately 14km. The DCB was sited with bunkers and a densley laid mixture of mines and improvised explosive devices. In spite of all these defences and stiff resistance by the terrorists, the Sri Lanka Army was able to capture the DCB on 20 April 2009 and rescued over 170,000 innocent civilians.

CHAPTER
Fifteen

Creating the Chance to Succeed

It was 13 February 2017 when I sat down to draft this chapter, and bitterly cold outside. Number 13: is it a lucky or unlucky number? For me it is lucky as in the summer of 1955 I entered the examination hall at Bedford School to sit O-Level Latin, for the third time, which was all I required to seal my place at St Catharine's College, Cambridge. To this day, I remember the master in charge of giving candidates their registration number and, to his horror, awarding me mine, which was 'Number 13'. I said to him: 'Don't worry Sir, I have tried twice before with ordinary numbers and failed so maybe this will be my lucky day.' It was. I passed.

Sri Lanka is deeply immersed in astrology, which I confess I am not. Nevertheless, I am a realist. I celebrated my eightieth birthday on 25 November 2016 at The Carlton Club, St James's, London along with about one hundred friends, including some from Sri Lanka. Being realistic, I must admit the body clock is ticking, but I still maintain a rigorous work ethic and have just returned from an intensive week in Colombo.

I was there in the capacity of an official guest, but it was I who set the agenda and planned the meetings, in order to probe, in as much as depth as was possible, just how much progress had been made since the end of the Civil War and change of president. The backdrop for this visit was that former President Rajapaksa had chosen to call an early election in 2015 for the presidency which he need not have done. He had clearly thought that on the back of his triumph in defeating the Tamil Tigers he could persuade the electorate to extend the two-term maximum rule to three. History is littered with examples of this type of tactic and the results are often unhappy ones, as it was this time for Rajapaksa. He lost the election, but the real loser was Sri Lanka which had not just lost a good president at a crucial time for the country but had to endure a coalition, with all that meant for compromised policies and indecision, as we found in the UK with the Cameron Government. The new president was President Sirisena, who, on being sworn in, stated that he intended to have a government of national unity. This was to be the coalition of the two main rival parties: the SLFP (Sri Lanka Freedom Party) and the UNP (United National Party). My visit in January 2017 was planned to be two years after this coalition had begun, and thus time to see what progress had been made.

The coalition began with a one hundred-item programme to demonstrate to the citizens of Sri Lanka – as well as to the questioning Western powers – a way forward on so many controversial areas of policy. It would be followed by a dissolving of Parliament on 23 April 2015, later postponed but followed by a general election which took place on 17 August and which was won by UNP Front for Good Governance (UNFGG) with UNP taking 106 seats and UPFA (United People's Freedom Alliance) taking 95, which together gave them the sought-after two-thirds majority in a Parliament of 225.

I had visited Sri Lanka in January 2015 and saw that the new President's strategies were well-received, even if they were viewed with some scepticism by the West. This scepticism was principally from Obama's Government, handled by Secretary Hillary Clinton and from the UK under Prime Minister Cameron and his Foreign Secretary, William Hague. This was founded on their knowledge that the UN had, at their insistence, tabled a highly critical motion on Sri Lanka alleging war crimes, lack of Justice, torture, lack of Freedom of the Press, lack of reconciliation and a host of other critical challenges. These had all been highlighted by the diaspora, somewhat ironically often led by former members of the LTTE. The motion had been referred to the UNHCR (UN Refugee Agency) in Geneva, who called for evidence. At that time, I had taken great care to submit a detailed report to the enquiry, despatched in good time, but there was never any response to it. I even offered to give evidence in person at my own expense. Later I learned that certain parties who also knew Sri Lanka were called to give evidence. Of course, who gives evidence or what the content of that evidence is, is never published. Transparency is not the hallmark of UN enquiries. Additionally, assertions are made that cannot be challenged and suppositions stated, none of which would ever stand up in a Court of Law. My own report of my 2015 visit states that this UN report, with the OHCHR (Office of the High Commissioner for Human Rights) evidence, was hanging over all Sri Lanka as it was due to take place in March 2015.

The report was indeed published in March 2015 under the name OISL (Office Investigation on Sri Lanka). From Sri Lanka's point of view, it was an unmitigated disaster but it could not be ignored. Key conclusions in paragraphs 1266, 1267 and 1268 (all points which had been raised earlier), were:

> 1266: The last phases, the intense shelling by the armed forces caused great suffering and loss of life among the civilians. Lack of food, water and medical treatment 'BECAUSE' [my emphasis] of strict control of supplies into the Vanni by the Government caused additional deaths.

This was all totally inaccurate, as I had put in my evidence to the UNHCR in my submission dated 20 October 2014. Of course, there was shelling in a war to destroy the terrorist artillery carefully positioned next to civilians and hospitals. As for food and medicines being in short supply, it was again totally inaccurate, as there was no policy of restricting supplies, only the challenge of supplies being destroyed by the enemy who sunk the ships which brought them in. In addition, the UN itself had stopped their own supply lines as their people fled the battlefield, unlike the ICRC.

Paragraph 1267 of the document, which addresses the question of casualties amongst civilians includes, 'there is no doubt that thousands, and likely ten of thousands lost their lives'. We now know from the UK Defence Attaché in Colombo, Lt Col Gash, from his despatches, that civilian casualties were between 5,000 and 6,000, at most. I say 'at most' as the Sri Lanka census undertaken by Tamil officials says between 6,000 and 7,000 but that also includes the deaths of Tamil Tigers. Even more confusing is the satellite imagery which shows graves for around 2,000 people. What is clear is that it was never, ever, anywhere near 'tens of thousands' or the minimum of 40,000, as claimed the UN in the Darusman Report. It is also clear that the UK Government knew by 19

May 2009 – the end of the war – that 40,000 was a hopeless exaggeration but never said so. I wonder why.

Paragraph 1268 refers to 'the over 250,000 deprived of their liberty in military run, closed IDP camps for months while security forces filter out LTTE cadres'. Hardly surprising, when it turned out that those cadres totalled over 11,000, a potentially huge threat to peace. Add to this that these refugees had nowhere to go as their land was littered with unmarked mines which had to be cleared; work on which is still on-going today in early 2019. As previously stated, my wife and I visited the Manik Farm camp in its latter stages and certainly all those still there were eternally grateful for a safe temporary home with good medical facilities, adequate food and education for the children; all this ignored by the UN team.

It will surprise no one to learn that the report contained 245 closely typed pages covering almost every conceivable violation of human dignity and stated that the Sri Lanka Government was either guilty or should have prevented or should have anticipated the problems. Rarely is the finger pointed at the terrorist group, the LTTE, and its merciless drive for Eelam regardless of the cost of human suffering or death to ordinary men, women and children of all faiths and castes as citizens of Sri Lanka.

As a result of the report and finding itself under pressure from the UK and the USA once again, the UN produced an action plan based on a resolution co-sponsored by the UK, USA and crucially the Sri Lanka governments. It read: 'Encourages the Government of Sri Lanka to develop a comprehensive plan and mechanism for preserving all existing records and documentation relating to human rights violations and abuses and violations of international humanitarian law, whether held by public or private institutions.'

The key phrase which the Government of Sri Lanka should never have accepted was: 'Violations of Human Rights law'. This ignores the self-evident fact that this was a war between the democratically elected and legitimate Government of Sri Lanka and a terrorist group, the LTTE Tamil Tigers. The law that must operate is the law of armed conflict otherwise known as International Humanitarian Law. The European Convention on Human Rights upon which the British Human Rights Act is based is wholly inappropriate for application in combat and battlefield conditions. The fact that the UK and USA ignored this is understandable as both Messrs Cameron and Obama were under intense pressure from dissident Tamil diaspora, many LTTE sympathisers and indeed some actual LTTE activists, all of whom were voters. This does not alter the law and in my judgement is a pretty shabby tactic, not least when one thinks about the suffering of the ordinary citizens of Sri Lanka from all ethnic groups.

In my visit of February 2015, just before the damning report was published, I had a one-to-one meeting with President Sirisena during which he had promised the people of Sri Lanka that he would deal with all the issues raised by the UN but it would take time and require understanding. However, even at this early juncture he was adamant there should be no role anywhere for foreign judges. I do remember coming away from my meeting thinking he was a politician of true traditional Eastern style. A thinking, measured man, not able to speak English but one with steely determination not easily put off by the needs of public relations or what seemed the easiest way out, as I have witnessed in so much of UK policy to Sri Lanka. He clearly believed that all my involvement over the previous forty years in the UK Parliament had been really helpful and he demonstrated this at the Independence Day celebrations by seating me in the place of the head of the diplomatic corps: a rare honour.

This was the background to my 2017 visit: I did my homework (as I always do), I had gone back over all my reports and findings and went on a mission to discover what had happened in the intervening two years and whether it was what had been promised. Of course, there had been extra demands arising from the UN following the publication of the OISL, the visits from UK junior ministers who had virtually no understanding of the complexity of the situation, the steady stream of representatives of the USA, UK and European Commissions, as well as the observations of key critical NGOs like Amnesty International, Crisis International and Freedom From Torture; all this in addition to the voice of diaspora. Every time I go on a fact-finding visit to Sri Lanka I make a point to contact two particular friends to give me an overview both of the political situation and the economy – to give the everyman's version of events and who have seen them first-hand.

I arrived in Sri Lanka at 12.35 pm on 2 January after an excellent flight on a SriLanka Airline's new airbus with its excellent individual beds in Business Class. My dear friend, Nathan Sivagananathan, CEO of MAS Group had arranged a dinner party that evening with some of his Tamil business friends. My dear hostess, Priya, a lawyer, had produced a sumptuous dinner. Inevitably the conversation turned to politics and inevitably both Brexit and Sri Lanka were discussed. There was a lukewarm feeling towards the Sri Lanka Government: the general feeling was that there was a slightly strained unity but it was good enough to take matters forward, which had been happening, albeit in the view of those gathered around the dinner table it was happening too slowly. However, there was deep concern over the lack of inward investment; indeed any economic trading strategy. They were absolutely bemused why there was so little investment from the diaspora, anywhere in the country but particularly in Jaffna. They raised the issue of GSP+. I was able to tell them of a meeting that Ranil Jayawardena, MP and I had with the junior minister in London at which we had raised and pushed the GSP+ issue (The Minister of Foreign Affairs at his meeting in London on Thursday 12 January 2017 with the UK Foreign Secretary Boris Johnson was formally told there was a recommendation going to the European Parliament March Meeting to lift the embargo). Long flights are tiring but a stimulating evening is the ideal for a good night's sleep, and this certainly was.

The next morning, before I started my official calls, I wanted to meet my second oldest friend Bradman Weerakoon, former Secretary to President J.R. Jayawardena. All politicians know there are a few outstanding senior officials in the civil service of any country and Bradman is one of them. I still vividly remember how swiftly and humanely he handled the tragedy of the riots against the Tamils in 1983. Bradman is in his late seventies now and continues to help out at the Ministry of Prison Reforms, Rehabilitation, Resettlement, and Hindu Religious Affairs. Physically, he is pretty frail, but his mind is as sharp as ever. It is so wonderful to find someone like Bradman still helping his former colleagues and his country through its challenges; I do not remember anything similar in the West and, my goodness, we could with it in departments such as health, which is floundering.

We got down to business. I asked him what, in his opinion, was the outstanding achievement of the current administration? Without hesitation, he said for the first time since Independence there was unity in the government, which is a credit to both the President and the Prime Minister who are from different parties. Add to that complete freedom of the press. However, on all the other issues he admitted Sri Lanka continues to make progress but frustratingly slowly. We then discussed the contentious issue of war crimes. We both were of the same opinion that the only really feasible option was to hold a proper Truth & Reconciliation Commission. As I left the building to meet with the leader of the Muslim Party in Parliament, Rauff Hakeem, I could not help wondering whether I would ever see the frail Bradman again, a truly wonderful man.

I have also known Rauff for over thirty years and he, too, is a remarkable man. He has steered the Muslim community through all the pressures and tensions in the Middle East and has also supported his community through a number of domestic tragedies, including the 1990 expulsion of around 100,000 Muslims almost overnight from Jaffna and Mannar by the LTTE. Having known each other so long we have an immediate rapport. He, too, recognised progress on some key issues: unity in government, which had facilitated developments being made on the issues of the separation of the Northern and Eastern Provinces; a new Counter Terrorism Bill and much of the list of UN issues were being addressed. However, he was still concerned over the slowness of the IDP resettlement, some religious discrimination from the hard-line Buddhists and in his words, 'Buddha statues appearing everywhere'. He ran through my list of challenges and stated that he felt progress was being made, but the issues were challenging and needed time. Incidentally, he too did not want foreign judges ruling in Sri Lanka – he felt that the nationals would not trust them and feared that if they were forced upon the country, rioting would erupt all over the country, leading to thousands more dying. I thought to myself how good it was to have such a measured response. We said our goodbyes and as we did so, he said: 'Michael, we owe a lot of thanks to you too.'

My last meeting before lunch was with the State Minister of Defence, Ruwan Wijewardene, who I had met before but did not really know well. We discussed the issues of land that had been requisitioned by the military during the war being handed back and trading activities by the military. He hoped that all the land that could be, would be returned by September 2017 and the hotels run by the military in the absence of anyone else would go to the private sector imminently. I raised the issue of signing the Ottawa Accord about never using mines again. He said the Defence Minister and he were in favour of signing it, as was the Chief of the Army in the Northern Province. The overall Army Chief had reservations but they thought these could be met. Personally, I thought they would sign and indeed they did the following year. I also raised the key issue for me: the number of civilians who escaped the clutches of the Tigers by going through the lines in the period between January and May 2009. I was confident this would prove once and for all that there never was a policy regarding the killing Tamil civilians. I made a recommendation to my government that the UK should consider helping Sri Lanka set up a retraining scheme along the lines of the best practice in the UK after World War II. With the UK giving 0.7 per cent of GDP to aid, this relatively modest proposal seems to me a 'no brainer' but time would tell.

Finally, in terms of meetings on the first day I went to see my host, the Hon. Mangala Samaraweera, MP, Minister of Foreign Affairs, on whose shoulders fell the heavy burden of facing up to the demands of the West and to see his country through to calmer waters. We went through my list of issues and progress made which, in areas such as missing persons was significant because of the preliminary work done by the ICRC and the Paranagama Commission. We concentrated on the prospect of the war crimes allegations supposedly covering the LTTE Tigers and the Sri Lanka Government armed forces.

My personal feelings at that time, and still to this day, stem from my knowledge that the only way forward should be for a Truth & Reconciliation Commission. This is something I have thought about deeply and I came to this conclusion some years ago. The most obvious framework which provides an example of how this can work is South Africa. However, we now have the example of Columbia, where a fifty-year internal war has ended with the combatants agreeing to a Truth & Reconciliation Commission with no courts or prosecutions (unless it is proved someone has lied). This procedure has been approved by Ban Ki-moon, Secretary General of the UN, agreed by Obama and the West, and interestingly involves no foreign judges.

Since this is now de facto, it seems to me the reality is that the law for this type of armed conflict has changed dramatically. Add to this the Second Mandate of the Paranagama Commission prepared after having obtained international legal and military opinion. It has strongly justified the killing or capturing the LLTE leader Prabhakaran during the final phase of the Vanni offensive. The Commission faulted UN's Secretary General, Ban Ki-moon's Panel of Experts (PoE) for failing to examine government strategy to free civilian hostages and bring an immediate end to three decades of war.

The membership and background experience stands up to any International scrutiny. It comprised Sir Desmond de Silva, QC (UK), Sir Geoffrey Nice, QC (UK) and Professor David M. Crane (US). The Commission had the support of a panel of experts including retd. Maj. Gen. John Holmes. The minister knew all, this although Columbia had happened after the UN resolution. I did not expect the minister to open up to me but it is interesting that we said to each other: 'Well there is now a new President – totally different to Obama – so who knows what President Trump's views are?'

Additionally, I pointed out that the new Secretary General of the UN, António Guterres, was a former Prime Minister of Portugal, who must therefore have some knowledge and understanding of Sri Lanka, as the Portuguese were the first Europeans to colonise the west coast of Sri Lanka. Mangala just smiled. As I was about to leave, he said: 'I gave certain commitments to the UN about changes Sri Lanka would make and these are beginning to come to fruition.'

As if the day had not been long enough I was told by the protocol team looking after me that we were to drive halfway to Jaffna as there was no aircraft available. So we set off in two cars and just four hours later we arrived in the ancient capital of Anuradhapura where I had been several times before. Our hotel was modern and fine but it lacked the charm and colour of the rest house in the grounds of the ancient city, at which I had stayed with my family. It has more monkeys playing around than anywhere else I know.

The next morning we were on the road by 7.00 am and joined the

A9 (the equivalent of the M1 in the UK – a long, straight road totally renovated by the Rajapaksa Government, together with the railway which runs alongside it, all part of the brilliant post-war infrastructure rebuilding). After about two hours we stopped at Elephant Pass, the scene of much heavy fighting between the Tigers and the army. There is a memorial to a very brave Lance Corporal Kularathna who single-handedly tackled a LTTE armed bulldozer with a crew of four, all chained in and the vehicle stuffed with explosives. He tackled it from the rear and though wounded he climbed up and threw grenades inside the cab, killing all the occupants and stopping the vehicle. He died of his wounds. I wrote a few suitable sentences in the memorial book but noted no one had recently done so, as the war was already drifting into the past.

On resuming our journey, I noticed two interesting things as we approached Vavuniya. First, children were going to school, beautifully turned out in white with black rucksacks. Secondly, as we passed the military headquarters at Vavuniya I looked at the bund surrounding the headquarters, which was interspersed with pillboxes but not a soul in any of them. We arrived in Jaffna in good time for a series of meetings, first with the District Secretary/ Government Agent and then with His Lordship the Bishop of Jaffna, Justin Gnanapragasam who I had met in 2015. I also met the relatively new Governor, Reginald Cooray, before spending the evening as the guest of Major General Mahesh Senanayake.

Two years previously, in 2015, I was conscious of a mood of resignation. There was gratitude that the A9 road was open, the railway was restored, the electricity worked normally and people could go wherever they wanted but there were still complaints of the amount of land being held by the military, the slow pace of house-building and the tension between the army, the Governor and the Chief Minister. This time, in 2017 almost all these issues were well on the way to being solved and at a national level the TNA (Tamil National Alliance) was working with the government to agree a devolution settlement. In theory, people should have been more positive about the future but they were not. There was little or no diaspora investment money coming in; tourism was growing but tourists were not being made welcome on the adjacent islands or even on some other parts of the peninsula. The old cement works which I saw in the distance when visiting a house-building project is a monument to the disaster of the war for the people of Jaffna. I asked everyone about employment, especially for the young men and women. There was much shrugging of shoulders. There also seemed to be a reluctance by the local politicians to encourage outside investment almost on the grounds that it would undermine their power base. Unfortunately, at the time of my visit the Chief Minister was abroad but I sensed from the Governor that he was really anxious to get things moving on projects like the restarting of salt production in the lagoons. This had been a big and successful industry when I worked in Sri Lanka in 1963 and had only stopped because of the war.

The next morning I left Jaffna to return to Colombo on an Sri Lanka Air Force transport plane, which took just under an hour compared to the eight hours' drive we had endured at the protocol team's suggestion! My busy day was supposed to include a meeting with the President but as luck would have it he was not too well and all meetings had to be postponed. Sadly for me it could not be rescheduled. I was also supposed to meet the Prime Minister but I did not expect that to happen, and it did not. I think he was of the view that since David Cameron had said he was one of his best friends I was not needed. Of course, Cameron was no more at this point – he had disappeared off the map entirely – and I was still actively trying to help. But I sense it was not just me that felt displeased with the Prime Minister: there was a clear undertone that Wickremesinghe was not really performing in contrast to President Sirisena who was greatly respected.

I had arranged lunch with our High Commissioner, James Dauris. I thought James might start by giving me an overview, but none of it. He asked: 'Now, how can I help you?' So I had to ask a series of questions. The most interesting were about Tamils returning to Sri Lanka from the UK. Did the relevant authorities have a list of those who were returned from UK and were they given the telephone number for the High Commission in case of difficulty? The answer was yes to both – and nobody had called. Next question: what was the position on Brexit, were they taking any initiatives locally? Answer: not at the moment as there were no Sri Lanka Government funds for new projects. Question: what about incoming delegations from Chambers of Commerce? Answer: we are not aware of any. And so the lunch progressed staccato style. We finished on the question of visas for Sri Lankan businessmen. Yes, this had been quickened up with a premium-priced turn around service of five days. However, there were still problems as sometimes the office in Chennai (Tamil Nadu) refused to give visas, without giving reasons, and when that happened it was passed to someone more senior but this was not working. I suggested the Colombo High Commission to check and report, and this was met with stony silence! I was only there for an hour but it seemed longer.

Next I was driven out to Parliament, with outriders in attendance, to meet another old friend, the Leader of the Opposition and the MP for the TNA (Tamil National Alliance), Mr Sampanthan. He was eighty-three years old and a bit hard of hearing but was very warm in his welcome. 'I have news,' he said. 'We are working closely with the Government to find a form of real devolution that will work in a Unitary State and it does not include joining the Northern and Eastern Provinces but it should be a format applicable to every province.' We then talked about Scotland and Northern Ireland. I mentioned the increased suggestion for devolution in Wales as well. In my judgement, it was a crisp, clear and successful meeting.

It was then back to Colombo, complete with cavalcade, to meet the Head of the ICRC, Claire Meytraud, a French lady who was delighted I greeted her in French and passed some other observation in French which set the tone for a very frank and worthwhile meeting. I asked specifically about torture. She reminded me that I had asked the same question two years previously and she said the answer was still the same: no, the ICRC had not found any torture, as defined by the Geneva Convention. I then asked whether the ICRC had access to every prison, military camp, detention centre and police station, as well as the Immigration Investigation Centre at the airport. The answer was emphatic: yes. Once again, there continued to be some evidence of some heavy-handling, possibly, but not much. This led me to refute again the recent UN Report published in December 2016. In my view those Tamils alleging torture may be experiencing tough questioning if suspicions are aroused but torture is not happening. I am afraid organisations such as Freedom from Torture and fellow travellers from Amnesty International and Crisis International are just undermining their own credibility.

We also discussed the Missing Persons Commission where ICRC had done a huge amount of field research concerning claims of up to 30,000 missing persons, of which 14,000 had been traced, leaving 16,000 still to find. This vital work was now to be handed over to the Missing Persons Commission but the ICRC would continue to help. This is the third time I have had a one-to-one session with the head of the ICRC. I pay a real tribute to its leadership, impartiality and dedication to whatever it is undertaking. I marvel at it.

I rounded off the day with a good meeting with the tourism team who gave me the welcome news that UK arrivals in 2016 were up 16 per cent. My evening was spent with a backbench government MP, Seyed Ali Zahir Moulana, who I had previously met in London at a conference on Select Committees. He is MP for Batticaloa and was the interlocutor for the transfer of the former LTTE leader Karuna to switch sides and join the government side. He is a backbencher after my own heart: dedicated to his constituents and not afraid to hold minsters to account and yet in one single action he did more to change the result of the war than any other single person. For me it was an absolutely fascinating evening.

The next day, Friday, was to be my last full day, with seven engagements. I had asked to see the former President Mahinda Rajapaksa with whom I had always had a good relationship. I must say his welcome this time was particularly warm, with television cameras in attendance. Although he was not the official Opposition, he did have a block of fifty-three followers and if I were to wager, I would imagine that this number would increase in ones and twos, as the Prime Minister upset a few more. By any yardstick Mahinda was (and continues to be) an astute politician, much loved by many in the country who still understandably look upon him as the leader who defeated the Tamil Tigers. Having won the war he restored the ruined infrastructure of road, rail and electricity to the north. Unfortunately, some of the Coalition Government senior ministers ignore this huge achievement and now bait him in meaningless media challenges, which is just more propaganda for Mahinda. Why the Prime Minister even bothers to join in the baiting is beyond me but he seems unable to resist. Fortunately, the President stays above it all. Personally, I remain deeply concerned that there are certain parties in the West who see him as a de facto dictator despite being elected in free and fair elections, and want to see him tried for war crimes. I was able to show Mahinda the bundle of heavily redacted despatches from the UK's Military Attaché, which, if the redaction were removed, would prove beyond doubt that there was no policy to kill Tamil civilians. He did not see any of them to read but I stated I would persist as I thought he was totally innocent. On the current issues in Sri Lanka he was pleased with the progress on missing persons, critical of the neglect of the agriculture sector and happy with the new prevention of terrorism proposals. However, he knew that whenever provincial council elections were held his new Party would do well, which is why these elections were continually being postponed. Clearly he was sitting, watching and waiting.

From politics on to defence, prisons and an organisation called SCRM (Secretariat for Coordinating Reconciliation Mechanisms). There were no new issues on defence, as I had seen the Minister of State earlier in the week. However, I did ask to visit the Rehabilitation Hospital / Home for those badly wounded in the conflict. I did this at the end of the day, visiting every ward and talking to the disabled men. I was moved by the whole experience: the home was situated in a beautiful setting, perfectly apt and deserving for the men who had shown such courage and determination both in their wartime experiences and in the private battles in their recoveries. It was good to see Sri Lanka looking after its war heroes. I have not visited our centres in the UK but I doubt they are better than Mihindu Seth Medura, Attidiya and Dehiwala.

On the subject of prisons, I was impressed by the minister D.M. Swaminathan who recognised that prison conditions, just like in the UK, left a lot to be desired. However, he had good news of a major new prison to be built on the edge of Colombo for which the land had already been purchased. He was wrestling with a huge number of minor offenders in prison, as there was no equivalent to community service in Sri Lanka. I asked about the number of LTTE still in prison. The minister stated there were ninety-three people in prison awaiting trial at that time, and between thirty and forty in rehabilitation, aimed at preparing them to live in normal Sri Lankan society. I could not help but reflect that this was an issue that needed urgent attention. The UN, at its session in March 2019, recognised that a good start had been made, which was encouraging.

My final formal meeting was with Mr Mano Tittawela who had come from the private sector to head up SCRM, the organisation focused on reconciliation in terms of helping people who had lost trace of a family member. This linked in with the work of the Paranagama Commission and the ICRC. The Missing Persons Commission was ready to start and the appointment of a Commissioner was imminent but he or she would have a challenging task of compensating, where appropriate, the 14,000 families whose loved ones were now accounted for. Even more challenging would be to continue the work to trace the 16,000 for whom little, if anything, is known. Clearly it is a Herculean task but for once I was reasonably confident it would happen. If it did, it would be a blueprint for the rest of the world to follow, and hopefully would be recognised by the United Nations. It has been successful in that the work is now happening and resources have been made available.

I now just had Saturday before flying back to the UK at the crack of dawn on Sunday.

One my oldest friends is the Hon. Karu Jayasuriya, whom I first met when he was the outstanding Mayor of Colombo. At one time he was tipped to be leader of the UNP but never made it; a lost opportunity for the party in my opinion. He was now Speaker of the Parliament of Sri Lanka, respected by all parties, which is vital in what is a boisterous and argumentative parliament. Karu was optimistic about the future but longed for the day when the ever-oppressive West and UN stopped dictating to his country. We discussed a wide range of issues over a long, lingering luncheon: I felt totally relaxed and engaged.

I never had the chance to be elected Speaker at Westminster because I lost my seat when the tidal wave of disillusion hit the Conservative Party in 1997, resulting in the fall of the Major Government. I had been Chairman of Ways and Means for five years as well as First Deputy Speaker, so would have been in the running, but losing my seat at Northampton South by 744 votes put paid to that. I lost because of the general swing against the Conservative Party and the specific intervention of Jimmy Goldsmith's anti-European Referendum Party, whose candidate in my seat polled 1,405. I knew Sir James a bit from the days of selling Goya beauty products and pitching for the Sutton Seeds account, both of which he owned. I kick myself in not going to see him early on to explain as Deputy Speaker I was handicapped, as I could not campaign until the election was called. Although over 500 of his candidates lost their deposits, analysis of the result shows that the intervention of the Referendum candidate caused twenty of us Conservatives to lose our seats. Karu reflected that I, too, must have had a noisy and boisterous Parliament to manage for the twenty-five days of the committee stage of the Maastricht Bill.

The evening of Saturday 7 January is one I shall never forget. I was invited for dinner at the home of the former President Madam Chandrika Bandaranaike Kumaratunga. This wonderful lady is the power behind the throne of the present Unity Government. She had invited me for 6.30 pm – a full forty-five minutes before any other guests were invited, so that, in her words, 'we could have a chat'. Actually, it was painless but the most thorough interrogation I have ever had! I have the deepest respect for Chandrika both as a politician and a person. She tried so hard to find a way forward for the citizens of Sri Lanka where all would be treated with respect and dignity. Sadly, the terrorist LTTE was never willing to give even an inch in its demand for Eelam. She patiently brought in the Norwegians to try to achieve a peace process but it was always undermined by Prabhakaran. At times she was making progress amongst the moderate Tamils but Prabhakaran would never allow it to develop, which is why there was an attack on her life, resulting in an injury leaving her blind in one eye. The dinner was a scintillating affair with a number of senior retired diplomats from Chandrika's period as President, which created a vibrant atmosphere with much debate about a range of subjects affecting the world today. For me it was a fitting climax to a demanding but ultimately successful visit.

CHAPTER
Sixteen

Freedom of Information Act

First they ignore you
Then they laugh at you
Then they fight you
Then you win
Mahatma Gandhi

I have been in Parliament for well over forty years but I had never had cause to look at The Freedom of Information Act 2000 until the summer of 2014. At that time I had working for me a young man who had ambitions to get into politics at some point in his future. His name was Jack Goodman. I wondered what work I could give him which would be interesting and challenging, and therefore suggested that he and I might have a close look at what I had been doing as Chairman of the All-Party Parliamentary British Sri Lanka Group.

As background reading, I gave him the reports on my visits as well as a summary of the UN resolution A/HRC/25/i. This had been co-sponsored by the UK and USA governments and adopted in March 2014, with the aim of 'Promoting reconciliation, accountability and Human Rights in Sri Lanka'. I explained to Jack that the motivation for the resolution had been due to huge pressure from a myriad of diaspora groups, both in the USA and the UK, which included not only many Human Rights groups, but also, and importantly, many former LTTE members. Some were members of the military, some financiers but all of one mind that the war may have been lost but the cause of Eelam was most definitely alive and well. I also briefed him on media coverage around the country both in Sri Lanka and the West.

The United Nations Human Rights Council (UNHRC) had requested:

[the] UN High Commissioner for Human Rights to undertake a comprehensive investigation into alleged serious violations and abuses of human rights and related crimes by both parties in Sri Lanka during the period covered by the Lesson Learnt Reconciliation Commission (LLRC), and to establish the facts and circumstance of such alleged violations and crimes of the perpetrators with a view of avoiding impunity and assuring accountability with assistance from relevant experts and special procedures mandate holders.

Unsurprisingly, this had not been supported by the then Sri Lanka Government led by President Rajapaksa who maintained this was not an international matter but a purely internal one, to be dealt with by the democratically elected sovereign government. Unfortunately, President Rajapaksa made a huge mistake in calling the presidential election early, in late 2014, and managed to lose it to a coalition of part of the SLFP (Sri Lanka Freedom Party) and all the UNP (United National Party) whose candidate was the moderate Maithripala Sirisena. In the meantime, the UN machine had moved on by producing a resolution now co-sponsored by both the UK and Sri Lanka governments and adopted by consensus at the UNHRC in October 2015.

This stated the following in Paragraph 15:

Encourages the Government of Sri Lanka to develop a comprehensive plan and mechanism for preserving all existing records and documentation relating to human rights violations and abuses and violations of international humanitarian law, whether held by public or private institutions.

This was the context developing in the summer of 2014 as my researcher and I discussed how I might help Sri Lanka. Then I remembered that during my visit in January 2009 I had met Lt Col Anton Gash, the British Military Attaché. As previously mentioned, we had met one morning at the Hilton Hotel. I had booked a room but for security reasons I changed it at the last minute, as I feared the room might have been bugged. As a result, I am confident that Lt Col Gash spoke freely to me during our meeting. He certainly was very frank and stated that at the time he was surprised at, and impressed with, the new-found efficiency of the Sri Lanka armed forces. In his view they were now well trained and equipped for the task to take on the Tamil Tigers. He also expressed surprise at the number of Tamil civilians escaping through the lines from the LTTE to the safety and sanctuary of the Sri Lanka Army. He explained that extensive leafleting was being carried out, behind the LTTE lines, to reassure the Tamils who were trying to escape that they would be safe. It appeared that almost every night, and sometimes even during the day, people were coming over. As I listened I drew the firm impression that the Sri Lanka armed forces were, at that time, a force to be reckoned with, and with the equally important dimension of showing the care and attention to look after the Tamils fleeing from the persecution of the LTTE.

Jack and I had a brain-storming session and then it came to me: 'Who is best briefed, best- qualified and above all the most independent person to provide a daily overview of what was actually happening on the ground as the war progressed?' Answer: the British Military Attaché, Lt Col Anton Gash. Furthermore, if we could get his despatches published, this would give the most objective assessment possible. Of course, there was still a risk that there would be something incriminating in the despatches but in my judgement that was a risk I had to take. In any case it did not seem wise to mention this idea to anyone in Sri Lanka. I did not wish, at this early stage, to run the risk of setting up barriers anywhere. I believed the political and military leaderships in Sri Lanka when they stated that they had no objective to kill Tamil civilians. Indeed, since more Tamils live peacefully in the south than in the north, it never, ever stacked up as a policy. Why would any government or authority authorise the killing of a significant part of its population?

Parliament's summer recess was fast approaching, so I asked my researcher to send a Freedom of Information (FOI) request, on my behalf, to the Ministry of Defence to whom we incorrectly assumed Lt Col Gash reported. This was duly sent on 14 August 2014. It requested:

Details of the despatches written by Lieutenant Colonel Anton Gash, the Defence Attaché of the British High Commission in Sri Lanka, to the UK Foreign Office during the period January 2009 to May 2009. These despatches described his assessment of what he had seen during this period of the Sri Lanka civil war.

I did not expect an early response from the Ministry of Defence, as it was the summer recess, and in any case I knew FOI requests always set off alarm bells. I did a little thinking myself: maybe as soon as Parliament returned I should put down a written question to the Foreign & Commonwealth Office on the same subject but approaching it from a different angle, namely relating it to the UN enquiry and their call for evidence. This I did on 26 September 2014:

> To ask Her Majesty's Government whether they intend to submit the despatches from the United Kingdom Defence Attaché in Colombo for the period June 2008 to June 2009 inclusive as evidence to the United Nations Office of the High Commissioners for Human Rights' Investigation on Sri Lanka.

The reply took a little longer than usual and was published on 31 October, answered by the Minister of State for the Foreign & Commonwealth Office, Baroness Anelay of St Johns. The content surprised me and made me think. It read:

> The UK strongly supports the establishment of an independent Office of the High Commissioner for Human Rights (OHCHR) investigation on Sri Lanka and, if requested to provide assistance, we will give such requests careful consideration. We continue to urge the Sri Lanka government to co-operate with the investigation in line with recent calls made by Zeid Ra'ad Al Hussein, the UN High Commissioner for Human Rights.

In its 22 September 2014 oral update, the OHCHR (Office of the United Nations High Commissioner for Human Rights) stated 'that a more fundamental and far-reaching accountability process on Sri Lanka, addressing both past and on-going violations, is absolutely necessary for Sri Lankans to come to terms with their past, end impunity, achieve reconciliation between communities and strengthen the rule of law. In March 2015, the OHCHR will provide a comprehensive report of the investigation to the UN Human Rights Council.' This seemed to me to be nothing more than a holding reply and that it was trying to buy itself more time.

Foolishly, I had thought my written parliamentary question was tight and precise. It was, but the answer did not reflect the question. Since the UK was party to the original UN motion I would have thought it would automatically have offered the evidence of the despatches but clearly this was not the case. So, I thought, if they are not going to offer them I had better try an FOI on the Foreign & Commonwealth Office in addition to the one requested of the Ministry of Defence. This I did on 6 November in identical terms to the request to the Ministry of Defence.

Meanwhile, the UN had not been idle and in September called for evidence on what was termed 'OHCHR investigation on Sri Lanka'. Evidence had to be submitted by 30 October. Not long, but I set to work and submitted a tight but lengthy submission with headlines answering the following charges:

1. Charge: The President & Sri Lanka Government deliberately set out to kill Tamil civilians.
2. Charge: The President & Sri Lanka Government deliberately starved Civilian Tamils after the capture of Kilinochchi.
3. Charge: The President & Government of Sri Lanka set up No Fire Zones to congregate the Tamil civilians in order to kill them by shelling.
4. Charge: The President & Government of Sri Lanka deliberately ignored International opinion.

I added a second section headed 'Post War' which covered the issues of Infrastructure, De-mining, Language, Property & Land, Democracy, Torture, Numbers killed, Disappearances. I produced a list of twelve comprehensive conclusions and highlighted several serious issues, which included the need for the UN to review their estimate of 40,000 killed. I always urged, in as strong terms as I could, that the UN must make clear to the Tamil Groups around the world that espousing the cause of Eelam was illegal, as the LTTE was a proscribed organisation.

I even offered to attend the hearing in person at my expense. The submission was sent by post on 21 September, was signed for but absolutely no response was forthcoming.

Of course, I assumed the FCO would be tuned into what the UN was about but I fear I was wrong.

All I received from it was a letter, dated 3 December, acknowledging receipt of my submission, which had been dated 6 November, confirming that yes, it did hold the information but it would take until 5 January to process my request as it would have to consider specific exemptions covering specific sections of the Freedom of Information Act, namely section 26: Defence, section 27: International Relations and section 31: Law enforcement.

On 9 December I decided that having to wait two months for a reply was unacceptable, so I complained to the senior Minister of State at the Foreign Office, pointing out that the OHCHR enquiry was on-going and these despatches were highly relevant. I received a reply along the lines of: 'The delay, while regrettable, reflects the careful consideration that is taking place.'

Then, bang on time, a letter from the FCO arrived, dated 5 January 2015, two months after the original request. I tore open the envelope to find a two-page letter explaining to me that both under section sections 27 and 31 there were exemptions so, in effect, a refusal. Under Section 31(1) (a), (b) and (c) no action could be taken because:

The United Nations High Commissioner for Human Rights is presently investigating alleged serious violations and abuses of human rights.... It is essential the investigation remains independent and impartial. On balance, we believe the premature public disclosure of information held by the FCO could wrongly influence that investigation and could prejudice the administration of justice.

In a phrase, the Foreign & Commonwealth Office had refused to grant any part of my Freedom of Information request. The only helpful part of the letter was to say that if I was dissatisfied I could seek an internal review from the FOI and DPA (Data Protection Act) team at the Foreign Office. Furthermore, if still dissatisfied, I could complain to the Information Commissioner.

It will not surprise readers that on 14 January 2015 I submitted my appeal but not just baldly. I thought I should add some meat to it, so I wrote a considered letter to a person called Esther Lawrence, the Desk Officer for Sri Lanka, re-emphasising how it was in the public interest, not least for the near 500,000 British citizens of Sri Lanka origin. I added that that if the UK Government consistently and consciously withheld information then it would appear to be guilty of undermining the Human Rights of those accused.

On 19 February, despite all my protestations, warnings and challenges I receive a letter stating that all the exemptions had been carefully reviewed but they had been correctly applied. Ever helpful, the Foreign Office stated that if I was still unhappy and I felt the internal review had not been correctly handled, I could apply directly to the Information Commissioner. Frankly, I do not think I had ever heard of the Information Commissioner but that was my fault. I did still feel very aggrieved at the total lack of concern and understanding shown by the Foreign Office and so, yes, I decided, I would take the whole issue to the next stage. Three months had passed since I had started my dealings with the Foreign Office but in reality it was six months since I started this assignment.

Then I had second thoughts: the officials did not really know me in any depth, or my involvement and knowledge of Sri Lanka, so I would make a personal appeal to the senior official who had been dealing with my case, Sarah Wrathall of the Foreign Office. I wrote to her on 16 March. It was a helpful, balanced letter, pointing out that the UK Government had been supportive of the war to defeat the Tamil Tigers and there was now a new co-operative government in Sri Lanka. Furthermore, the UK and the USA had set up the formal enquiry (OHCHR) so it would be incredible if the UK Government knowingly and consciously withheld material evidence such as these key despatches. I finished by stating she should consult with the Foreign Secretary, Philip Hammond, MP, before coming to a final decision. The general election then intervened but a letter dated 7 May arrived from the Deputy Leader Sri Lanka Team, Michael Cockle, reaffirming their views; no mention of consulting the Foreign Secretary and telling me again how to contact the Information Commissioner.

In the meantime, whilst my correspondence with the Foreign Office continued, I finally received a letter from the Ministry of Defence dated 4 February 2015. This was in response to my sending the identical FOI submission way back on 14 August 2014, which had been chased up on 11 September. So, suddenly out of the blue I received this letter which stated that the issue raised fell into the exemption categories but I could appeal to their internal review. As it had taken the Ministry of Defence nearly six months to get to stage one, I felt there did not seem much point continuing to deal with them.

When I reflect on all the time and trouble I took to produce balanced and in-depth information I do feel aggrieved that all the Foreign Office did – both its ministers and its officials – was look for reasons not to publish anything at all, which is hardly in the spirit of the original Freedom of Information Act. On top of this, Sri Lanka is a friend of the UK with tens of thousands of their citizens having dual British/Sri Lanka nationality, let alone the young who are born in the UK. We forget too easily that the UK beseeched Sri Lanka to help the UK at the United Nations when we faced an aggressive motion on the Falklands. Indeed, at the request of the then Foreign Secretary Douglas Hurd, MP, I made a telephone call to President Jayawardene who promised to review their intended vote with the non-aligned countries. Sri Lanka was just one of seven nations that voted for us. Is this really how we repay friendship?

I started this assignment in August 2014. Six months had now passed. Was I going to give up? No, I was not! Who knows, maybe someone at the Information Commissioner's Office would listen. I sent a long and considered two-page letter to the Information Commissioner on 6 June; I suggested the question for him to consider was whether I was right in asserting it was in the public interest to publish the despatches and I backed it up by spelling out six points. At the risk of being tedious, these points are worth repeating in summary form:

1. There are about 500,000 British Citizens of Sri Lanka origin.

2. Surely the deciding moments of the war are relevant to the people of Sri Lanka?

3. The UK is a prime mover of the UN inquiry, surely it has a responsibility to supply the evidence of the despatches?

4. Since alleged war crimes are involved and almost all the Tamil Tigers are dead, how can it be possible to withhold key independent evidence?

5. The UK claims it cannot publish because it would affect international relationships but this involves a friendly fellow member of the Commonwealth.

6. This FOI request is to find clarity about the end of the war. This is in the interest of all parties: UK, UN, and Sri Lanka.

I added a newspaper cutting taken from the *New Statesman* (5-11 June 2015, p. 24) written by my colleague Baroness Helena Kennedy about the Magna Carta. She asked the question: 'Whose power now needs constraint? Who seems to enjoy power without much consequence or restraining? Who operates above the Law? The straight answer is that arms of government still act in ways that ignore the law.' I thought to myself that these were very pertinent questions in relation to my FOI request. At the very least the Information Commissioner would realise that I was deadly serious about getting these despatches published.

A month later, almost to the day, a letter arrived dated 7 July, asking for clarification about both the Ministry of Defence and Foreign Officer requests, which I answered on 11 July. A couple of weeks later I received a letter dated 24 July stating, 'We are now able to progress your complaint and can confirm your case is eligible for consideration.' I really was encouraged by this as it seemed something may happen, and I was heartened when a colleague in the House of Lords commented that the ICO do a thorough job.

Two months passed and I thought to myself that it was time for a letter to the Chief Executive of the ICO, so I sent a pleasant letter dated 22 September. I pointed out just how long ago I formally started this inquiry – namely November 2014. A few days later I received an encouraging letter, dated 29 September, which led me to believe the Chief Executive had had a meeting with the team allocated to me to ensure something happened one way or another. I reviewed my original submission and decided it would do no harm to highlight the key issues, so I wrote again on 19 October. November passed quietly, Christmas was looming and so, reluctantly, I accepted that I would have to be patient until January.

The House of Lords rose on Tuesday 22 December and literally on the day before I received an email at home from the Foreign Office, of a copy of a letter to me, also dated 21 December, with a huge attachment of twenty-six pages. It was unsigned, and just said 'South Asia Department'. I hardly bothered to read the letter because there in front of me, as an attachment, were twelve despatches covering the twenty-six pages, some of them heavily redacted. I thought to myself, can it really be that at last I have in front of me the despatches I have fought so hard to obtain?

I did not have the time to read the despatches carefully at this time, as Parliament was rising and, in any case, I was committed to helping my daughter at her kitchen shop, wearing my uniform apron embroidered with the word 'Kitchenalia'. I stood at the entrance in the traditional US role of 'Greeter'.

After Christmas, I read the letter carefully, noting that it was stated that the reason for being able to release the despatches in part was that the OHCHR enquiry could have been influenced by the despatches but now that it was over and reported upon on 16 September, the material could be released. I had to take a deep breath, reflecting that I was dumbfounded, because this was the whole purpose to get the UN to take into consideration these despatches from an independent informed source.

Just as I was reflecting on what to do, I received a letter from the Information Commissioner dated 6 January 2016 and I quote the key part:

> I can confirm that after some delay, the FCO has now provided me with a substantive response to my enquiries, including a copy of all of the information falling within the scope of your request. I also understand that in late December the FCO provided you with some of the information, falling within the scope of your request that it had previously sought to withhold. Based upon your previous submissions, I am assuming that despite this disclosure of

the information, you will still wish to pursue your complaint with the ICO.

It did not take me long to decide on a two-pronged response.

First, I wrote to the Information Commissioner pointing out, amongst other things, the following:

> Since so much is blacked out how do I know whether the Foreign Office has met any requirements you may or may not have laid down. You will see from the 26 pages of attachment that there is a strange numbering system, so I do wonder if all the despatches of Colonel Gash have been sent to me blacked out or not. You will also note that after March 12th only one was sent in April on the 22nd and one in May on the 12th. Both April and May were two of the key months towards the end of the war so I find it hard to believe there were just these two despatches.

Secondly, I decided it was time to try to put on some political pressure, so I wrote a personal but formal letter to the Foreign Secretary. I sent my two letters to Philip Hammond and to the Information Commissioner on the same day, once again outlining my FOI request and explaining how, all of a sudden, twenty-six pages of redacted material had been sent to me almost out of the blue. I went on to explain in some depth my unique involvement with Sri Lanka, asked for a personal meeting and attached five questions as a sort of agenda for such a meeting. I covered the material from the actual despatches: the numbers killed, as the despatches seem to suggested less than 10,000 compared to the UN's 40,000. Why was the OHCHR not given access to the despatches? Had the despatches been made available to any third party? And, finally, why did the UK Government appear not to have given to the OCHCR any evidence about those British/Sri Lanka subjects that appeared to have been involved in the war particularly those affected by alleged war crimes?

The Information Commissioner was now fully committed and charged up, raising my questions with the Foreign Office, together with some of his own, in a tough letter of 19 January. I wrote a personal letter to him to thank him.

The Foreign Office responded on 5 February – a record in itself! Most of the response appeared to be self-justification of the stance it had taken but eventually in its fourth point there was a chink of light as three more despatches had come to light. On 9 February the ICO wrote back about these three new despatches and also raised a question about an attachment to one of the other despatches. And so, finally, on 23 February the missing three despatches were found and delivered covering twelve pages, some heavily redacted. It is clear to me that had I not carefully checked the dates and put myself in Lt Col Gash's shoes, these three would never have surfaced covering 7, 25 and 26 April (but nothing more for May which mystifies me to this day).

I wrote to the ICO on 1 March, thanking it for its help but still questioning the extent of the redaction. Examples of four typically redacted pages are in Appendix VII. Some pages were entirely redacted. I sent a further letter on 23 March, asking about progress. On 29 April the ICO wrote that a draft decision notice was with a senior official awaiting review and I would hear soon.

The decision arrived on 4 May 2016, all fifteen pages. It covered the history of the whole appeal from the time of original referral on 6 June 2015 at which point nothing had been obtained at all from the Foreign Office. I now had fifteen despatches – claiming to be all there were – covering thirty-eight pages: quite an achievement in itself. However, the extent of the redactions irked me from the start. Sadly the Information Commissioner, having been such a help to this point, felt there was nothing more he could do to challenge the Foreign Office's application of what is called section 27(1)(a), which essentially is that if certain material is published that would be detrimental to the UK's foreign relations, it can be redacted.

I was disappointed of course but I did understand and accepted the ICO had moved the whole project forward and had been really understanding and efficient. However, I still wrestled with the extent of the redactions. I re-read the second paragraph about the decision: 'If you disagree with the decision notice, you have the right of appeal to the First Tier Tribunal (Information Rights).'

Well I did disagree, so decided to appeal.

In the meantime I needed to evaluate the political situation, not least in the light of my letter to the Foreign Secretary of 11 January 2016, seeking a one-to-one meeting as I had previously had with a former Foreign Secretary, Douglas Hurd, on a difficult matter affecting Sri Lanka. His reply on 11 February indicated that my letter had fallen on stony ground. It acknowledged the serious concerns I had, said it was up to the Information Commissioner to make a decision but in the meantime, and to quote: 'I do not think it would be appropriate to comment further.' No mention was made of the importance of the UK's relationship with Sri Lanka or any attempt to answer any of the questions raised by me. Clearly being in the Lords where one does not see ministers who are in the Commons is a singular disadvantage.

The appeal process to the First Tier Tribunal was pretty straightforward. The form told me I had twenty-eight days from the decision of the ICO, which I met by sending it in on 31 May. Did I have a representative? Answer: 'No.' Not least as I could not afford a barrister; in any case I was not confident he or she would perform any better than myself. It did make me think that ideally I should take a knowledgeable friend with me when the time came for the hearing. I was asked for the grounds of appeal, so I sent a three-page letter, a copy of which is in Appendix VIII. There are two key paragraphs responding to the Foreign Office's basic argument which maintained that the effect of publication would be to undermine international relations specifically between Sri Lanka and UK, and by implication between the UK and other countries.

The first point I was keen to maintain was that this was a spurious argument. The issue here was war crimes and specifically if there was a policy 'to kill Tamil civilians'. I then covered the history of the UN motions but pointed out that by withholding Lt Col Gash's despatches that the UN enquiry was denied vital evidence. Later in the letter I quoted Prime Minister Cameron's statement on the UNHRC's resolution: 'Today's resolution is a crucial step in uncovering the truth about alleged war crimes in Sri Lanka.' I wrote in my submission to the tribunal that, 'The disclosure of information submitted in Lieutenant Colonel Gash's despatches would not only aid the process of promoting reconciliation, accountability and human rights in Sri Lanka but would serve to assist the process of truth seeking that is essential for this task.'

Finally, I was asked: 'What outcome I was seeking from my Appeal'.

I wrote: 'The publication in full of the despatches from the UK Defence Attaché Lt Col Gash in Colombo Sri Lanka sent between January 1st and May 19th inclusive in 2009 when the war between the Government of Sri Lanka's armed forces defeated the LTTE (Tamil Tigers) but with minor redaction to protect the names of junior personnel.'

Ironically, the primary appeal was against the Information Commissioner's refusal to instruct the Foreign Office to remove the redactions from the despatches that we had extracted from the Foreign Office. Technically, the ICO had the right to respond to my appeal which had been lodged by me in time on 1 June. It did respond, at length, in a letter over seven pages as it wrestled with the conundrum which it rightly said boiled down to two issues: 'Would disclosure of the information be likely to prejudice international relations and if so, does the public interest in maintaining the exemption outweigh the public interest in disclosing it?'

Of course, having come this far the ICO maintained that publication would not be in the public interest and that it would be for the tribunal to decide.

I read the ICO submission carefully, marking it up as I went. It then occurred to me that this did not relate to what was happening on the ground in Sri Lanka so I penned another letter on 24 June to the tribunal highlighting the press release of the Head of the British Diplomatic Service and the Head of UK DFID (Department for International Development), which stated: 'The UK will continue its programme of support for Sri Lanka to help the government fulfil its goals on reconciliation, human rights and strengthening democracy.' My view was clear, so I wrote, 'there can never be true reconciliation whilst these despatches, now openly known to exist are kept solely for the UK government'. I just hoped the tribunal would recognise that no one in Sri Lanka was the least bit likely to be upset, as these despatches would almost certainly be solid evidence to refute the charge that the Sri Lanka Government and its armed forces had a policy to kill Tamil civilians.

Just as I thought matters would now move forward smoothly, I received at the beginning of July an email telling me the Foreign Office would also be fighting my appeal, so I now faced two powerful, entrenched opponents, wishing to hold the line and not remove the redactions. And by now I had also learned the hard way that appeals rarely move forward expeditiously but I would never have guessed that it would take another ten months for the actual hearing to take place. The final decision was received virtually a year after my lodging my appeal, made on 31 May 2016 and a decision reached on 3 March 2017. Readers may well ask how this came about? The main culprit was the Foreign Office.

It took from the end of May until 10 August to make its response to my appeal, although there was no basic change in it from when I had started my initial investigations back in 2014! Its whole position relied on the parameter that 'the public interest in maintaining the exemption outweighs the public interest in disclosing the information in the context of damaging the bilateral relationship between the UK and Sri Lanka as well as harming international relations'. Then, to the surprise of all parties including, I suspect, the officials of the First Tier Tribunals, the Foreign Office calmly sought a sixty-day stay of the proceedings. Thankfully the registrar would have none of it and rejected the request on 12 August.

Whilst awaiting the Foreign Office's response, I decided to do a little creative thinking. I was in luck as the House of Lords decided to have a 'Take Note Debate' on the Iraq Inquiry, commonly known as the Chilcot Report, taking place on 12 July. It was too good an opportunity to miss. I put my name down to speak and was called at 6.16 pm. My contribution appears in full in Appendix IX. I drew attention to what was then my two-year-old Freedom of Information request. However, almost my last words were the most prophetic, when I said: 'I ask the Foreign Office to reflect carefully on the full implications of Chilcot, namely that we should treat each situation separately and recognise that the truth will get out. It is better to publish evidence than to hide it.'

Following the debate, I wondered what had happened about redaction in relation to the long-delayed and infamous Chilcot Report. I sought the help of the House of Lords Library over the extent of redactions in the report. Clearly there were redactions under: 'The protocol between the Iraq enquiry and HMG regarding documents and other written and electronic information.'

Looking at the extent of the redactions they were clearly far less than I had experienced with Lt Col Gash's despatches. I decided these findings were sufficiently important to bring them to the attention of the Tribunal, so I wrote to the clerk on 3 August asking him to do so.

Just before I wrote the letter I noted a report in the *Telegraph* stating that the Foreign Office had, in effect, made a huge mistake in its assessment on Human Rights in Saudi Arabia over the Yemen war, switching from a statement that 'our judgement is that there is no evidence that International Human Rights has been breached' to 'we have been unable to assess that there has been a breach of International Human Rights by the Saudi-led Coalition'. A complete volte-face. I just wondered if at some point in time the Foreign Office might decide to do the same volte-face over Lt Col Gash's redacted despatches.

Time passed and the Foreign Office evidence was duly received and raised no new issues. That is until 24 October when it tabled a 'Rule 14 Application', which meant in effect that certain evidence was so sensitive that it could only be shared between the tribunal, the ICO and the Foreign Office – but excluding me, Lord Naseby. Interestingly in paragraph 11 of the application it stated: 'it is also required in order to evidence the way in which Her Majesty's Government has cooperated with the Office of the High Commissioner for Human Rights investigation on Sri Lanka (OISL). This is sensitive.'

I reacted to this immediately: time and again I had been told that Her Majesty's Government thought it would be improper for it to intervene or interfere with the work of OISL which was supposed to be independent. Of course, many observers know the UK authorities are closely involved since the UK was the driving force behind the original motion.

I was still mulling it over when I received a second 'Rule 14 Application' dated 18 November entitled 'Publication of details concerning Col. Gash'. In paragraph 3 it stated, 'in an attempt to resolve these proceedings without further litigation the FCO shared with Appellant (who is a parliamentarian and Privy Counsellor) certain information, given on strict conditions of anonymity and confidentiality'.

My response was sent on 14 December (my eightieth birthday celebrations had prevented me from attending to it earlier) but still, my reply was robust and was based on a meeting I had with the senior Foreign Office official, following a letter from Alok Sharma, MP, Minister for Asia & Pacific, dated 13 October 2016. I quote: 'I know this has been a long-running process which is now going to Tribunal. I would like to discuss a particular element of your Appeal with you. Unfortunately, I am travelling from 19 October but I have asked the Head of South Asia Department, at the FCO to meet you on my behalf.' And handwritten: 'I know XX will be in a very good position to discuss this issue.' No mention of 'in confidence' or 'on Privy Council terms'. My previous, pre-parliamentary career had been in advertising and served me well with a good grounding in business protocol: there had been a strict rule that whoever went to a client meeting must produce, as soon as possible after it, a contact report itemising what was discussed, what was agreed and whether any parts of the meeting were confidential. I remain totally adamant that my contact report from the meeting with the Foreign Office official is 100 per cent accurate and sent the day after the meeting. Furthermore, the official made no response, despite being given the opportunity. Frankly, I was furious. It was insulting to be told to keep things confidential when the FCO had not done so previously. I felt sure it was just using it as a weapon in the 'fight' that was the tribunal, and at the same time undermining my professionalism at the meeting.

It put the tribunal in a difficult position and it was decided that a judge should adjudicate. The judge recorded there was a difference of opinion of the status of the meeting at the Foreign Office but for the moment confidentiality must remain. I shall never forget the underhand way the Foreign Officer official covered up her own inadvertent error.

Just prior to my birthday I had a discussion with my brother who is a lawyer in Vancouver Island and was over to celebrate with me. Up until this point the hearing had all been done by correspondence, which had been a huge challenge for me with no secretary or any other help.

Since it was clear we were now approaching the home straight, I pondered on whether to go for an oral hearing. My brother was quite clear and said: 'Why not? You have nothing to lose and possibly much to gain, not least the sympathy of the tribunal judges.' So the decision was made and communicated to the registrar who sent out an email which read:

Lord Naseby no longer consents to a paper consideration; therefore this matter will be dealt with at a hearing.... Would all parties please by 24 November 2016 provide their dates to avoid for the

period 16 January 2017 to 31 March 2017; the Tribunal will then
set a suitable hearing date.

I thought to myself: 'Wow!, we are really approaching the final lap.' I
sent in my request for the hearing to be heard in the second half of
January, as I was going to Sri Lanka in the first week of January, which
would bring the benefit of my being fully up to date with the current
situation in the country when the hearing was heard. But it was not to be,
as the other two parties, the ICO and the Foreign Office were incredibly
busy. Eventually a date was fixed for Thursday 23 March at 10.00 am in
Court 5 at Fleetbank House, 2-6 Salisbury Square, London.

I decided to ask my close friend and advisor Amal Abeyawardene on
matters Sri Lanka if he would join me, which he readily accepted. The
tribunal was held in a small court and heard by three judges. Both the
Foreign Office and the Information Commission (ICO) had senior QCs
acting for them. On reflection, since I am not a lawyer, I should have
found a QC to go through all the mountain of material. I brought with
me my files and a bound file from the ICO.

Whilst Amal and I sat outside flicking through the file, there to our
amazement were the thirty-nine pages of the despatches – unredacted!
This created a massive dilemma for me. Should I keep quiet or should
I hand them in? I am a senior politician having been in Parliament for
forty-two years. I think I am respected. I certainly believe in the Rule of
Law and in my country. With a very heavy heart I decided that I could
not keep the unredacted copies.

Just as I came to this conclusion, the Foreign Office's QC came over
to introduce himself, saw what we were looking at and said there had
been a terrible mistake by the ICO in sending this unredacted folder
inadvertently to me and that I must extract them from the folder
immediately and hand them over to him. I did so, saying that I believed
in the Rule of Law but that someday they must be shown fully in public
if there are ever to be any cases of war crimes made against the former
President, senior ministers or the military in Sri Lanka. The QC was
visibly shaken and expressed his sincerest thanks to me, which was
witnessed by Amal Abeyawardene.

The court hearing took about two hours with opening statements, then
the questioning of the Head of South Asia Department, who I thought a

weak and unconvincing witness. All parties then summed up their cases. The Foreign Office continued with its claim that the redactions were necessary to protect its relationships with other friendly countries. If the redactions were removed it would demonstrate to our allies that the UK was untrustworthy with confidential information.

I challenged this assertion in the specific case of the Government of Sri Lanka, who I was confident would welcome the full publication even if it was sent in confidence. However, the Foreign Officer remained adamant there could be no exceptions. I also emphasised to the judges that it was not just Sri Lankan citizens who wanted to know the contents but also the 500,000 UK citizens of Sri Lankan origin.

The judges retired but came back fairly quickly. The Chairman was kind enough to say I had made a powerful case, which, along with the doggedness I had shown, was much to be admired. However, the judges, without dissent, had decided the security of the country was paramount and the appeal was rejected.

My feelings at the time, and which remain unchanged today, are that I had exhausted all possible routes to get the despatches published in full. However, there was still within them, even in their heavily redacted form, a considerable amount of factual evidence that ought to defeat the prospect of any war crimes cases. I also left with a totally clear conscience that I had not taken the unredacted despatches with me. Personally, I continue to pray that I made the right decision. Perhaps one of my relations or the relations of those involved in Sri Lanka will petition under the Thirty Year Rule to see what these important despatches – with no redactions – did actually record.

This picture shows cages used by LTTE Tamil Tigers to put captured Sri Lanka Army personnel without water in the sun to die.

CHAPTER
Seventeen

War Crimes: Allegations Against the Sri Lankan Armed Forces

There is nothing more emotive or serious for countries or their armed forces, at any level, particularly for their leaders or individual heads of state, than a charge of alleged war crimes.

However, in assessing the situation of whether Sri Lanka should be tried for war crimes during the period between 1 January to 19 May 2009, I am compelled to propose a few facts to give a context to these allegations. The first of which is the challenge to determine the true nature of the engagement between the armed forces of the elected Government of Sri Lanka and the LTTE Tamil Tigers.

The LTTE did not represent the Tamil people, nor did it ever represent more than a small portion of the Tamil people living in the Northern or Eastern Provinces. Its objective was to achieve, by force, an independent state of Eelam, thereby totally destroying the unitary state of Sri Lanka. The method of achieving this was to murder any competing Tamil leader who disagreed with its strategy. However, it did not stop there (as we will see in detail in Chapter 18). Suffice to record, the LTTE was quite ruthless in its killing of all who stood in the way, be they presidents, senior politicians, the civilian police or thousands of innocent civilians. Eventually the leading nations of the world recognised that this was no less than unadulterated terrorism on a scale probably never seen before. The result was the proscribing of the LTTE Tamil Tigers in thirty-two major countries.

In relation to the war crimes' allegations, the question should have been: was the war an engagement to be governed by the law of armed conflict – otherwise known as International Humanitarian Law – or was it governed by Human Rights legislation created by The European Convention on Human Rights? For me, the definitive ruling came from Sir Desmond de Silva, QC, the late former chief prosecutor of a UN-sponsored war crimes tribunal who stated, in writing, that accountability in war is best dealt with by applying law that is specifically designed for war conditions. His published statements applied on separate occasions to war generally and to Sri Lanka specifically.

I have listed in Chapter 18 the horrors of what the LTTE Tamil Tigers did to innocent civilians.

This chapter is only concerned with the allegation of war crimes against the armed forces of Sri Lanka. However, to understand properly what its enemy did, I do need to highlight some of the horrors.

It is estimated that the Tamil Tigers Army, for what it termed 'the final war', consisted of about 5,000 hardened fighters, aided by possibly as many as 10,000 Tamil civilians: a mixture of civilian supporters and forced conscripts of all ages, some as young as fourteen (others may have been even younger). Alongside these were no less than 300,000 to 350,000 Tamil civilians who had been forced at gunpoint to move with the Tamil Tigers. The main objective was to use them as supplementary fighters, as a human shield or bargaining counter, or just to make it hugely difficult for an advancing army not to kill civilians. To this has to be added a highly sophisticated armoury of mobile artillery and a clever use of terrain with defensive bunds. In addition to all this was the notion amongst the Tiger leadership that the West would not stand by if it saw the possibility of a massacre of civilians and would therefore force a ceasefire. Indeed, Lt Col Gash, in his despatch of 28 January 2009 says: 'The LTTE appear to have no options left, and the language on TamilNet and other similar platforms is clearly striving for international intervention to force a cease-fire on the Government of Sri Lanka?'.

Against this background, here specifically are the war crimes allegations made against the Sri Lanka armed forces:

1. A claim that President Rajapaksa had a stated policy to kill Tamil civilians

There is not a shred of evidence anywhere to support this allegation, which is still peddled to this day by certain groups of diaspora living in the West. Indeed, all the evidence from Lt Col Gash clearly shows the trouble taken by the Sri Lanka armed forces to look after the Tamil civilians who had escaped from the LTTE. The numbers were not minimal: Lt Col Gash reports on 2 March 2009 that 37,197 had already arrived overland. Additionally, there is no clearer evidence than the despatch from Lt Col Gash about the injured Tamil civilians rescued off the beach by the ICRC (International Red Cross) and the Sri Lanka Navy and taken to Trincomalee for care.

2. A claim that the setting up of the five No Fire Zones (NFZs) was a conscious policy to congregate civilians so that they could be killed

In reality, there is clear evidence that the ICRC (Red Cross) was informed at every stage that the objective was to safeguard civilians. According to the rules of armed conflict, a NFZ only becomes effective if all warring parties agree its details. The LTTE did not endorse it, presumably because it undermined its human shield strategy. To make matters worse, from the moment the NFZs were named, the LTTE moved artillery and mortars into those zones and starting firing at the army. It also carefully positioned its weaponry next to hospitals. The response from the Sri Lanka Army was clear: the LTTE was not respecting the rules of the NFZs and so continued as if there were none in place.'

Major General Holmes, in his 'Expert Military Report' to the Paranagama Commission makes clear that the army had briefed all its units over the concentration of civilians, hospitals, UN/NGO facilities and humanitarian convoys within their area of operation. Maj Gen General Holmes continued that Rules Of Engagement did not mean there would be no collateral damage or civilian deaths, even with the most well-equipped and trained armies. He concluded with an example from the UK that 'the inherent right to self-defence will always apply'. The Paranagama Report was published in August 2015.

3. A claim that the Government of Sri Lanka was out to starve both the Tigers and the civilians

Evidence now is quite clear that there was sufficient food and medicines held by the government agent who followed the policy of maintaining six months stock of key requirements. This had been helped by a bumper harvest locally and seaborne supplies which had reached the affected areas. All of this was conveniently not mentioned in the British Foreign Secretary's challenge to the Sri Lanka Government, and quickly taken up by others, including the UN. Indeed, on 19 May 2009, the day the war ended, the warehouses under the control of the government agent still had stocks of fuel, food and medicines. The question which remains unanswered is: were the civilians denied adequate supplies by the LTTE?

4. The kernel of the war crimes claim centred on 'genocide'

The Darusman Report of 2011 claimed the civilian death toll could have been as high as 40,000. Other so-called 'objective' commentators, such as International Crisis stated 40,000-147,000; Frances Harrison, BBC correspondent, stated 50,000-101,748; the US State Department stated 7,700. The British Military Attaché who was 'on the ground' for the whole of the war stated about 7,000. In addition, he reported that 20 per cent of this figure was LTTE cadres who had thrown away their uniforms to hide their true identity and claimed to be civilians, making a truer figure of Tamil citizen deaths approximately 6,000. The latest Sri Lanka Government census was carried out by Tamil civil servants in 2011/12 and stated the figure of 7,400 in a category called 'due to unidentified sources'. However, these were civilians, which, in the Department of Census & Statistics' definition, included all LTTE fighters killed as well.

Finally, Dr Shanmugarajah, in a legally valid affidavit, based on his role as a Senior Medical Officer working close to the LTTE operation centre, stated the figure of 2,500 civilian deaths (up to 14 May 2009). All the reliable sources therefore, in effect claim between 5,000-7,000, which, whilst regrettable and sad, certainly do not warrant the term 'genocide'. Indeed, there is still a conundrum in that the satellite images from Amnesty International clearly only finds about 2,500 graves, which makes me think that Dr Shanmugarajah may be nearer the truth than most people think. The one remaining source which could yet throw more light on the situation is The Commission of Missing Persons. Who knows what it may uncover? The census categorised people who were previously thought to have been killed as 'unidentified other causes'. I wonder how many may turn up to be well and very much alive overseas.

5. The UN's Darusman Report identified the camps where all the 295,000 Tamil citizens rescued from the LTTE were considered 'Detention Camps'

Indeed, some wild journalists and politicians suggested they were more like concentration camps.

However, since the ICRC had access from Day One, these claims do not stack up and I find it not just galling but irresponsible of those in authority to use such emotive terms with all their negative connotations. Of course, all the well-meaning NGOs wanted to get in on the act but free access was simply not possible until a thorough screening of all the people – to root out the members of the LTTE – was completed.

I followed the stories carefully, as I had been to refugee camps in other parts of the world. Ann and I visited Manik Farm in April 2012 and we had private conversations with those waiting to leave as soon as the mine clearance programme allowed them to go home. Far from complaining, almost all were relieved to have reached the safety of the camp and praised the staff and the facilities.

I could go on through all the other claims about alleged war crimes peddled ad nauseam by sections of the diaspora lobby groups but it seems to me much more beneficial to explore how to achieve reconciliation.

Too easily do we forget that the key people are all the citizens of Sri Lanka, resident in Sri Lanka.

It does not include the diaspora who have chosen to live in another country, nor the former LTTE fighters and leaders who may have escaped, such as Mrs Adele Balasingham. There is some similarity with the British ISIS fighters who now want to return and influence UK policy: in my view, totally unacceptable. I question the objectivity of the UK Government and the UK political parties who all too easily are tempted to court Tamil support in key marginal areas. I had a marginal seat in Northampton South. I engaged my Irish community but refused to support its claim in any way for a United Ireland. I question, too, all the Tamil lobby groups in the UK: Global Tamil Forum (GTF), British Tamil Forum (BTF), Provisional Transnational Government of Tamil Eelam (PTGTE), Tamil Eelam People's Alliance/ Tamil National Alliance (TEPA/TNC) to name just a few – there are others.

Personally, I believe that at the end of the day there will have to be a Sri Lanka Peace & Reconciliation Commission. I have studied both the South Africa and Columbia case histories. The key element is there should be *no overseas judicial involvement*. All political parties and ethnic groups should sign up and support it. There must be no witch-hunt of the Sri Lanka military. There is a huge lesson to be learnt from the UK Army's experience in Iraq and Northern Ireland where, for decades after the event lawyers are still attempting to prosecute soldiers who were following orders whilst their then enemy goes free. There should be an invitation to those LTTE leaders scattered around the world to come and express their regrets, apologies or whatever is seen as appropriate. The Tamil lobby groups around the world should agree to cease any lobbying for a Tamil homeland or Eelam.

The achievement of this will demand true leadership but the cause is so vital to the future of Sri Lanka that it should be attempted. It may well be that external parties could help with the structure. Reconciliation will not come from tinkering at the edges, nor from the involvement of the United Nations or any overseas government, including the UK. How wonderful it would be for Sri Lanka if, following the examples of South Africa and Columbia, it were to be the third success.

The sheer genius at creating deadly naval equipment out of nothing.

CHAPTER
Eighteen

LTTE: Tamil Tigers and Other Groups
Supporting Eelam

As I reflected on the content of this book on my life with Sri Lanka, I asked myself whether I should specifically cover the LTTE Tamil Tigers as a subject in itself. I contemplated that I had only knowingly met one member of the LTTE, the de facto joint leader and theorist, Anton Balasingham, a UK citizen, in his office in London. I say 'knowingly' because I must have met others, particularly in the UK, at the many meetings held on Sri Lanka. Nobody knows how many former activist LTTE cadres there are in the UK, but it would not surprise me if it were anywhere between 300 and 400. The more I reflected, the surer I became that it would be appropriate. After all, the LTTE had murdered my two closest Sri Lanka friends, Gamini Dissanayake and Lalith Athulathmudali, and I felt they deserved the exposure for this.

Gamini, leader of the Opposition and a presidential candidate, was blown up by a suicide bomber on 24 October 1994. I looked upon him as a really close friend; he even stayed at my home in Sandy, Bedfordshire. It was not just politics that united us, it was our joint love of cricket. In my judgement he was the outstanding UNP politician in Sri Lanka. Without his commitment and drive I doubt that the Victoria Dam project would have been the success it is. The world does not have too many natural leaders but he was definitely one. What a waste of talent his murder by the Tamil Tigers turned out to be.

Lalith was different, a politically astute strongman, undoubtedly a potential Leader of the UNP, gunned down on 23 April 1993. This was not the first attempt on his life, as he told me of the occasion when a bomb had been planted in a meeting room. I can only wonder what passed through his mind as the bomb rolled down the table before failing to explode. Lalith knew about my campaigns in the very marginal seat of Northampton South, and how I won it against the odds in February

1974 and then held it in the second election in October 1974, despite the swing against the Conservatives. Additionally, he was fascinated about my involvement with Airey Neave, MP, helping with the campaign he masterminded to get Margaret Thatcher elected Leader of the Conservative Party in the summer of 1975.

Sadly, Airey too was taken away by a terrorist bomb. A car bomb exploded as his car tilted, going up the ramp of the House of Commons underground car park. This was a huge loss to Margaret Thatcher, to the Conservative Party and to me personally as he was my mentor, anxious to ensure I got a junior ministerial job. But with my mentor gone, it was not to be.

In the case of all three, a massive loss of talent. Two taken away by the LTTE Tamil Tigers and one by the IRA. For Sri Lanka the tragedy was a double blow, as both Dissanayake and Athulathmudali were potential leaders. One has to ask, and for what end?

These personal cases strengthened my case for including this chapter and outlining the atrocities of the LTTE. After all, what other terrorist organisation dominated life in its own country for nearly thirty years and was proscribed in thirty-two countries? I find it astounding that even today there are sympathisers in the UK who are openly proud of Prabhakaran and what he stood for, symbolised by the antics outside the Sri Lanka High Commission on Independence Day in 2018 where men were wearing T-shirts espousing Eelam and Prabhakaran. All strictly illegal but the UK authorities seem blinded into inaction. Furthermore, this is only a snapshot of the still worldwide movement now transposing Eelam into a 'Tamil homeland of Tamil speaking people'. Consider the constant campaigning by a number of MPs, including myself, to get the LTTE proscribed in 2001 in the UK; in fact, it took at least two years longer than it should have done. Even then there was no officially led campaign to root them out, to stop their illegal fundraising, to crack down on the money laundering through petrol stations, to prevent the bogus shipping line from operating and to stop the generosity of people being hoodwinked by illegal charities such as White Pigeon. Worse still was the sheer scale of intimidation of ordinary Tamil families, particularly those working in professions and with money. Almost every Tamil family in the UK had relations in Sri Lanka who they were told would be harmed unless substantial sums of money were donated to the 'Eelam Cause'. The same was happening in the USA, Canada, Germany, France Switzerland, Norway, Australia and probably in all the thirty-two countries where the LTTE was proscribed.

One wonders why no one faced up to the reality of the LTTE with its global funding, certainly from 1983 onwards. It was happening in almost all the major financial capitals of the world, as well as at grass roots level. It is estimated that from 2002 onwards the LTTE was raising at least US$200m annually. Such a tragedy, and all to finance a terrorist organisation run without a thread of democracy by a demagogue. Amazingly, fundraising under a variety of different guises still seems to be happening today by a plethora of Tamil operations across the world. It is possible that the extortion dimension has greatly weakened, as there are far less opportunities to implement it.

So I actually see it as my duty to put down in black and white what I believe the LTTE was all about; not an exhaustive catalogue of atrocities but enough to make the case that its actions must never be accommodated, nor can there be any case for anyone to perpetuate the myth that its members were just 'Freedom Fighters' seeking a so-called independent Tamil homeland.

Let me reiterate the scale and horror of the atrocities.

Child soldiers

It is illegal to recruit either forcibly or voluntarily children under the age of eighteen. Furthermore, under the Rome Statute of the International Criminal Court, the recruitment of children is a war crime. I was a boy of four at the start of World War II and nine in 1945. Sure, when I was seven we used to play war games in Pinner, Middlesex. What little boys do not? But that is a world apart from being a forced or even becoming a voluntary joiner of a terrorist army. And this is what happened with children – boys and girls – aged as young as seven years old, recruited by the LTTE Tamil Tigers.

How many? Thousands, certainly. UNICEF stated that between April 2001 and September 2004 there were no less than 4,250 cases of underage recruitment by the LTTE. I emphasise that these were the numbers UNICEF were able to verify, so the reality is likely to be far higher. On 31 July 2005 UNICEF stated that a total of 5,081 underage children had been recruited; 40 per cent were girls and 60 per cent boys. The LTTE enticed children to become members of 'The Baby Brigade'. A member of the Brigade who survived the war stated: 'It was the "in" thing to be a member. I too wanted to "belong". We were told we would be "martyrs". My parents would belong to "great hero families".' For a low caste Tamil child this was the perfect deal, a prize too great to resist.

It is estimated that since April 1995 60 per cent of LTTE personnel killed in combat were children. This huge casualty rate is hardly surprising when one looks at the role children combatants played and considers the fact that the LTTE strategy was to use the child soldiers at the very front of the frontline. I give two examples, quoted in Shenali Waduge's book, entitled *I Am Free*:

18 July 1996: Assault on the Mullaittivu military Complex by LTTE. 300 Sri Lanka troops surrender, disarmed by child soldiers and gunned down by them.
1 February 1998: Kilinochchi/Paranthan forward Defence line attack by LTTE Baby Brigade makes heavy losses. 200 child fighters were killed'.

The 40 per cent of child soldier who were female had been trained by Adele Balasingham, who called them 'Freedom Birds'. Wife of Anton Balasingham and one of the key LTTE leaders, she is clearly a major candidate for any war crimes cases but today she continues to reside comfortably in the south of England.

By the end of the war, of the near 12,000 LTTE fighters who surrendered, just 594 of them were the surviving child soldiers. Each of them was given a Presidential Pardon with the state of Sri Lanka viewing them as victims rather than perpetrators. Was this ever noted by the West? I wonder.

Years ago, I used to look after the advertising for Save the Children. I still cannot understand why the myriad of NGOs, particularly the Human Rights activists such as Amnesty International, Crisis, Human Rights Watch et al, were quite so ineffective in preventing or at least curtailing this appalling use of children. Statements were made over the years but, as ever, nothing practical was done. Personally, I pay tribute to Shenali Waduge for this book on child soldiers, which gives real insight into their plight.

Sri Lanka citizens

Every child has a parent and from 1973 onwards, every family in Sri Lanka was acutely aware of the ruthless and arbitrary attacks carried out by the LTTE on mainly (but not exclusively) Sinhalese civilians. Villages were regularly attacked by the LTTE, which used guns and sometimes, even more horrifically, swords and machetes. No one was ever spared: not the old, the sick, the children or even the babies. Over one hundred attacks were made between November 1984 and April 2009, starting with a fishing village in the north called Dollar Farm, Welioya, where thirty-three fisher-folk were slaughtered, to Okanda near Ampara which reported five dead. It is estimated that in the intervening years over 9,800 civilians were murdered and more than 10,000 were injured.

As time moved on the LTTE became increasingly more daring and aggressive in its attempts to disrupt normal life in Sri Lanka. There were attacks on the central bus station in 1987, killing one hundred. In 1996 a truck bomb targeting the Central Bank killed ninety-six and injured over 1,300. Buses, trains, train stations and places of religious worship were targeted with ruthless efficiency, killing hundreds upon hundreds. Is it any wonder that many of the better-off emigrated whilst those less fortunate had to suffer decades of fear?

Undermining the economy

It started with transportation, particularly trains, as they were the easiest to attack, but as time moved on the LTTE grew bolder. In 1995 it attacked the oil refinery at Kolonnawa, followed by attacks on some ships. The most daring and hugely damaging attack came on 24 July 2001 at Bandaranaike Airport (today we know it as Katunayake). The attack was made by just 20 LTTE cadres who hit the poorly defended airport. The damage was not just in the loss of key aircraft, both civilian and military, but also in Sri Lanka's standing in the world: tourism collapsed almost overnight and investors shied away as Sri Lanka was categorised 'High Risk' the world over.

Although further economic target attacks took place up to the end of 2008, nothing reached the scale of the airport attack.

The cold-blooded killing of key individuals, leaders in democracy
I have been in politics for over fifty years. I can think of no other democratic country where so many political leaders have been murdered from right across the ethnic, religious and political divide. Many of them I knew personally and as I write this their faces come out of the memory bank. I did not know the Tamil Mayor of Jaffna, Alfred Duraiappah, whose shooting on 27 July 1975 heralded the beginning of the atrocities to come over the next thirty-four years until 18 May 2009 when the war ended and the perpetrator of all the atrocities, Prabhakaran, was announced dead.

However, I did know Mr Amirthalingam, the moderate Tamil leader and Secretary General of the TULF (Tamil United Liberation Front). In fact, I clearly remember going to his residence in Colombo to share my experience of Northern Ireland with him. He was gunned down on 13 July 1989. Incredibly, almost all the leaders of the Tamil Democratic Parties have been murdered, be they from the TULF, EPRLF, PLOTE, EPDP, TNA. The one person to have escaped was Douglas Devananda, another Tamil politician whom I know personally. On 7 July 2004 a female LTTE suicide bomber was arrested in the ante-chamber to the office of Douglas and blew herself up. Douglas shared with me the chilling internal camera shots of the incident. He is a remarkable man and a Tamil voice of considered reason. These were all Tamil politicians wanting to work through democratic means. Each murdered for their beliefs.

The targets for Messrs Prabhakaran and Balasingham themselves started at the top:

President Premadasa (UNP), killed by a suicide bomber on 1 May 1993; President Chandrika Kumaratunga (SLFP) an abortive attempt on her life on 18 December 1999 leaving her blinded in one eye; Lakshman Kadirgamar, Foreign Minister, killed by a sniper in his own compound on 12 December 2005. All three people I knew well and had met with, talked, laughed and discussed policy with them. They were all human beings trying to do their best for all the people of Sri Lanka. Two are gone but thankfully the third, Chandrika, is still working hard in her own unique and dedicated way. Of course there were many more assassinations of senior military personnel, other senior ministers whom I did not know personally. Their only crime was working for the country they loved.

It was not just Sri Lanka that suffered but India too, with the tragic assassination of the former Indian Prime Minister Rajiv Gandhi on 21 May 1991. Ironically, he was out attending an evening rally campaigning for the Tamil cause in Tamil Nadu as part of his campaign to be re-elected. Although security was tight, it appears the female police were not provided with metal detectors, allowing a lone, bespectacled woman wearing a shalwar kameez to enter. She approached Rajiv and, encouraged by Party helpers, placed her sandalwood garland around his neck. As he leaned forward she went to kiss his feet and once prone activated her bomb, killing Rajiv and sixteen others, as well as blowing off her own head. Shock reverberated around the world. In all probability this was one atrocity 'too far', as it undermined forever the close linkage between the LTTE /Tamil Tigers and the political leaders of Tamil Nadu who would never again countenance an independent Tamil homeland in Sri Lanka or indeed any concept of a homeland involving the unification of the Northern and Eastern Regions of Sri Lanka.

The forced ethnic cleansing of Sri Lanka Muslims

Ethnic cleansing is a concept alien to civilised societies, unknown too in Sri Lanka until October 1990 when approximately 75,000 Muslims resident in greater Jaffna were ordered to leave their homes in just forty-eight hours. There were no exceptions for the elderly, sick, dying, pregnant or infants. All jewellery and money had to be handed over. This was the most disciplined action of ethnic cleansing but it was not the end of persecution of Muslims. I recount just three:

3 August 1990: the cold-blooded killing of 300 Muslims by LTTE cadres whilst in the prostrate prayer position at the Kattankudy Mosque.

29 April 1992: the massacre of 130 Muslim civilians in Alanchipothana.

15 October 1992: the massacre of 146 Muslim civilians in Palliyagodella.

The forced ethnic cleansing of Sri Lanka Sinhalese

The LTTE Tamil Tigers' strategy was to drive out all Sinhalese residents from the Jaffna Peninsula, beginning in the early 1980s. In the 1981 census, 19,334 Sinhalese were recorded as resident in the Northern Province. A few years later almost none were recorded.

The forced herding of around 300,000 Tamil civilians to act as a human shield

In the latter days of 2008, the LTTE Tamil Tigers forced at gunpoint virtually the whole population of Jaffna Peninsula, numbering around 300,000/350,000 Tamil civilians, to follow the Tamil Tigers to Kilinochchi and then into the Vanni. Their purpose was primarily to create a human shield that would confuse and restrict the armed forces of the government, thus slowing them down. Even in the last days of the conflict in May 2009 a human shield of about 200,000 remained. When the end of the war was clearly imminent, the human shield just disintegrated, fleeing from their so-called liberators into the safety of the government armed forces; a dash made with Tamil Tiger bullets whistling over and into them.

The rejection of the No Fire Zones when offered by the Sri Lanka Government

This was not only a rejection which in itself negated the whole concept of No Fire Zones but indeed a conscious policy of placing artillery as close as possible to the hospital to entice retaliation. In the later stages of the war, there was the ever-more conscious, callous policy of firing on the LTTE's own hospitals, claiming it to be the actions of the Sri Lanka Army. Finally, in the last few days of the war, came the absolutely horrific decision to blow up the buses temporarily housing the LTTE's own wounded fighters and civilians. If these actions seem indescribably awful, then they are nothing compared to what it did to captured Sri

Lanka army troops: killing with no mercy or putting them in a metal cage without water in the hot sun until they died where they stood. I literally shuddered as I stood in front of one of these cages in January 2017 at the place where the LTTE armaments had been collected near to Nandikadal lagoon.

The fabrication of news
The Tamil Net World Wide News Service pumped out fabricated news day and night, appealing to the gullibility of parts of the West's media, including the UK's Channel 4, the correspondent for *The Times*, the late Marie Colvin, and a host of others including, sadly, the BBC. Prabhakaran was the messiah/leader of all the atrocities but who was it that really championed his cause through such an effective PR machine? It seems to me it was Anton Balasingham, the one-time clerk at the British High Commission in Colombo who seemingly was granted UK citizenship based on his good work in Colombo. Balasingham worked away unmolested. His output heavily focused on alleged Human Rights abuses of the Sri Lanka Government exploiting and abusing the Tamil people in what he termed the Tamil Homeland of the Northern and Eastern Provinces. Of course, he was not the first to coin the phrase. I believe the most persuasive orator of the cause was Mr S.J.V. Chelvanayakam, the founder and leader of the Lanka Tamil State Party who, on 26 November 1947, had said in the Ceylon House of Representatives: 'If Ceylon is fighting to secede from the British Empire, why should not the Tamil people, if they feel like it, secede from the rest of the country?'

The issue was not really promoted again forcefully until the election of 1977 when the election manifesto of the TULF (Tamil United Liberation Front) in its first resolution stated

'The territory from Chilaw through Puttalam to Mannar and thence to the North and from there covering the East stretching to Kumana in the South through Trincomalee and Batticaloa was firmly established as the exclusive homeland of the Tamils. This is the territory of Tamil Eelam.'

After Margaret Thatcher's premiership, UK politicians had steadily become sensitive to all issues of Human Rights and believed every story created in Sri Lanka: be it allegations of gross discrimination, economic discrimination, religious discrimination or language discrimination. The whole campaign was primed by the so-called asylum seekers flooding the UK Home Office with applications. This was wonderful fertile soil for Mr Balasingham to till and he was good at it.

I wonder, too, about his relationship with the British Government. He was taken ill in February 1999, somehow went to a Southeast Asian nation – possibly Malaysia – where tests were undertaken, resulting in a diagnosis for diabetic nephropathy, a progressive disease which would ultimately kill him. However, of more immediate relevance was an obstructed kidney, which had to be removed. Why is this relevant? Well, apparently Mr and Mrs Balasingham had entered the UK illegally and decided they needed to leave legally. Mrs Balasingham must have had a dual UK/Australian as she was from Australia and apparently the Australian High Commission in London provided a new passport for her. Even more intriguing was that someone somehow persuaded the Foreign Office to issue a new passport for Mr Balasingham, the arch guru and motivator of the LTTE Tamil Tigers. One wonders how this could possibly be seen to be in the interests of British/Sri Lankan relationships.

Independent Sri Lanka had never in its short life had to face anything like this barrage of criticism from around the world. It was not helped by India and particularly the politics of Tamil Nadu, the Indian state of 60 million Tamils and just a mere 40 miles from northern Sri Lanka across the Palk Strait. I say the politics of Tamil Nadu from two points of view. First, the fact that for most of the near thirty-year LTTE uprising the ruling party in Tamil Nadu funded, trained and protected the LTTE. Second, that India's central government was a coalition dependent on support from Tamil Nadu, so the Central Government of India did not and probably dared not rein in the LTTE. And so it continues to this day, in the sense that it remains a safe haven for those who escaped by sea. One wonders how many of the missing persons are either hiding in Tamil Nadu or used it as a sort of safe transit camp?

The heavy criticism of, in essence, all the Sri Lanka governments created a favourable climate for asylum seekers, particularly the Tamils who mostly spoke good English and were either professionals or had a skill that was sought by the UK. The net result was a constant flow of Tamils into the UK, which today amounts to approximately 300,000. I cannot blame any Sri Lanka citizen, particularly the young and ambitious, for wanting to come to the UK. Life was challenging in Sri Lanka and, in any case, Prime Minster Blair had a policy of welcoming immigration to supplement the UK workforce. The only problem for the UK was that hidden in the genuine immigration and, indeed, possible asylum applicants were a significant number of LTTE activists. I have no proof but I suspect Mr Anton Balasingham, the arch strategist, had a clear strategy to infiltrate into the UK a number of key LTTE activists. I am afraid the UK immigration authorities were no match for him.

I also wonder whether it was sheer chance that many of the new arrivals congregated in what are termed by the UK political parties as 'key marginals'. Certainly, it is perfectly normal for immigrants to follow those who went before and maybe as a UK politician I am too suspicious. However, it is interesting to note that the Tamil professionals who came to progress their careers included many who could be influential, including doctors, dentists, accountants and of course the lawyers! After all, Tamil lawyers have a reputation for being loquacious and have a tendency to litigate. This is by no means a criticism; indeed, my dearest friend was the late Sir Desmond de Silva, QC who did so much to help the UK over the troubles in Northern Ireland and justly earned a reputation for thoroughness, understanding and fairness.

In his last years he tried so hard to help his Mother country when President Rajapaksa asked him to assist with tracing the Missing Persons. As a result, he became perhaps the leading member of the Paragama Commission, charged with researching in depth what happened to those listed as missing. In my judgement, and that of many others, this work was done with real commitment, indeed as good as anywhere in the world. Why the incoming coalition Government of President Sirisena and particularly Prime Minister Wickremesinghe chose to ignore this work in general and Sir Desmond in particular is beyond me. We shall never know why. It was a huge and unnecessary loss to Sri Lanka. Indeed, I recall, all too clearly, the disappointment felt by Sir Desmond that the Prime Minister would not listen to him. I find it incredible that as I write this the Paragama Report has so far only been published in English. Certainly, I shall lobby for it to be translated into Sinhalese and Tamil. One can only wonder what is going on.

However, thousands did come and they did settle in the inner cities where they became a strong minority voice and voter. I understand this, as I sat for twenty-three years in the key marginal of Northampton South with two strong ethnic voting communities – the Irish and the Bangladeshi – and therefore I have some experience of the challenge that faces an MP in this situation. As already explained, I fought both 1974 elections: the first in February when the gurus in Central Office stated I had little chance of winning. They were wrong, as I used all my experience as both a senior advertising man and as a former Conservative Leader of the London Borough of Islington, long-thought to be a Labour stronghold. The net result was a triumphal majority of 179 after three counts. The second election in 1974 was expected at any time and actually took place in the October. Harold Wilson was an astute politician who knew enough of the populace would respond to his plea for a working majority and so it turned out with a swing to Labour.

However, to return to Northampton South with an anticipated swing to Labour and defending a majority of just 179. I had a large Irish Community with, it was said, an IRA cell in my constituency. I certainly did not ignore it; indeed, I went out of my way to listen and to give a commitment to look after those individuals who needed help but I made it quite clear I was not prepared to take up the Irish cause. They tried hard to twist my arm and promised the Irish vote but I resisted. I also had a large Bangladeshi community. Of course, they did not know initially that in the 1960s I had worked in northern India, based in Calcutta, a stronghold of the Bengalis. I had learned Hindu by going to the *munshi* every weekday morning with about six other young British executives. The teaching was intensive but good, not least having to learn how to write the Hindu script. Anyway, I passed the equivalent of an O Level. However, once I discovered there were a significant number of Bengalis on the voting register, I sought out the leaders, including the local Iman. My Hindi was not a great help, as they spoke Bengali or Urdu, but nevertheless it demonstrated a genuine commitment to India on my part. Out of this initiative I built a great friendship that lasted all my twenty-three years as an MP. It was their support that gave me my first win in February 1974.

Ironically, I must have upset the Irish, as I received a death threat at the beginning of the October 1974 General Election campaign from the

IRA; a threat that was taken seriously by the authorities. I say again a special thank you for the help, protection and advice given to me at the time.

I recount this story again as it does, I think, demonstrate that even in a marginal seat an MP does not need to pander to supporters of a terrorist or quasi-terrorist group. It is a mystery to me why any MP would countenance the idea of setting up a racially focused group from another country but that is what happened in the UK in relation to Sri Lanka. We had the All-Party British Sri Lanka Parliamentary Group, set up on my initiative in 1975, approved by the Commonwealth Parliamentary Association, which covered all aspects of Sri Lanka including the Tamil community.

Indeed, we took up issues like language discrimination to good effect and investment in the Northern Province but this was not enough for some MPs who wanted to corner the Tamil vote in their constituency. Virtually without adequate notice a new All-Party Tamil Group was founded. It did not stop there as it was followed by Labour for Tamils and then Conservatives for Tamils.

Why no one in authority could see that this was no more than a front for LTTE propaganda, particularly for Tamil Eelam, is beyond me. Certainly, Prime Minister Cameron was more than happy to meet these Tamil groups and listen to their propaganda. The contrast with the handling of the Northern Irish troubles is stark. Here the UK Government involved both Conservative and Labour, working hard for peace and reconciliation. Such a tragedy that Prime Ministers Brown and Cameron sided, in effect, unintentionally with the terrorists.

It does not stop there with these political pressure groups in the UK. Today there are a myriad of Tamil groups all over the world but mainly in the West, mostly headed by former LTTE activists or those who support the so-called Tamil homeland concept. None of them are proscribed, indeed almost the reverse, as I witnessed under the government of Prime Minister Cameron who seemed to welcome and almost encourage these insidious Tamil homeland groups, presumably because of the significant Tamil vote in marginal seats, without ever thinking that the UK was undermining the legitimate government of another friendly state. Sadly, I still recall a meeting I had managed to obtain with Prime Minister

Cameron on 8 November 2013 to meet with two senior directors of the Conservative Friends of Sri Lanka: Amal Abeyawardene and John Rajan Yorke. The meeting was in the Prime Minister's office in the House of Commons. He was running late. He thundered into the room and allowed us to make some brief introductory remarks on the need of the UK to help with the restoration work following the war. He then exploded, stating that he had just been shown the Channel 4 Killing Fields film thanks to one of the Tamil groups and there was no way the British Government would help until the perpetrators of the war crimes were brought to justice. I suppose one can acknowledge that he never changed his tune; never understood the fraud of the films.

Cameron demonstrated this on his arrival in Colombo at the time of the CHOGM (Commonwealth Heads of Government) meeting in Sri Lanka. I was ashamed at his rudeness and indifference to the leaders of the Sri Lanka, a friendly government, President Rajapaksa and the little girls who wanted to garland him on arrival, a tradition in Sri Lanka. He just ignored them. When he went to Jaffna he again ignored the welcoming party and went to visit a refugee camp. He then chastised the Sri Lanka Government for failing, after eight years, to rehouse the refugees, completely failing to understand that the homes of the refugees were in a minefield awaiting clearance. I was angry that there was no offer of extra financial help or even a comment on the excellent work that Halo, the UK charity, was doing in helping the mine clearance. Mr Cameron has now gone, but I fear there is still no real understanding in Whitehall of either the extent of the challenge of de-mining nor an appreciation of the extent and depth of the Tamil activist groups worldwide.

There are, I think, five key groups of LTTE/ Pro LTTE organisations operating in the Western World, particularly in Canada, the USA, the UK and several other European countries. They are: Provisional Transnational Government of Tamil Eelam (PTGTE), Tamil Eelam Peoples' Alliance/ Tamil National Alliance (TEPA/ TNC), Global Tamil Forum (GTF), and British Tamil Forum (BTF) Ex-combatant/intelligence group.

As far as I can see, none of them have or are helping Sri Lanka settle down after such a long and terrible war; none of them are helping to create the stability so necessary for inward investment and none of them are helping with any kind of reconciliation and understanding. Far from it. All they are doing is stoking the fire of Eelam, sometimes under the title of 'Tamil homeland'.

I suppose few UK officials know the source of the cry for a Tamil homeland, which I outlined earlier. For those really interested in what happened in the millennia when the Cholas from South India invaded, I refer them to an excellent publication, *Myths and Realities of Sri Lanka: Abuse of an Island's History*, by J. Jayasundera, published by the Campaign for Peace & Unity in Sri Lanka. There is absolutely no valid historical base of evidence of anything pertaining to be a Tamil homeland. Yes, previous Dutch and British colonial governments did authorise slave indentures of supplementary labour from Tamil South India, which undermined the indigenous Muslim and Sinhalese communities in both the north and east, but this does not amount to a 'Tamil homeland'. Just because the Eastern Province is predominately Tamil-speaking, this is no valid reason to join together the Eastern and Northern Provinces. In fact, it goes deeper because there are significant number of Tamils in the North Central Province and another million or so in Colombo district – all living alongside their Muslim and Sinhalese compatriots harmoniously.

Some may argue that Scotland has achieved a degree of 'homeland' with its devolved Assembly but with each day that passes we see the economic unviability of the current situation despite the over-generous Barnett formula, which in effect means the rest of the UK is subsidising Scotland.

On top of all this is the known fact that India would most definitely never countenance another second attempt at Eelam.

It is time the world community woke up to the real threat emanating from all these innocent-looking Tamil groups, nearly all of which, in their many different guises, are in fact trying to achieve Tamil Eelam. If my analysis is correct, Sri Lanka must never lower its guard and allow itself to be coerced into substantially reducing its armed forces or closing or withdrawing from its present, strategically vital military locations: all too often with the cry from certain Tamil quarters of returning the land to its original owners. Of course, proper financial compensation must be paid where it was requisitioned by the Ministry of Defence.

Would it not be far better for the West to recognise the pool of talent the young people of Sri Lanka offer? What better epitaph to all the young people, be they child soldiers or young government soldiers, sailors or airmen, indeed young and not so young troops on all sides who gave their lives and were killed in the line of duty, to defend the unitary state of Sri Lanka?

The intrepid 'Biggles' on fact finding safari.

CHAPTER
Nineteen

Reflections

The motivation to write this book was to record my experiences of a country which captivated my imagination over fifty years ago. That captivation grew and grew over the years as I dug deeper, became more involved and spent more time thinking, reflecting, studying, reading and, above all, visiting Sri Lanka. My guiding principle was a determination not to back any particular political party, or ethnic or religious group, and to resist the temptation to get involved in some fascinating businesses. I was driven by one simple principle: wanting to help the people of Sri Lanka. What a journey those Sri Lankans of my age have had, whether they are Sinhalese, Tamil, Muslim, Christian or of no particular religion.

Independence, with all its hopes, was achieved from the UK quite early in 1948; hopes that sadly did not bear the fruit that so many wished for as the pure socialist era of the husband and wife Bandaranaike presidents somehow failed to deliver. The period of President J.R. Jayawardene was more successful, as he understood the need to create a vibrant, competitive economy, thereby achieving good economic growth. Sadly, this potential success was undermined by a failure to fully meet the aspirations of the Tamil community, particularly in terms of language. The final tragedy was in July 1983 with his fatal wavering before bringing in a curfew in Colombo after three days of rioting against Tamils caused by the killing of thirteen soldiers in Jaffna by the LTTE Tamil Tigers.

I have recorded, discussed and analysed the genuine efforts of all the subsequent presidents to find a solution to the challenge of the LTTE Tamil Tigers. Sadly, all failed until Mahinda Rajapaksa realised the only solution would have to be a military one. It took him a full four years to be ready for the final assault commencing in January 2009 and completed on 18 May 2009.

So the real question remains will it all deteriorate again?

Can Sri Lanka find the leadership, tolerance and understanding that are key for the country to remain a unitary state with every single citizen of Sri Lanka treated as equal? After all, there have been far too many failed states of recent times, including the divided Cyprus, Libya, Iraq and Zimbabwe. It seems to me the common denominator for state failure has been too much interference from the outside – particularly the West. There has also been too much involvement from the United Nations and too much so-called Human Rights involvement from NGOs, as opposed to genuine aid help. Add to this too much tolerance by certain Western countries of illegal activities, such as those Sri Lanka diaspora groups who want independence with the creation of a separate state Eelam for their ethnic group. An ambition almost certainly not supported by the majority of Tamils residing in Sri Lanka.

Once the war was over, Sri Lanka faced a barrage of criticism, principally from Western governments amazed that against all the odds the Sri Lanka armed forces, having waged an all-out war against the LTTE Tamil Tiger terrorists, actually defeated them.

As a boy I was evacuated from London during World War II, only returning in 1943 with victory for the Allies still two years away. When the six-year war was won against Germany and the Axis forces there were huge celebrations and joy. By way of contrast, the defeat after nearly thirty years of the LTTE Tamil Tigers, proscribed as a terrorist group in over thirty-two mainly Western countries, was hardly welcomed anywhere at all except in the whole of Sri Lanka and her allies in the East. Was there rejoicing around the world? Amazingly there was almost the opposite, as the worldwide diaspora and Tamil Tigers who had escaped joined up in a media campaign vilifying the Sri Lanka forces with accusations of atrocities of every possible nature from the starving of civilians and herding those who escaped into quasi concentration camps, shooting captured members of the Tigers and raping extensively.

Almost immediately the UN decided, regardless of sovereignty, that it needed to investigate the atrocities with or without Sri Lanka's Agreement. The UN ignored that this had been a war and that meant the laws to be checked concerned the Geneva Convention or specifically International Humanitarian Law. Unilaterally it decided that it was all about Human Rights and they came under The European Convention on Human Rights. A three-person Investigative Commission was set up to take evidence without the agreement of Sri Lanka and without access to Sri Lanka from any party with the promise of anonymity, so that the evidence and sources would never be published inside thirty years: hardly a formula for getting or validating the truth. The lack of access to Sri Lanka inevitably meant that the evidence tabled came mainly from the LTTE element of the diaspora.

The Investigative Commission paid lip service to the known crimes of the Tamil Tigers who had: recruited several thousand child soldiers; herded about 300,000 Tamil citizens to follow them into an ever-diminishing area known as the Vanni, shooting those who tried to escape; placed captured Sri Lanka army personnel in metal cages to die of thirst as they fried in the hot sun; and finally blew up the coaches containing the wounded civilians. However, there were few Tamil Tiger leaders left to prosecute, so they virtually ignored this challenge. Charges were laid that the Sri Lanka forces had carried out numerous war crimes: genocide, killing civilians, raping, shelling hospitals, and starving the civilians and members of the Tamil Tigers, with the result that at least 40,000 civilians were killed with some reports quoting up to 100,000.

These charges seemed to me so unreal, so exaggerated that I set about trying to find the truth. The key source turned out to be The Freedom of Information Act. I asked the UK Government to publish the despatches of the UK Military Attaché in Colombo particularly for the period 1 January to 19 May 2009. It took two and a half long years of persistent pressure to eventually get at the truth as seen by Lt Col Gash, albeit with extensive and serious redactions. Nevertheless, we do now have those despatches, which bear testament to what he saw, with all his experience.

We now know that there was not a 'genocide' of 40,000 or more civilians killed.

Lt Col Gash suggests maybe 6,000, of which maybe 20 per cent were Tamil Tigers who threw away their uniforms, making a real civilian total of 4,800. There is now a question mark over that figure of 4,800 thanks to the work of the Sri Lanka Census Department. Great lengths were made to appoint Tamil enumerators and these good people have taken great trouble to record deaths and missing persons. As far as the census records are concerned, there is no distinction made between ordinary civilians and Tamil tigers – they are simply recorded as deaths. In addition to this, there are still satellite images showing graves which barely account for 2,000 people, corroborated by Dr Shanmugarajah, the government-appointed Senior Medical Officer forced to work with the LTTE. This continues to remain a mystery for the moment but further research may yield a more definitive reason unless it is nearer the truth than anyone thinks.

What we do know now is that there was absolutely no massacre of Tamil civilians. And we also now know that civilians were looked after kindly by the Sri Lanka Army. We also know there was no starvation amidst the civilians, not least as the government agent had stocks of food and medicines despite what the British Foreign Secretary David Miliband said at the time.

Of course, the UK Government, at the time under Prime Minister Brown, knew all this and more as it had the Gash despatches without any redactions. It just chose to keep them secret to the detriment of Sri Lanka's interests and that is how matters still stand today. Only it knows the full content or maybe the OHCHR (Office of the High Commissioner for Human Rights) knows as well, for I believe at some time Colonel Gash's despatches were shared with the OHCHR in Geneva, in preparation for the OHCHR Investigation on Sri Lanka (IOSL) report.

Even today few people understand the scale of the impact of the Tamil Tigers on all the people of Sri Lanka: two presidents murdered; tens of government ministers murdered; hundreds of police officers killed – including 600 killed in cold-blood after surrendering; thousands of innocent civilians from all ethnic groups callously killed; 100,000 Muslim and Sinhalese ethnically cleansed out of the Northern Province.

Even today, every time Sri Lanka is discussed or assessed in relation to the UN motions there are continuing allegations of torture – even in the recent 2018 Foreign & Commonwealth Report. I find this strange because during my last three visits in 2012, 2015 and 2017 I have repeatedly asked the Head of Mission of the ICRC whether they had found, seen or been informed of any cases of torture and each time the answer is 'No – None'. Heavy-handling sometimes, but no acts of torture, as defined by the Geneva Convention.

In 2018 there was the House of Commons Report, dated 28 June 2018, from the 'Intelligence & Security Committee of Parliament', headed: 'Detainee Mistreatment & Rendition 2001–2010'.

This is a scathing report from senior UK politicians about the part the UK Government played in the rendition of terror suspects, particularly at Guantanamo Bay. No heavy-handling here, but reports of real torture. How on earth can any UK Government now remain the sponsor of a critical motion on Sri Lanka? The other party to the critical motion is the USA but it has pulled out of the UNHCR. Is it not ironic that all this was taking place at the same time as Sri Lanka was fighting the Tamil Tigers? In my judgement both the UK and USA should recognise their own failings, particularly over torture. Sri Lanka should now be left to its own devices. Maybe the country needs help but genuine, friendly countries should wait until asked. In any case, the miserly £6.5m of aid given over three years from the UK might as well cease, except for the mine clearing. I saw little point in Prime Minister Cameron strutting around, chastising the Sri Lanka Government for not rehousing enough refugees but never offering a penny to help.

How many other countries have been through a near thirty-year war and recovered as well as Sri Lanka? If the West really wants to help then it must cease listening to the hardcore LTTE sympathisers and former Tamil Tigers who escaped and still hanker over a separate state Eelam. The key countries are UK, Canada, USA, Germany, France and Australia. Even India, who has most to gain or lose, has stated it has no wish to see a separate state of Eelam. Indeed, India has helped financially with rehousing; far more than the West.

Yes, I am still frustrated at the time it took to set up the Missing Persons Commission, the slowness to revise The Prevention of Terrorism Act, and the creation and reality of a Truth & Reconciliation Commission. Above all I sincerely believe this is the key that could unlock the door to real reconciliation. These have to happen, but they have to be done in a manner that all Sri Lankans living in Sri Lanka can buy into and not some creation of the West with foreign judges. I emphasise the phrase 'living in Sri Lanka', because those who have left the country and settled elsewhere have no locus to be consulted or reassured.

Yes, I acknowledge some real successes in Sri Lanka, like the handing back of 92 per cent of private land to the original owners held by the security forces during the conflict, and the signing of the Ottawa Convention on mines and cluster bombs. Indeed, the outgoing UN High Commissioner for Human Rights, Zeid Ra'ad Al Hussein, commended Sri Lanka in June 2018 for its co-operation and the progress it had made.

We must never forget that Sri Lanka is a democracy where there have been, and continue to have, regular provincial and general elections. I am certain these will continue. People do vote in Sri Lanka and with a conviction far exceeding anything achieved in the UK, USA or in Europe. Even in the hiatus of the Parliament challenge and counter-challenge as to who was in charge between the Executive President Sirisena and the Prime Minister Ranil Wickremesinghe in November /December 2018, there was an Appeal to the Supreme Court whose unanimous decision was accepted by all parties. Nothing could more clearly demonstrate that the decision of the highest court in the land was accepted without any challenge or negative backlash. The passion was every bit as excitable as the UK Parliament over Brexit but respect for the written Constitution held sway in the end, a real tribute to the Sri Lanka parliamentarians.

In the draft to this chapter I had written Sri Lanka had now had nearly ten years of peace for the first time in thirty years, with no bombs and no real discrimination in terms of language, education or opportunity. Sadly, this was shattered by the 2019 Easter Sunday bombing of churches and hotels by radicalised Sri Lanka Muslims. These tragedies happen, as we in the UK know all too well from our experience in Northern Ireland and on mainland Britain, but they do not alter the fundamental progress of a nation.

Time to reflect and commemorate the thousands of young military men and women who gave their lives in the pursuit of peace for their own country, the island of Sri Lanka.

Time the West backed off and allowed the unitary state of Sri Lanka to fulfil its own destiny based on 'peace building'. It is also time to reflect that since both Sinhalese Buddhists and Tamil Hindus value, respect and venerate the lotus flower with its symbolism of purity of body, speech and mind, is it really too much to ask the religious leadership of both faiths to come together in the cause of a lasting peace? That would do more than anything to create a real paradise.

Time to recognise that the pendulum of truth and reality is swinging back to Sri Lanka, as we saw at the Geneva UNHCR review meeting in March 2019.

Time that those Tamil diaspora who still seek revenge and their mission of Eelam recognised the truth that the LTTE Tigers were an evil terrorist group who in essence tried to totally undermine a sovereign state, including its Tamil citizens, ruthlessly killing its leaders and forcing some 300,000+ to be used as human shield.

Time to accept all the evidence from multiple sources that the civilian casualties were never 40,000 to 100,000 but at most around 5,000 (and possibly even less).

Time for the UN to make it quite clear to all Human Rights activists that the practice of serving private warrants alleging war crimes whilst abroad on senior members of the former Rajapaksa Government be they civilians or military is unacceptable. Genuine alleged war crimes can only be settled by a Truth & Reconciliation Commission or by the Court at The Hague.

Time these activists stopped spending Tamil people's money and resources, presumably some if not all from LTTE extortion rackets. What a waste to spend money on propaganda films like Callum Macrae's latest film *No Fire Zone* which appears to be a rehash of his films *Sri Lanka's Killing fields*, and *Sri Lanka's Killing fields: War Crimes Unpunished*: shot down in flames at the time for their inaccuracies, misinformation and total lapse of journalistic standards.

Time to reflect and ask the powers in the West, the United Nations and even the international NGOs to recognise that reconciliation is not just needed in Sri Lanka but must be promoted around the world. This means all the Tamil Eelam, quasi Eelam and Tamil Homeland groups should be disbanded and the LTTE treasure chest of funds handed over to Sri Lankan-based charities from all the ethnic groups. Currently it is frozen in EU countries but it appears there are no constraints on the use of LTTE funds elsewhere in the world, particularly in the USA, Canada and Australia.

Time to put these financial and human resources into investment in the Northern Province for the benefit of the whole, mainly Tamil, community, young and old.

Time to allow the undoubted talent of the young people to be fulfilled.

Time for the newly elected Executive President Gotabaya Rajapaksa to re-establish Sri Lanka as a dynamic creative economy with his proven leadership.

Time for him to sort the difficult economic landscape.

Time for him to be allowed to prove his engagement with all minorities particularly the Muslims and Tamils.

Time may well prove this event to have been a ground breaking moment for all Sri Lankans.

The potential is all there. It just needs the catalyst of leadership to take it forward. Leadership that should recall Abraham Lincoln's wise words; 'A house divided against itself cannot stand.'

If it is grasped and I hope and pray it is, then this wonderful country – which it really is – and its creative people will truly have regained 'Paradise'. Anyone who has any real thought for the future good of this tremendous country should leave it alone. Let the citizens of Sri Lanka choose themselves how to rebuild this paradise island.

When one takes on a project/ mission as I have done for over fifty years with Sri Lanka, one never ever thinks of recognition. Whatever I did was to try to help this beautiful, unique country break the bonds of persistent uprisings for forlorn causes that are of no value to the ordinary people of Sri Lanka. I took it upon myself to speak out at Westminster and even in Strasbourg to ensure Sri Lanka got a fair hearing. It was a huge surprise in autumn 2005 to be approached by the then serving High Commissioner in London, who informed me that I had been awarded the Sri Lanka Ratna (Titular), the country's highest honour for non-nationals conferred on me by President Kumaratunga.

I am beginning to wonder if my wonderful journey as a campaigning friend of Sri Lanka is coming to an end; every journey has a beginning although we may not recognise it at the time but also there must be an end. Why do I feel this now? Primarily because I had my eightieth birthday in November 2016. I reflect, too, that for our Golden Wedding Anniversary I gave my wife a ring and matching earrings centred on blue sapphire stones from Ratnapura, the gem city of Sri Lanka. Stuart

Devlin, goldsmith, created this unique gift and for me this set will forever remind me of the sparkle and excitement that Sri Lanka has brought to my life.

I say thank you to my many, many Sri Lankan friends across all sections of society.

However, it might never have happened had not my dear late friend Ananda de Tissa de Alwis played tennis, given me dinner regularly and discussed his prospects of standing for election to the Parliament; later successfully becoming the Speaker of the Sri Lanka Parliament. I only became First Deputy Speaker in the UK Parliament but he 'lit the lamp'.

Methinks I see in my mind a noble and puissant nation arousing herself like a strong man after sleep, and shaking her invincible locks.

Methinks I see her as an eagle mewing her mighty youth, and kindling her undazzled eyes at the full midday beam.

From John Milton's *Areopagitica*, 1644

APPENDICES
Section 1:
Appendices referred to in the narrative
of the book

APPENDIX I

Prime Minister Thatcher's speech at the opening of the Victoria Dam

1985 Apr 12 Fr
Margaret Thatcher

Press Conference in Sri Lanka

Document type: Speeches, interviews, etc.
Document kind: Press Conference
Venue: Presidential residence, Kandy, Sri Lanka
Source: Thatcher Archive: COI transcript
Journalist: -
Editorial comments: 1445-1600.
Importance ranking: Major
Word count: 3623
Themes: Commonwealth (general), Conservatism, Defence (general), General Elections, Privatized & state industries, Foreign policy (general discussions), Foreign policy (Asia), Foreign policy (development, aid, etc), Foreign policy (International organizations), Leadership, Media, Race, immigration, nationality, Terrorism, Strikes & other union action

Prime Minister

May I say that it was a great privilege today to have the honour to join in the ceremonial commissioning of the Victoria Dam Hydro-electric Scheme. This makes my first visit to Sri Lanka a truly historic and memorable one, because I know how much it means to Sri Lanka's future development; and I am also proud that Britain has played such an important role in the project, both in terms of our £130 million aid and through the participation of British companies, Balfour Beatty, Nuttall & Wessell (phon.) and the Consultants, Alexander Gibb and Preece Cardew & Ryder. This underlines the immense role that Britain can play in helping the emerging countries to realise their ambitions for their people.

I shall never forget the tremendously colourful spectacle which was laid on this morning for the commissioning, and I am sure it gave as much pleasure to those taking part as the thousands of spectators, as the dam will bring new life and prosperity to Sri Lanka.

As you know, I have still well over half my programme in Sri Lanka to complete, including the state banquet this evening; my Address to Parliament tomorrow, followed by the opening ceremony of the Mahaweli Centre. But already I feel I have got off to a most useful start, both by setting [end p1] the seal on the largest single overseas aid project ever undertaken by Overseas Development Administration, and second, by getting a largely bird's eye view of your lovely land: third, through the friendly and constructive talks with President Jayewardene, which have yet to be completed.

Once again, I have seen a beautiful country of great potential. Britain would like to play an even bigger part in realising that potential. [end p2]

APPENDIX II

Lord Naseby's speech to the House of Lords, January 2000

12 January 2000

6.36 p.m.

Lord Naseby

My Lords, I want to concentrate my remarks on South Asia and what is known as the SARC region. As many noble Lords will know, I have lived and worked in Pakistan, India and Sri Lanka. Most of my remarks will concern Sri Lanka, which I have known intimately for nearly 40 years.

First, I want to speak about the Maldives, one of the smallest countries in the region, a country that has the great benefit of a consistency of government in that Abdul Gayoom and his foreign minister, Mr Fathullah Jameel, have been in power for a great many years, which has given stability to that part of the region.

In day-to-day terms all seems peaceful there, with tourism, fishing and the merchant marine. However, I remind your Lordships that just a six-foot rise in the tide level would mean that the Maldives would disappear altogether as a nation. My first question to Her Majesty's Government is: what are the Government doing today to ensure that the United Kingdom keeps up pressure on global warming? Unless we remain proactive in that field, nations such as the Maldives will cease to exist.

683 I now turn to Sri Lanka, which is one area of the world where there is significant conflict. It has particularly close ties with this country. I do not know whether I should declare an interest, but I am joint chairman of the British Sri Lankan parliamentary group.

I hope that all noble Lords will give unreserved condemnation to the recent acts of terrorism committed by the LTTE. The recent bomb attacks on 18th December—just before Christmas— injured President Chandrika Kumaratunga, killed 21 people and left 110 severely injured. There was another bomb on 5th January outside the office of the Prime Minister, which resulted in the death of 12 more people and injured another 20. Understandably, such acts of terrorism have, for the moment, stalled negotiations aimed at progressing the peace process.

Despite the bomb attack on the president, in which she lost an eye—I do not need to remind your Lordships that her father and her husband have been assassinated—the presidential election went ahead, which is a true reflection of the strength of democracy in that country. Even after that, in her acceptance speech having wan the presidential election, she was brave enough to say, I urge you to use every ounce of influence at your disposal to bring Mr Prabhamaran to the negotiating table without further delay. I urge you to persuade with every conceivable argument anyone who is a member or a supporter of the LTTE to renounce violence and join us in establishing peace". That was not just a message to those in Sri Lanka; it was a message to the world. There are significant numbers of Sri Lankans in the United States, Canada, Germany and not least in this country. I hope that those in this country, who are known to support the LTTE, will heed those words.

In that speech she put out a hand of friendship to Ranil Wickremasinghe whom I have known, I guess, for some 20 years. He is the leader of the main opposition, the United National Party. She sought from him a bi-partisan approach to finding a peaceful solution to the problem. Despite the understandable political differences which we have across this Chamber sometimes, there are occasions when we work together. Her Majesty's Government could help in trying to ensure that

that message is conveyed to the government and opposition in Sri Lanka. This country is held in the greatest respect in Sri Lanka and I am sure that we can assist in that regard.

I turn to the international situation in Sri Lanka and the international community and ask the question: is it not now time for the international community to put pressure on Mr Prabhakaran to hold talks with the government of Sri Lanka? And, on the invitation of that government, I feel that the international community could play a significant role to advance the peace process.

Those in government who listened to the interview of the Secretary General of the Commonwealth on the World Service, to which I listened, will know that he was involved in the mediation attempts in 1997, and more recently Norway has been involved. I hope I do not express too partisan a wish in my belief that the 684 United Kingdom could play a significant role in bringing some pressure on Mr Prabhakaran and all other parties to get together. When I read about and listen to the Secretary General telling us that he only communicated with Mr Prabhakaran, I feel that that is not satisfactory. Whoever is in that role must see the man face to face; it is not enough to have an intermediary.

In recent days Britain signed the United Nations Convention for the Suppression of Terrorist Financing. Indeed, I pay tribute to the Government for signing that on the very day it became available for signature. But I hope it is not just a piece of paper but that action will flow from it. In this country it is known that the LTTE is collecting funds. I do not mean a charity day with a flag; I mean protectionism; money being extorted from Sri Lankans living in this country. Unless they pay up, as your Lordships know only too well, their families will suffer. That is the way terrorism works. Many in this Chamber have as much experience of it as I have.

I speak personally now: I find it repulsive that tonight, in Camden, there is an office of the LTTE. That is not acceptable. Given that we passed the new terrorist Act in the last Session, which gives us powers to prevent parties from carrying out, planning or preparing terrorist activities, I hope that high on the agenda—leaving aside the Sikh problem—will be the LTTE. I realise that it is not the responsibility of the foreign minister, but there is evidence that junior officers of the LTTE are seeking asylum in this country in order to keep the conflict going. The Home Office should pay some attention to that problem.

I want to end on a positive note. Sri Lanka is a highly literate society. The people are pro-British. Nevertheless, it is a developing country, though it is not the poorest country by a long shot. However, there are great challenges to be faced in that part of the world. Its growth runs at around 5 per cent a year. Understandably that growth is stifled by the fact that 5 per cent of GNP goes to cover the cost of war. If the United Kingdom, in the international community, could find a solution, it would allow a further 50 per cent growth. That sort of growth is so significant that it would have an incredible effect on all the people of Sri Lanka, be they Tamil, Sinhalese, Muslim, Burgher. That is a power well worth striving for. I ask Her Majesty's Government to recognise that this is a problem to which we must find a solution. It is a key problem. It has been going on for nearly 20 years and urgently needs resolving. It is time that this Government played an active role in the international community to get that moving.

APPENDIX III

Lord Naseby's speech to the Sri Lanka-United Kingdom Society, February 2000

The Rt. Hon. the Lord Naseby P.C.

House of Lords

London SW1A 0PW

SPEECH ON FRIDAY 18 FEBRUARY AT HILTON HOTEL, COLOMBO BY THE RT HON THE LORD NASEBY, FORMER MEMBER OF PARLIAMENT AND DEPUTY SPEAKER OF THE HOUSE OF COMMONS

Mr Chairman, distinguished guests, friends in Sri Lanka, Ladies & Gentlemen

It really is wonderful to be in Colombo again as the Guest of the Sri Lanka UK Society. You only have to get off the plane at the airport to be hit by the temperature to know you are back in the East. And it was ever thus. Ann and I remember so clearly arriving at Ratmalana Airport from Calcutta in April 1963. The family consisted of we two, our eldest son Julian and the dog Twinkle. That was 37 years ago and now we are celebrating 52 years of Independence.

What do I remember of those days? Firstly my joy at leaving a rather depressing Calcutta and arriving in such a lush, beautiful country where everyone seemed so friendly. I had received promotion from Reckitt & Colman to Marketing Manager and been issued with a car and driver. The only slight challenge was the car – a Ford Anglia, hardly the size of car for a driver. As an aside, that was the last time I had a driver until I became Deputy Speaker of the House of Commons in May 1992.

We had a first floor flat at Turret Road, overlooking the gardens. I used to have my hair cut on the veranda by an old boy who did an excellent head massage as well.

Phone - House of Lords Message Bureau 0171 219 5353
Fax - House of Lords 0171 219 5979

I still have my hair cut at home. Ann was a trained doctor, but one of the little prejudices at that time was that foreign doctors were prohibited from working – however she did help our Dr Chinatambi at her family planning clinic.

I, of course, was Reckitt's commercial man operating out of E.B. Creasy's office in the Fort. They were our main distributors, but the Goya range was handled by Lalvani Brothers in the Pettah. I love visiting the Pettah and indeed have already been there to place a small order with our favourite jeweller at New Centre Jewellery Stores.

Life wasn't exactly straightforward as there were enormous shortages and the bush telegraph used to tell us when meat, cheese and honey were 'in' at Elephant House. Indeed, you might have guessed it was coming by the number of ships that used to wait outside Colombo harbour. I wonder if the new P&O privatisation deal to build a modern container terminal will mean the end of waiting. I hope so because the opportunities for Colombo to be the trans-shipment port for the whole of the Indian sub-continent are legion.

I was a marketing man then, indeed I still am. The only way a marketing person can fully understand a market is to get out and see what is going on. I still have the reports at home. The roads were good in those days and whilst there were next to no hotels, there were the circuit bungalows. Leaving aside the markets of Greater Colombo, I remember four key circuits. The south coast with a series of wonderful bungalows set on the seashore: I took the family on one trip and we still have clear memories of those beautiful sunsets at places like Bentota, Galle and Tangalle.

2

There was the Hill Country tour finishing up at the Hill Club. The tour that took in Sigiriya, Polonnaruwa, Trincomalee and a diversion to Batticaloa. Again, how wonderful it would be to return to that bungalow at Trinco, overlooking the harbour with the bougainvillia if it were still there. The Northern tour taking in Anuradhapura, Mannar, Elephant Pass and Jaffna. How privileged I have been to visit almost the whole island and how sorry I feel that the opportunity is no longer there for any Sri Lankans to do the same.

Sri Lanka has had a huge impact on my life. It was all the fault of the late Speaker Ananda de Tissa de Alvis - then at J Walter Thompson, ad. agency in Colombo – he was their manager. He had become interested in politics – who is not interested in politics here? It is in your blood. At any rate, my tour was coming to an end, Ann went home to find a house and job and I was alone. Ananda and I became close friends. I caught the bug and on returning to the UK sought to join the Conservative Party in 1964.

I wondered if I would ever return and then in February 1974 I was elected MP for Northampton South with the princely majority of 179. I soon found that there were all sorts of Commonwealth Country groups but none for Sri Lanka so in 1975 I started the British-Sri Lanka Parliamentary Group and have been its Chairman ever since, except when I had to give it up for the period as Deputy Speaker 1992-97. But I am back again now.

3

Since 1975 I have been on many visits, some official, some private. I have written a pamphlet and overseen elections and YET here we are tonight with a shadow over us of an internal conflict of monumental proportions.

It is not for me to apportion blame but clearly there have been and are faults on all sides. In so far as I have been a friend of yours for 38 years, like any true friend, I hope I can speak my mind, not to interfere but with a genuine desire of helping to bring an end to hostilities that have cost thousands of lives, uprooted millions of people and denied to all Sri Lankans the opportunity to join in the real success of South and South East Asia.

You have already proved to the World that you can be the best in the world with your cricket performance of winning the World Cup. Now somehow, somewhere, we have to find the key to peace.

We have seen great changes in the UK in recent years, indeed my own family has seen great changes. I am no longer Michael Morris but am now Lord Naseby. Naseby the key battle of our civil war on 14 June 1645. A battle which saw Parliament and democracy defeat the autocratic king of the day – a battle just outside Northampton that was to shape our history. We became a republic between 1649 and 1660. Some terrible things took place on both sides, the worst being the beheading of the King. And yet, out of it all came a Parliamentary democracy within a bicameral system headed by a titular monarch and a chamber that became the Mother of Parliaments. So out of horror, great and lasting success can come.

4

Few people and almost no politicians in the UK have looked at the three devolved structures we have, to see what lessons can be learned, to compare and contrast each and to reflect on whether those structures could be a catalyst for solving other problems.

What have we got? In its most simplistic form, we have a Scottish Parliament, a Northern Ireland Assembly and a Welsh Assembly. The Scottish Parliament and the Northern Ireland Assembly have primary legislative powers over many areas, whereas the Welsh Assembly is limited to secondary legislative powers.

The electoral systems that created these bodies are different almost beyond comprehension, yet the driving force behind each is such that one can conclude they are there to ensure the survival of the unitary state, but in a manner that will ensure proper in–depth representation of all the strands of political and ethnic colour.

You could argue that the strength of Scottish nationalism under the banner of the Scottish National Party might lead to Scottish Independence – yet this has been anticipated in circumscribing what the Scottish Parliament might and might not do. You could worry about the checks and balances of the ethnic dimension and the protection of human rights in the Northern Ireland Assembly and yet these are circumscribed by ensuring an interlock between the Chief Minister expected to be a Unionist and the Deputy Chief Minister expected to be a Nationalist. To be elected to these positions, one needs a majority from each party and from the Assembly – furthermore if either resigns voluntarily or otherwise, both must be up for re-election.

6

How is the Nation's interest preserved? – very simply in our case because the First and Deputy Ministers are appointed by the Queen BUT on the basis of nomination from the constituent Assembly and Parliament. Although in our case the Scottish ministers are required to take an oath or affirmation of allegiance to the Queen – there is no such requirement in Northern Ireland. Here they make a "pledge of office". This includes commitment to non-violence, to serve the people equally, to operate within the framework of an agreed programme of Government and to act in accordance with decisions of the Executive Committee and the Assembly. There are yet further checks as we go down the ministerial appointment scale to ensure cross-community support. Scotland has a further check in that although the First Minister is appointed by the Queen, it also has to be approved by the Lord Advocate and Solicitor General for Scotland. I, too, see this legal check as vital.

Both Scotland and Northern Ireland are, as I have said, able to make primary and secondary legislation in all areas of public policy where they have legislative competence. It is even tougher in Northern Ireland where they may not legislate if it would discriminate against any person or class of person on the ground of religious belief or political opinion. Tonight is not the night to look at the detail of what is devolved and what is reserved BUT someone might legitimately ask what happens if there is a disagreement between the devolved power and the centre.

So much of the minutiae of the interface between the devolved power body and Westminster are covered by mutual understandings. In technical terms, these are termed concordats. They set the ground rules and, of course, they can be amended.

7

I know Ranil Wickersinghe well, I know the President but I have never met Prabhakaran, in fact it seems few people have.

If it is true he believes in Thimpu principles and I appreciate their strength. If he recognises that he has no Turkey like Northern Cyprus to help him and if he has the future of Sri Lanka Tamils truly at heart, then I believe at some point he will want to come to the negotiating table. At this time he will come with some strength and considerable respect for his abilities. Equally he must know that the big powers be they the Western Countries or Australia or the USA or South Africa, each are slowly but surely doing two things. They are and will increasingly tighten the screw on the LTTE activities, which will inevitably make life more difficult. Secondly, there is, thankfully, a much wider recognition that for peace to succeed there must be a firm financial commitment that in the devastated areas there will be immediate and huge financial investment in infrastructure, schools, universities, hospitals, housing etc. This is why I appealed to the UK Government to give a lead. I don't blame the LTTE for wanting to see the colour of the prospective money.

What makes it happen is someone - some persons - to act as a catalyst. To create confidence on all sides much like Senator Mitchell did and Kissinger in earlier days.

What is the prize – it's enormous, not just peace but a reuniting of a nation that has so much to offer South and South East Asia and maybe even the World. Remove the War and the drain it is on the Exchequer and the growth rate of the economy could move from 5% to the average 8% of South East Asia. Remove the war and reintegrate the talents of the Tamil people and you have a potential powerhouse here in S Asia.

9

You have a bilateral agreement with India which opens the door to inward investment here – you have your privatisation strategy that, like the Colombo container port investment, will put Colombo back where it always was as the key port in South Asia. You have proved with winning the World Cricket Cup that you are dedicated, professional and can succeed.

It is my earnest wish that these few but deeply thought-about views might ignite a helpful move to peace. Peace is like deep sleep after many months of interrupted nights. Peace is the culture of the Buddah and Hinduism and Christianity and Allah. There will still be challenges like the de-commissioning of weapons BUT if there is hope and faith on both sides, it can happen. I remember in the UK Parliament so clearly in 1994 the Maastricht Committee stage; 25 days of debate night and day – over 500 amendments and all I could do as Chairman was keep calm, be patient but make some progress. You will need to keep calm, be patient and try to make progress and find the art of judicious compromise.

I hope I have not been too sombre this evening for it should be and is a joyous occasion. We had a wonderful entry into the Millennium in the UK – mostly families getting together. How joyful it would be if what is said to be the true Millennium, that is January 1st 2001, were the announcement of peace in Sri Lanka.

10

A breakdown of costs to run Project Galle for six months

Project Galle 2005 - monthly costs

1. Project Galle Management Team	Monthly Cost
Group Co-ordinator	2000
Human resources	1500
Information manager	1500
Information assistant	1000
Receptionist	150
Team Administrator	1500
Head of Field Operations	1500
Facilities manager	1500
Warehouse Manager	1500
Communication Manager	1500
Fund Raiser	1000
Total	**14650**

2. Support staff and sub-contractors			
6 Field Operatives 7days a we 20$ day			3600
2 Cleaners			150
Watcher			50
Cook			800
2 Warehouse Labourers			1200
5 Warehouse Pack Assemlers			325
Book Keeper			120
Catering	30 people	at 2 per day time	1800
Drivers and transport	local vans	5 at 35	4550
Legal fees			200
IT expert			300
Total			**13095**

3. Properties	
71 Pedlar Street	
Rent	1000
Electricity	150
Water	100
Drinking Water	100
Phones	500
Computer rentals	700
Walkers Building	
Inclusive Rent	800
Total	**3350**
Grand total 1,2,3	**31095**
Total Funding needs for 6 months	**186570**

APPENDIX V

Lord Naseby's letter to Andy Hayman, Assistant Commissioner of Metropolitan Police, New Scotland Yard, February 2007

Andy Hayman
Asst Commissioner of Metropolitan Police
New Scotland Yard
10 Broadway
London
SW1H OBG   6.2.07.

Dear Commisioner Hayman   ref: LTTE – Tamil Tigers

I write as Chairman of the All Party British Sri Lanka Parliamentary Group.

We have been monitoring with ever deepening concern the activities of varying LTTE front groups who seem to be flagrantly flouting the proscription of the LTTE & the Terrorism Acts particularly Section 12 & 13 of the 2000 Act & Article 2 of the 2006 Act.
My colleagues & I have been waiting patiently to see what action Scotland Yard would take over the flagrant flouting of the terrorism Acts arising from the Black July Remembrance Rally at Speaker's Corner , Hyde Park on 25th July 2006.

I understand that the Rally was booked by Councillor Mrs Elisa Packiadevi Mann in the name of the The Tamil Youth Organisation , a known front organisation for the LTTE. The key stagers of the event were: Councillor Daya Idaikadar , Mr A.C. Shanathan, & Mr Jayanathan Wijeyanesah
The event was attended by over 3,000, collections on a substantial scale were made for the LTTE, banners flown in LTTE colours , placards displayed of The Tiger Leader Prabhakaran & an 18ft stand up Portrait of him at the side of the stage..The whole proceedings were broadcast worldwide on TTN. I understand that you & your officers have been fully briefed on this event.

There is little point in Parliament passing Terrorism Legislation when it can be so openly flouted. The Police have hard concrete evidence .May I on behalf of my Colleagues ask what exactly is preventing the four persons mentioned above from being prosecuted.
I look forward to speedy response.

Yours Sincerely

c.c The Commissioner of Police
    The Home Secretary

APPENDIX VI

Queen's Speech for opening of Parliament, 2009

19 November 2009

2.45 pm

Lord Naseby

My Lords, I wish to speak exclusively on Sri Lanka, mentioned by the noble Baroness, Lady Kinnock. I have been involved in that country for 46 years and for the whole of my political life of 35 years. There has never been a period under both Labour and Conservative Governments when relationships were as difficult as they are. I wish to make an appeal for a new start and a completely new look at the relationship between our two countries.
Some Members will have noted that at the Remembrance Sunday ceremony the eighth high commissioner to lay a wreath was from Sri Lanka, representing the eighth country in terms of losses in the Second World War—Ceylon as it was then. Not many Members of your Lordships' House will know that when the vote was taken in the United Nations criticising the United Kingdom over our relief of the Falklands, only nine countries voted for us. I had the privilege to speak to the then Sri Lankan President, JR Jayewardene, and make a personal appeal on behalf of the All-Party Group for Sri Lanka to support the United Kingdom. It was not just my words that led to that support, but perhaps they added a little bit. That country stuck its neck out in support of this country, against the wishes of much of Asia, because our friendship goes very deep.

There needs to be an understanding of the results of 25 years of terrorism in any country, particularly Sri Lanka. The last war took place when I was a small boy, and it lasted for only five, not 25, years. Specific challenges, particularly regarding the resettlement of refugees and building up that economy, need to be addressed. GSP Plus is a specific issue; it is an arrangement to allow apparel and other products from Sri Lanka to enter the EU at an advantage. Two days ago, a decision was taken in principle to remove it and, in effect, impose sanctions on Sri Lanka at this very difficult time. Many, not just me, will want to question why 200,000, mainly female, workers from the villages—a good proportion of whom are Tamils—should be thrown into unemployment, with another 1 million affected.

I wish to highlight certain points that I hope that the Government will take on board and reflect on. At the end of the recent war—a successful war in terms of Sri Lanka—284,000 refugees voluntarily went into refugee camps. They had been used as human shields. They had been pushed from the west of Sri Lanka to the far east. Many had been shot by the Tamil Tigers while trying to escape. The war finished towards the end of May. As of 9 November, when I received the latest figures, 126,000 people had been resettled in their homes and about 30,000 were with families and other relations. That leaves 147,000 people. They are leaving at a rate of approximately 3,000 to 5,000 a week. Sixty-eight UN and international NGOs have access to the remaining camps; 173 media personnel have been in and out of them. DfID has been there, along with representatives of the UN and, most importantly and recently, Members of Parliament from Tamil Nadu. Tamil Nadu has a very close relationship with the Tamil communities in northern Sri Lanka. If anybody was going to be highly critical, it would be the MPs from Tamil Nadu: but they came voluntarily, their report was produced by them alone and it said that they were comfortable with what was being done and hugely encouraged by the rate at which people were being resettled.

There remains the challenge of 2.5 million landmines, but reasonable progress is being made. The UK, through HALO and others, has helped. However, we are not high in the league of help-providers despite our long historic relationship. Now there is a major programme of infrastructure building. As we look at our relationship with Sri Lanka, it is strange that, having sold guns to the Sri Lankan army, we did not supply ammunition—like the Belgians not supplying ammunition for our guns in the first Gulf War, in which my son served. Secondly, we did not support the application for an IMF loan. Of course it went through, because others recognised that if you are going to rebuild an economy you must have the help of the IMF. I do not take these things personally, but I have made recommendations to Her Majesty's Government after all the visits that I have made. Sadly, none of my recommendations has been accepted. We also had the difficult episode involving the special envoy. However, that is all in the past.

Now we turn to the current issue. The resettlement is going well; de-mining is going pretty well; but overhanging it all is the cloud of GSP Plus. Two days ago, a decision was made by the European Union Committee—not the Council of Ministers—that the removal of GSP Plus should proceed. In about two months, Her Majesty's Ministers will have to say whether that should continue. We in Parliament have just been visited by the Catholic Archbishop of Colombo, leading Buddhist religious leaders and leading Hindu and Muslim leaders. They left a memorandum with Her Majesty's Government, and with me. The final paragraph states:

"As responsible religious leaders, we are saddened by the fact that our European friends with whom Sri Lanka has always cherished such excellent and cordial bilateral relations, have given a larger than necessary sense of attention to certain groups with vested interests who are intent on destroying this country and pushing it once again into an abyss of political and economic confusion and chaos. Therefore, we appeal to our friends to stand by us at this hour and to help us guide our leaders and people towards a greater sense of spiritual and material progress. We appeal to you to help us in this matter and thank you for any consideration given to this very deserving request".

The removal of GSP Plus would—this is no exaggeration—throw out of work 200,000 mainly young, female workers in the countryside, rather than in Colombo, many of whom are Tamils, not to mention the other people involved in that trade, who probably number 1 million. If they are to be disadvantaged and thrown out of work, what is the purpose? How does that help bring together the communities in Sri Lanka? Others will say that there are still political problems; but the Government know as well as I do that elections are coming, and it is for the new Sri Lankan Government to settle the political dimensions.

There are encouraging signs for all of us who are in contact with Sri Lanka. The Tamil community and MPs are talking to the President, to the governing party and to opposition parties. There are seeds of hope, and a general election should resolve some issues. However, if the EU proceeds to remove GSP Plus, all Sri Lankans of any creed and in all elements of society will increasingly wonder whether they should not look to China, Iran and those parts of the world that have helped them to defeat the Tamil Tigers. I appeal to Her Majesty's Government to open a new chapter and to help Sri Lanka in its hour of need rather than kicking the people when they are down. They helped us at the time of the Falklands when we were down. Surely it is not too much for us to help them now.

APPENDIX VII

Five examples of typically redacted pages

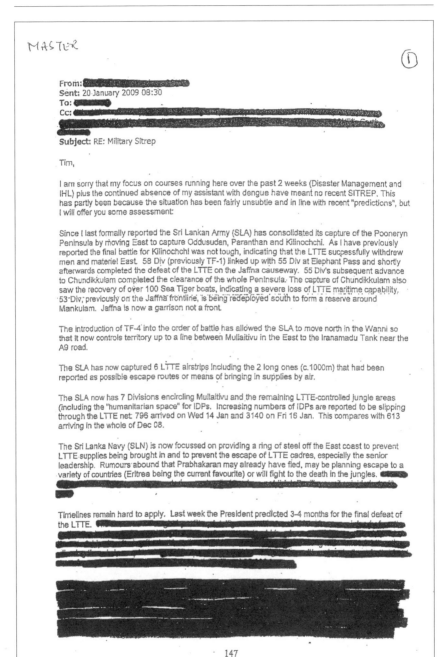

MASTER

From: ▓▓▓▓▓▓▓▓▓▓▓▓▓▓▓▓▓▓▓
Sent: 20 January 2009 08:30
To: ▓▓▓▓▓▓▓▓
Cc: ▓▓

Subject: RE: Military Sitrep

Tim,

I am sorry that my focus on courses running here over the past 2 weeks (Disaster Management and IHL) plus the continued absence of my assistant with dengue have meant no recent SITREP. This has partly been because the situation has been fairly unsubtle and in line with recent "predictions", but I will offer you some assessment:

Since I last formally reported the Sri Lankan Army (SLA) has consolidated its capture of the Pooneryn Peninsula by moving East to capture Oddusudan, Paranthan and Kilinochchi. As I have previously reported the final battle for Kilinochchi was not tough, indicating that the LTTE successfully withdrew men and materiel East. 58 Div (previously TF-1) linked up with 55 Div at Elephant Pass and shortly afterwards completed the defeat of the LTTE on the Jaffna causeway. 55 Div's subsequent advance to Chundikkulam completed the clearance of the whole Peninsula. The capture of Chundikkulam also saw the recovery of over 100 Sea Tiger boats, indicating a severe loss of LTTE maritime capability. 53 Div, previously on the Jaffna frontline, is being redeployed south to form a reserve around Mankulam. Jaffna is now a garrison not a front.

The introduction of TF-4 into the order of battle has allowed the SLA to move north in the Wanni so that it now controls territory up to a line between Mullaitivu in the East to the Iranamadu Tank near the A9 road.

The SLA has now captured 6 LTTE airstrips including the 2 long ones (c.1000m) that had been reported as possible escape routes or means of bringing in supplies by air.

The SLA now has 7 Divisions encircling Mullaitivu and the remaining LTTE-controlled jungle areas (including the "humanitarian space" for IDPs. Increasing numbers of IDPs are reported to be slipping through the LTTE net: 796 arrived on Wed 14 Jan and 3140 on Fri 16 Jan. This compares with 613 arriving in the whole of Dec 08.

The Sri Lanka Navy (SLN) is now focussed on providing a ring of steel off the East coast to prevent LTTE supplies being brought in and to prevent the escape of LTTE cadres, especially the senior leadership. Rumours abound that Prabhakaran may already have fled, may be planning escape to a variety of countries (Eritrea being the current favourite) or will fight to the death in the jungles. ▓▓▓▓
▓▓

Timelines remain hard to apply. Last week the President predicted 3-4 months for the final defeat of the LTTE. ▓▓
▓▓
▓▓
▓▓

147

273

CONFIDENTIAL LOCSEN

a.   The attack on the Sri Lankan cricket team in Lahore has attracted much domestic attention. There are persistent media rumours of an LTTE connection, ▮▮▮▮▮▮▮▮▮▮ ▮▮▮▮▮▮▮▮▮▮▮.

b.   The President presented 4 squadrons of the SLAF with Presidential Colours on 7 Mar 09. There is definitely a sense that the air campaign is winding down and the SLAF is being patted on the back for a job well done (except for air interception).

7.   Statistics. 2009 casualty figures are shown below. SLA figures for Feb 09 are rounded off. SLA MIA figures for Feb 09 are not available. The assessed figures for LTTE casualties represent the assessments compiled from SLA ground troops engaged in frontline combat; ▮▮▮▮▮▮▮▮▮▮▮ ▮▮▮▮▮▮▮▮▮▮▮▮▮▮▮▮▮▮.

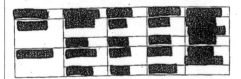

8.   LTTE.

a.   Assessing LTTE strength is difficult. ▮▮▮▮▮▮▮▮▮▮▮▮▮▮▮▮▮▮▮▮▮▮ ▮▮▮▮▮▮▮▮▮▮▮▮▮▮▮▮▮▮. Reports from the UN suggest that LTTE forcible recruitment, especially of women and children, has increased. It is likely that many of the casualties in the LTTE counter-attacks are unwilling recruits.

b.   There have been rumours that there have been clashes and disagreement among LTTE leaders over how to conduct the endgame to this campaign. There have also been reports that the senior leadership has been fighting in the front ranks – ▮▮▮▮▮▮▮▮▮▮▮ ▮▮▮▮▮▮▮▮▮▮▮▮▮.

9.   IDPs.

a.   As at 2 Mar 09 a total of 37,197 IDPs had arrived overland – 31,694 in Feb 09 alone. Over 200 LTTE cadres have been identified trying to infiltrate disguised as IDPs. 2564 IDPs arrived by sea in Feb 09, compared to 191 in Jan 09 and 783 for the whole of 2008 *Comment: GoSL announced on 12 Mar 09 a programme to reintegrate 300 cadres who had been extracted from the IDP population.*

b.   The LTTE has been consistently trying to prevent the egress of IDPs, other than the most seriously injured:

- On 9 Feb 09 a suicide bomber killed 9 civilians and wounded 41 at the screening centre near Puliyampokkanai.

- On 10 Feb 09 19 civilians were killed and 75 wounded by the LTTE as they tried to escape to Govt held territory. The UN reports civilians reaching ICRC medical facilities manned with gunshot wounds to the lower limbs –to prevent them leaving.

4

CONFIDENTIAL LOCSEN

Jan 09 observed SLA artillery killed 10 civilians next to the UN bunkers approximately 400m north of the A35. On 25 Jan 09 LTTE artillery killed 8 civilians in the same area.

The dead and injured are being concentrated at PTK hospital, around which a 1km no-fire zone has been declared, honoured so far by both sides. Arrivals over the past 3 days are:

25 Jan 55 dead, 102 injured
26 Jan 60 dead, 115 injured
27 Jan 45 dead, 80 injured   Total: 159 dead, 297 injured.

An attempt by ICRC/UN to bring out 200 sick and wounded failed on 27 Jan 09 when the agreed cease-fire broke down. A further attempt to extract will be made on 29 Jan 09. It is not possible to distinguish civilians from LTTE cadres, as few cadres are now in military uniform.

COMMENT

Securing the eastern seaboard will neutralise the threat from the Sea Tigers. The destruction of the SLN fast attack craft last week may have been the last flourish, or we could see a final attempt to mass suicide craft against the SLN before the coast is denied.

It is becoming increasingly unlikely that the LTTE will be able to use aircraft given the limited space available to them. It is surprising (to me) that they did not mount a final suicide mission as previously predicted. This could indicate that rumours of foreign mercenary pilots were correct (ie not ideologically motivated for suicide) or that the SLA has unknowingly destroyed the remaining Zlin aircraft.

Rumours about the LTTE leadership are rife; that ▮▮▮▮▮▮ has fled to Cambodia; that ▮▮▮▮▮▮ has fled to the south of Sri Lanka. Nobody knows. The most recent GoSL statements in the media have said that ▮▮▮▮▮▮ will be tried in Sri Lanka if he is captured alive, contradicting previous statements that he would be handed over to India. The expected attempts to distract from the GoSL offensive by destabilising the south and the east through terrorist attacks have not materialised. This may indicate a leadership vacuum. We continue to anticipate that the LTTE will switch their effort to insurgency against softer targets in due course.

The LTTE appear to have no options left, and the language on TamilNet and other similar platforms is clearly striving for international intervention to force a cease-fire on the GoSL.

Further civilian casualties are now inevitable as they no longer have options to move away from the combat zone. Without the presence of the IDPs the LTTE would be subjected to unrestricted air and artillery strikes, so have no incentive to release them. The SLA is exercising restraint but, without a change in political mood, will not hold back entirely.

ASG

A S GASH
Lt Col
DA Colombo

(6)

From: [REDACTED]
Sent: 04 February 2009 15:46
To: [REDACTED]

Subject: PTK Hospital

PTK hospital is now empty. 90% of patients left by themselves overnight; the ICRC and UN moved the last serious casualties this morning to the coast 4km east of PTK. During the move out the LTTE tried to seize the UN's vehicles but were dissuaded. The UN is now trying to arrange a sea or air lift from the coast for the patients and their own people.

[REDACTED] has apparently been sandbagging [REDACTED] this morning and afternoon in the strongest language ("legal reprisals" etc).

[REDACTED] has apparently said that the LTTE detonated 2 or 3 trucks of explosives near PTK hospital yesterday – I am not clear whether this is being linked to the attack on the hospital.

348

From:
Sent: Monday, February 16, 2009 4:44 PM
To:

Cc:
Subject: IDP Reception - Trincomalee 12 Feb 09

IDP RECEPTION - TRINCOMALEE

On Thu evening (12 Feb) I observed the arrival of 400 IDPs by sea to Trincomalee.

The operation started at 0630 hrs on 12 Feb with the transfer of the IDPs - stretcher cases plus some accompanying family members - to a vessel chartered by the ICRC. The transfer is believed to have been carried out by the LTTE, or at least with their agreement. Observers comment that the standards of boatmanship and discipline were very high during the transfer. All IDPs were in possession of "release" passes issued by the LTTE.

After a sea move to Trincomalee, during which patients were stabilised and prioritised by the ICRC, the Sri Lanka Navy (SLN) took control of the operation. SLN personnel boarded the vessel to continue medical prioritisation and to start the screening process; initially this was profiling by intelligence personnel and metal detector screening of personnel and bags.

From 1930 hrs (12 Feb) to 0300 hrs (13 Feb) the ship-to-shore transfer took place. (I was present 2200-0200 hrs). SLN small boats moved 3-4 stretchers plus their accompanying "bystanders" to a remote beach location within Trincomalee Naval Base. Reception consisted of a linear channel along the beach with the following stages:

Simultaneously:

- Physical search of baggage
- Physical (strip) search of the able bodied (separate and well-screened male and female areas)
- Immediate medical care for the injured (assessment, pain relief, redressing wounds, insertion of IV drips)

Then:

- Reuniting of personnel with baggage

Then:

- Registration Desk (ICRC had already provided statistics compiled onboard, so this was a quick confirmation)

Then:

- Refreshments (tea, water, biscuits)

Then:

- Transport (ambulances for the injured to Trincomalee General Hospital, buses for others to St Anthony's School holding area)

The operation was efficient and effective, but most importantly was carried out with compassion, respect and concern. I am entirely certain that this was genuine - my presence was not planned and was based on a sudden opportunity; I had free access to the 300m long stretch of beach over a 4 hour period and was able to observe upwards of 200 SLN personnel working extremely hard in difficult conditions. Their high morale was notable; they were enjoying the work and clearly finding it satisfying. There were constant examples of thoughtful assistance - looking after babies while mothers were being searched, helping elderly ladies or mothers of babies with their bags, cheerfully

208

APPENDIX VIII

Lord Naseby's letter of Appeal

The Rt. Hon. the Lord Naseby P.C.

House of Lords

London SW1A 0PW   30.5.2016

Dear Sirs,

I wish to appeal against the Decision Notice of the Information Commission Office, case reference FS 50585337 dated 4th May 2016 & giving me 28days to Appeal.

This case history commenced onAugust 14 2014 eventually leading to a formal request to the FCO in November 2014; subsequent rejections by the FCO lasted until 7th May 2015. An experience of delay, procrastination and reluctance to co-operate which resulted in an Appeal to the ICO on 10th June 2015.

At this point I should like to formally record my thanks to the ICO for listening to & understanding my complaint in depth. The ICO persuaded the FCO to comply in part with my request and on December 21st 2015 provided 26 emails mostly heavily redacted. After further pressure from me based on logic a further 3 emails from the key month of April were discovered, heavily redacted & sent to me.

The ICO have partially found in favour of my request as will be noted in para 46 with its emphasis on the word 'WHY' in capitals. In addition the ICO found in favour of me concerning Section 40 on personal data paras 48 – 59. However I still await the four items from the FCO highlighted by the ICO in item 3 of ruling page 2 although their 35 days is not quite up yet.

The only rejection and therefore the subject of this Appeal is on upholding Section 27/2 & Section 41(1) in para 60 i.e. the effect the total publication of Colonel Gash's emails with no redaction would have on International Relations specifically between Sri Lanka & UK plus by implication between the UK and other Countries.

I would maintain this is a spurious argument. The issue here is 'War Crimes' and specifically if there was a policy 'To kill Tamil Civilians' levelled against the democratically elected Government of Sri Lanka despite a huge number of Tamils living totally unmolested in Colombo & the South.. These are the allegations by certain Diaspora groups and many of the Human Rights organisation spread all over Europe & North America. This is despite the LTTE / Tamil Tigers being proscribed all over Europe & North America. There might just have been validity in the FCO claim had the UK not made two key decisions. Firstly along with the USA they co-sponsored a motion at the UN calling for an an inquiry including War Crimes to be held in Geneva. Secondly to consciously not make available even in confidence the emails from Lt.Colonel Gash, the only independent knowledgeable, unbiased and reliable party who had access to all the military aspects of the War from January1st 2009 until May19h when the war ended. The result was that a key UN enquiry was denied vital evidence which would undoubtedly have changed the findings & the recommendations that followed.

War Crimes allegations are at the pinnacle of crimes which if leading to convictions can dramatically affect an individual's life & livelihood. It cannot be right to consciously with hold absolutely key information even if I myself have never seen it.

I wish to summarise my key concerns as to non disclosure in the following way:
1.In its Resolution A/HRC/25/1, co-sponsored by the UK Government, and adopted in March 2014 on 'Promoting reconciliation, accountability and human rights in Sri Lanka, the United Nations

Human Rights Council (UNHRC) requested the UN High Commissioner for Human Rights to "undertake a comprehensive investigation into alleged serious violations and abuses of human rights and related crimes by both parties in Sri Lanka during the period covered by the Lesson Learnt Reconciliation Commission (LLRC),and to establish the facts and circumstances of such alleged violations and of crimes the perpetrators with a view of avoiding impunity ans assuring accountability with assistance from relevant experts and special procedures mandate holders."

2.The resolution, co-sponsored by both the UK and Sri Lanka governments and adopted by consensus at the UNHRC in October 2015, stated in operative Paragraph 15 the following:

"Encourages the Government of Sri Lanka to develop a comprehensive plan and mechanism for preserving all existing records and documentation relating to human rights violations and abuses and violations of international law,whether held by public or private institutions"

3.My Prime Minister Rt. Hon. David Cameron MP also welcomed the adoption of UNHRC's resolution by stating the following:

"Today's resolution is a crucial step towards uncovering the truth about alleged war crimes in Sri Lanka, ensuring accountability for the past and respect for human rights now and in the future.

Britain is committed to standing up for those affected by Sri Lanka's civil war, and has been instrumental in the United Nations investigation and adoption of this resolution. I welcome the Sri Lankan Government's commitment to ensuring those responsible are held to account and I encourage them to continue to work with the UN.

When I visited Sri Lanka, I was struck by the huge potential of the country and I urge President Sirisena to develop the work he has already started- to build a peaceful, prosperous and united country where every community has a voice"

4. The disclosure of information submitted in Lt.Colonel Gash's despatches would not only aid the process of promoting reconciliation, accountability and human rights in Sri Lanka but would serve to assist the process of truth seeking that is essential for this task.

The resolution was cosponsored by Sri Lanka and the UK with the UK Government being one of the prime movers of the resolution. Both Governments accept the need to establish the truth relating to the end of the conflict. Therefore,it is not clear how full disclosure of information would adversely affect relations between the two countries. Moreover it is submitted that the disclosure of the said despatches is more likely to facilitate and contribute positively to the process agreed upon by both governments rather than harm relations between two states. Moreover, information regarding troop movements, military strategies etc. are no longer issues of contention and is likely to be treated as despatches sent by any Military Attache in the course of performing his/her duties. If names of any Sri Lanka military officer/s providing this information are contained therein, such names may be witheld for obvious reasons.

5. As mentioned in the report of the OISL investigation (copy can be sent), it is stated that some of the crimes may meet the threshold of war crimes. Also, other allegations by different groups speak of genocide and crimes against humanity. It is generally accepted that these allegations, while still unproven, are egregious in nature and would be tantamount to a violation of " jus cogens" principles in international law with possible application of universal jurisdiction, if proven true. Therefore, there is a moral obligation on the UK Government to disclose information which may assist in establishing the truth of the matter.

24

APPENDIX IX

Lord Naseby's speech at the House of Lords 'Take Note Debate'

Debate 12 July 2016, Vol 774 No. 26
Lord Naseby Col 172–174 commencing @6:15 pm

My Lords, I associate myself with the words of condolence from both Front Benches to the families who lost loved ones in the second Gulf War. I can say that because I held a letter from my son in the first Gulf War which, thankfully, did not have to be opened as he came home safely. Nevertheless, I am quite clear: I supported the action that was taken in going to war against Iraq. I did it because of the environment at the time. We forget too easily what the environment was: 9/11, other atrocities against the United States, considerable evidence of chemical warfare and of provisions for chemical warfare and the evidence that was given to Parliament.

There is no way that Tony Blair is a war criminal or that he is guilty of war crimes. The action he took as Prime Minister was taken in the interests of our country. He was the democratically elected leader of our country, not a dictator. This maxim about democratically elected leaders must apply all over the world as far as leadership is concerned.

Others have commented on military equipment. Whatever one says, it was an absolute shambles and a total disgrace. Post-war planning was poor. Post-Brexit planning is poor. That lies with the Prime Minister of the day and his Cabinet.

Have we learned the lessons, or have we had to wait for Chilcot to learn them? As far as I can see, we have not. Why did we go into Libya? It is not at all clear to me. Why did we try to force democracy on Egypt? We must have known that the Muslim Brotherhood had been trying since 1921 to get "democratically elected". We supported elections there and what happened? It got elected, and then we discovered that it is almost as bad as Daesh, and the army in Egypt moved in again. Why did we not think twice about Syria? Why did those of us who know a little about that part of the world not realise that it is the fourth Sunni/Shia war? The only thing that is slightly different is that there are far more western-educated people on one side. That war had no real implications for the West. Why did we not check who the people supporting the new democracy in Syria were? Surely we should have been able to discover that the vast majority of them are jihadists.

I urge my noble friends on the Front Bench to get a proper communications strategy and action plan geared solely against Daesh and to work with Assad to implement it. If that does not happen, we shall once again be in terrible turmoil.

Action Aid and Christian Aid are right to raise the problem of the 3 million people — at least 3 million refugees, poor souls — with nowhere to live and no livelihood, wondering day after day what is going to happen to them. Have we in the West really got an action plan to deal with that? If we have, I hope that somebody is going to deploy it so that we can discuss it.

This may surprise most though not all of your Lordships but I need to relate Chilcot to the situation in Sri Lanka today. A press release on 7 June from our High Commission in Colombo after the visit of no less a person than the head of the British Diplomatic Service, Sir Simon McDonald, concludes:

"The UK will continue its programme of support for Sri Lanka to help the Government fulfil its goals on reconciliation, human rights and strengthening democracy".

That is fine, but there is a parallel with Iraq where the UK was, in effect, tackling terrorism in the form of weapons of mass destruction. A battle is undertaken. Here I refer to page 181 of volume 12 of the report under the heading "Battle Damage Assessment":

"Section 6.2 describes the main principles of International Humanitarian Law (IHL), also known as the Law of Armed Conflict … or the Law of War, how they were disseminated to those engaged in military action, and how they were reflected in the UK's Targeting Directive and Rules of Engagement. The key elements of IHL which apply to targeting of military objectives during a conflict are set out in the 1977 Protocol Additional to the Geneva Conventions",

and then it lists the four main principles.
The Chilcot inquiry's assessment was undertaken by British judges and members of the Privy Council. No foreign judges were called in to do this assessment. We see how well it has been done. In Sri Lanka, there was a war against the terrorists, the Tamil Tigers. However, instead of its being assessed against the Geneva convention, to which I have just referred, the UK and US Governments have endorsed investigation by the UN High Commissioner for Human Rights with the addition of foreign judges. This is wrong and misconceived. After all, there is a reasonable number of fair-minded judges across the ethnic groups who could undertake the task of judging what happened against the principles of the Geneva convention.

If the UK Government really want to help, they should release the full text of the dispatches of our military attaché there during the war, Lieutenant-Colonel Gash, containing his independent observations. The Ministers here will know that for two years I have been trying to obtain these under the Freedom of Information Act. However, so far I have received some 30 pages of those dispatches, provided reluctantly, some very heavily redacted. As I go to the next stage of the tribunal, I find the Foreign Office hiding behind policy that releasing these dispatches might undermine relationships with other countries such as Saudi Arabia, which is hardly a democracy.

I ask the Foreign Office to reflect carefully on the full implications of Chilcot, namely that we should treat each situation separately and recognise that the truth will get out. It is better to publish evidence that is available than to hide it. If in future we as a country follow that in any engagements that we may have, we shall be a country that can be proud of what we achieve democratically.

Parliament owes a huge debt to Chilcot for what he has done. It must be for Parliament to decide how to take it forward.

APPENDICES
Section 2:
Appendices of major parliamentary
debates on Sri Lanka

APPENDIX I

Hansard references to contributions from Lord Naseby (Michael Morris MP) in debates, oral and written questions in the House of Lords and House of Commons

---

List of *Hansard* references to Contributions (Debates, Oral Questions and Written Questions) of Lord Naseby in the House of Lords on Sri Lanka

Oral Question on 'Syria-Jordan Border: Rukban Camp', HL *Hansard*, 16 October 2018, cols 402.

House of Lords, 'Written Question: Immigration: Sri Lanka', 4 September 2018, HL9992.

House of Lords, 'Written Question: Asylum: Sri Lanka', 4 September 2018, HL9991.

House of Lords, 'Written Question: Asylum: Sri Lanka', 19 March 2018, HL6460.

Debate on 'Sanctions and Anti-Money Laundering Bill', HL *Hansard*, 6 December 2017, cols 1114-5.

QSD on 'Sri Lanka', HL *Hansard*, 12 October 2017, col 385.

QSD on 'Sri Lanka', HL *Hansard*, 12 October 2017, cols 373-6.

House of Lords, 'Written Question: Sri Lanka: Disaster Relief', 7 September 2017, HL1434.

Debate on 'Criminal Finances Bill', HL *Hansard*, 25 April 2017, cols 1323-4.

Oral Question on 'Bilateral Trade: Sri Lanka', HL *Hansard*, 28 February 2017, col 711.

Debate on 'Iraq Inquiry', HL *Hansard*, 12 July 2016, cols 172-4.

House of Lords, 'Written Question: Sri Lanka: Floods', 24 May 2016, HL284.

Debate on 'Syria: UK Military Action', HL *Hansard*, 2 December 2015, cols 1175-6.

Oral Question on 'All-Party Parliamentary Groups', HL *Hansard*, 11 November 2015, col 1991.

House of Lords, 'Written Question: Crimes against Humanity: Sri Lanka', 28 October 2015, HL3079.

Debate on 'Middle East and North Africa', HL *Hansard*, 16 September 2015, cols 1940-2.

QSD on 'Syria', HL *Hansard*, 24 June 2015, col 1660.

Oral Question on 'Sri Lanka: Presidential Elections', HL *Hansard*, 14 January 2015, cols 780-782.

QSD on 'UK and Sri Lanka: Bilateral Trade', HL *Hansard*, 11 December 2014, cols 2102-5.

Oral Question on 'Sri Lanka', HL *Hansard*, 24 November 2014, cols 669-71.

Debate on 'Azure Card', HL *Hansard*, 20 November 2014, cols 555-8.

House of Lords, 'Written Question : Sri Lanka', 26 September 2014, HL1913.

Oral Question on 'Sri Lanka', HL *Hansard*, 2 July 2014, col 1713.

Debate of 'Queen's Speech', HL *Hansard*, 11 June 2014, cols 413-4.

House of Lords, 'Written Question: Sri Lanka', 25 March 2014, HL6082.

Oral Question on 'Sri Lanka', HL *Hansard*, 26 February 2014, cols 919-21.

Oral Question on 'Sri Lanka', HL *Hansard*, 26 February 2014, cols 919.

House of Lords, 'Written Question: Asylum Seekers', 11 February 2014, HL5245.

House of Lords, 'Written Question: Government: Ministerial Meetings', 06 February 2014, HL4947

Debate on 'Commonwealth Heads of Government Meeting and Philippines', HL Hansard, 18 November 2013, cols 772-3.

House of Lords, 'Written Question: Commonwealth Business Council', 5 November 2013, HL3065.

Debate on 'Commonwealth', HL *Hansard*, 17 October 2013, cols 722-4.

Debate on 'Syria and the Use of Chemical Weapons', HL *Hansard*, 29 August 2013, cols 1786-7.

Debate on 'Queen's Speech', HL *Hansard*, 15 May 2013, cols 435-8.

Tributes on 'Death of a Member: Baroness Thatcher', 10 April 2013 cols 1186-9.

Debate on 'Sri Lanka', HL *Hansard*, 8 January 2013, col 23GC.

Debate on 'Sri Lanka', HL *Hansard*, 8 January 2013, col 16GC.

Debate on 'Sri Lanka', HL *Hansard*, 8 January 2013, cols 13-6GC.

Debate on 'Foreign Affairs: Global Role, Emerging Powers and New Markets', HL Hansard, 6 December 2012, cols 782-4.

House of Lords, 'Written Question: Immigration', 28 May 2012, HL277.

House of Lords, 'Written Question: Sport: Cricket', 7 July 2011, HL10662.

House of Lords, 'Written Question: Sport: Cricket', 21 June 2011, HL9831.

House of Lords 'Written Question: Sport: Cricket', 20 June 2011, HL9741.

Oral Question on 'Charity Commission: Bogus Charities', HL *Hansard*, 4 May 2011, col 453.

Oral Question on 'International Development Aid', HL *Hansard*, 7 February 2011, col 6.

Debate on 'Queen's Speech', HL *Hansard*, 26 May 2010, cols 90-2.

Debate on 'Queen's Speech', HL *Hansard*, 19 November 2009, cols 81-4.

House of Lords, 'Written Question: Sri Lanka', 21 July 2009, HL5028.

House of Lords, 'Written Question: Sri Lanka', 21 July 2009, HL5027

Oral Question on 'Refugees', HL *Hansard*, 13 July 2009, col 936.

Oral Question on 'Sri Lanka', HL *Hansard*, 17 June 2009, col 1060.

Oral Question on 'Sri Lanka', HL *Hansard*, 17 June 2009, cols 1059-60.

Oral Question on 'Sri Lanka', HL *Hansard*, 20 May 2009, col 1384.

Private Notice Question on 'Access to Parliament', HL *Hansard*, 12 May 2009, col 924.

Debate on 'Sri Lanka', HL *Hansard*, 30 April 2009, cols 387-8.

Oral Question on 'Sri Lanka', HL *Hansard*, 23 February 2009, cols 6-7.

Oral Question on 'Sri Lanka', HL *Hansard*, 23 February 2009, col 6.

Oral Question on 'Sri Lanka', HL *Hansard*, 12 February 2009, col 1231.

Oral Question on 'Aid Workers', HL *Hansard*, 27 January 2009, col 171.

Oral Question on 'Visas: Sri Lanka and Maldives', HL *Hansard*, 26 November 2008, col 1441.

Oral Question on 'Visas: Sri Lanka and Maldives', HL *Hansard*, 26 November 2008, cols 1439-40.

Oral Question on 'Maldives: Elections', HL *Hansard*, 14 May 2008, col 997.

Oral Question on 'Sri Lanka', HL *Hansard*, 30 April 2008, col 241.

Oral Question on 'Children: Infant Mortality', HL *Hansard*, 3 March 2008, col 862.

Oral Question on 'Sri Lanka', HL *Hansard*, 27 February 2008, col 649.

Oral Question on 'Health: Mixed-sex Wards', HL *Hansard*, 28 January 2008, cols 440.

House of Lords, 'Written Question: Sri Lanka: Navy', 29 October 2007, HL5677.

Oral Question on 'Terrorism: Tamil Tigers', HL *Hansard*, 9 July 2007, cols 1223-4.

Oral Question on 'Terrorism: Liberation Tigers of Tamil Eelam', HL *Hansard*, 3 May 2006, cols 462-3.

Debate on 'Animal Welfare Bill', HL *Hansard*, 18 April 2006, cols 995-7

Debate on 'Tsunami Relief', HL *Hansard*, 10 Feb 2006, cols 973-6.

Debate on 'Asian Tsunami: Emergency Relief', HL *Hansard*, 13 June 2005, cols 1112-3.

Debate on 'Asian Tsunami: Emergency Relief', HL *Hansard*, 13 June 2005, cols 1093-6.

Debate on 'Asian Tsunami', HL *Hansard*, 2 March 2005, cols 225-8.

Oral Question on 'Aid projects: Capital Equipment', HL *Hansard*, 2 February 2005, cols 229-30.

Debate on 'Water Purification Units', HL *Hansard*, 24 January 2005, col 999.

Debate on 'International Terrorism', HL *Hansard*, 14 September 2001, cols 63-65.

Oral Question on 'Ending terrorist activity in Sri Lanka and on the Terrorism Act', HL *Hansard*, 12 March 2001, col 513.

Oral Question on 'Illegal immigrants from Sri Lanka', HL *Hansard*, 20 February 2001, cols 591-2.

Debate on 'Representation of the People Bill', HL *Hansard*, 14 February 2000, col 922.

Debate on 'The International Situation', HL *Hansard*, 12 January 2000, cols 682-686.

Searches carried out on Parliamentary Search:

"sri lanka" type:"Members' contributions" date:01/01/1997..22/11/2018 author:"Naseby, Lord"

"sri lanka" House of Lords date 01/01/1997 to 22/11/2018 author: "Naseby, Lord"

"sri lanka" date:01/01/1997..22/11/2018 author:"Naseby, Lord"

Vol. 678

No. 104

Friday

10 February 2006

PARLIAMENTARY DEBATES
(HANSARD)

HOUSE OF LORDS

OFFICIAL REPORT

ORDER OF BUSINESS

£3·50

Tsunami Relief

4.03 pm

Lord Naseby rose to ask Her Majesty's Government what analysis has been undertaken of the results achieved and lessons learned in Sri Lanka and the Maldives from the aid moneys donated by private and public sources for tsunami relief and reconstruction since the disaster on 26 December 2004.

The noble Lord said: My Lords, my involvement in the Maldives and Sri Lanka goes back to 1963, when I worked for the Reckitt and Coleman Group and had responsibility for both those countries. I have also had the privilege of starting the all-party groups and of chairing both across the two Houses. I visit both countries very regularly, and when the tsunami hit on 26 December 2004, I and many millions of people in this country watched in absolute horror what was happening. The response from the British people was quite amazing, as was the way in which the money flowed in to help those poor people so very quickly.

It seemed to me that there was no point my being chairman of an all-party group and sitting at home wondering what was happening, so I decided that I would get out there and see whether I could help. My wife and I went out and, I believe, did some good work. We got there in early January 2005, and having made that visit and produced a report for Her Majesty's Government, I decided that it would be sensible to go back a year later and see what had actually happened on the ground, not least because there had been a fair amount of critical press comment about what was not, or what might not be, happening on the ground.

The Maldives was the smallest country of those affected, with just 300,000 people. In some ways, it was the hardest hit: not in numbers of deaths, because, thankfully, only about 100 people died, but 15,000 people out of 300,000 were made homeless. The key crunch area was the economic effect. I ask noble Lords to picture 1,192 beautiful islands, of which 199 are inhabited. They are no more than six feet high: the waves that came in were more than 12 feet high. Of the inhabited islands, 190 were hit. There was no power, no means of communication and some of the islands were completely flattened. There was nothing left on an island called Vilufushi, which I visited last year and again this year, where one-third of the population was directly affected. Tourism, which is the biggest industry, was brought to a halt with 21 of the 68 resorts knocked out. More than 200 fishing boats were destroyed. We should remember that these islands are miles away from the capital, Male. Everything has to go by sea: there are no motorways.

Phase 1, which provided emergency aid, worked well. Oxfam provided water. The Royal Navy and the Red Cross got generators going. We also provided a couple of landing craft. It was a job well done and well administered by the Government of the Maldives. Phase 2, restoration, took place during the past year. When I went back, I found good progress. Fishing is nearly back to normal. Only 10 islands are still closed to tourism. Occupancy is back up to around 75 per cent.

As I went from island to island, rehousing was bursting with activity, being led by the Red Cross. The various factions of the Red Cross will provide 84 per cent of the new housing. There is no Red Crescent representation, although I hope that there will be in the future. The British Red Cross is run by Jill Chambers. I watched the beginnings of 744 houses being constructed to a good design and which are liked by the potential occupants, who can choose the colour of tiles and the roof that they want. How nice to see housing that people want to live in. There is good consultation.

The press say, "Why did it take so long?". We forget that everything has to be imported. Even a warehouse had to be built, which takes an enormous amount of time. There is one big problem—the shortage of overall funding. That gap is calculated at £145 million. It behoves Her Majesty's Government, the Disasters Emergency Committee and the UN agencies to address that issue, for which I have two suggestions. The British Red Cross operation is running well. It would be a tragedy to wind it up after 744 houses, when at least another 500 are needed. I hope that the DEC and DfID can find a means of financing at least another 250 houses. I also ask DfID to look at the safe island policy, in particular with respect to education, and the materials for schools. The estimated cost is $5 million. I hope that we can provide all the materials. If we cannot do that, let us at a minimum adopt at least one island: I suggest Vilufushi. There is an efficient government and good progress. Since we have a special relationship with the Maldives, we should respond in their hour of need.

Sri Lanka was hit by the tsunami and 35,000 people were killed, 500,000 people were made homeless and there are 40,000 widows. However, the core of its economy is unaffected. Both last year and this year I went to the south because, on security grounds, I was not allowed to go to the east. Again, great work is being done everywhere that I went. During the emergency conditions, 900 camps were set up, which were tented accommodation originally. There was good, clean water, food, shelter and no disease. That is no mean achievement. Slightly more than 41,000 transitional housing units were built—they are not perfect, but they are not bad—and 9,000 simple, two-bedded, single-storey houses have now been built. I talked to some of the residents of the new houses—they like them. I talked to a fisherman, a tailor and a widow. I visited a village erected with Marks & Spencer money. It was actively built by its supplier, MAS, and overseen by CARE. It consists of 41 houses, a little shop and a small community centre. It is running on the ground and I hope that someone from the press will go and look at it.

Further, I visited Belgian Red Cross houses and more CARE houses around Hikkaduwa. Have enough been built? Not yet—but there is the inevitable problem of finding out who owns them, because when something is destroyed a number of people can claim that they own it. The work has been held up, of course, by the problems caused by the buffer zone. But at least

[LORD NASEBY]
that has been resolved and the matter has now been left to the local planning authority to sort out—and it is being sorted out.

Do I think I was hoodwinked? No, because I did not tell the Government where I was going. I know the country well and it seemed rather simple to get hold of a car to carry out the visits, and to ring up a few personal friends to ensure that I knew exactly where I was going.

As to livelihoods, it was a joy to see the fishing vessels, which are all brightly painted now. The only ones missing are the trawlers. It was nice to see some English names on the sides of the little fishing boats. The micro-industry work being carried out by Oxfam is very encouraging and Adopt Sri Lanka, a new charity, is doing good work in lace-making, tailoring and so on. I went to the port to check on the delays there. There were delays in February and March but the warehousing in the port is now empty.

There is a problem in the eastern area because of the security situation. I am afraid that the NGOs there are pulling out because of the number of bombings and so on. But, with the Geneva talks settled and due to start in 10 days, it is to be hoped that we will see an opportunity for those NGOs and the Government to go back in.

But there are two shadows overhanging any real recovery from the tsunami which affect each country in one way. The easier one is in the Maldives, where its people are grappling with a new constitution as part of the transition from a one-party state. There are now four political parties. One party has pulled out—the NDP—and I encourage Her Majesty's Government, which I know meets representatives of the NDP in the UK, to ask it to co-operate. After all, that is what democracy is about.

It is more difficult in Sri Lanka, where there have been troubles since 1983, when there was a war. We have had peace for the past three years, but no contact between the two parties. The LTTE is a problem. The Government can do two things. First, they can take an initiative to encourage the international community to provide housing and so on for the 400,000 displaced persons. Secondly, they have to recognise that the LTTE here is operating by extortion and money-laundering—every garage around London seems to be controlled by a Tamil with, I suspect, money-laundering underneath—and there is a bogus charity, the White Pigeon.

Above all, no one seems to be doing anything about enforcing prescription. There is now very worrying information that the LTTE—which is a past master at suicide bombings—has some link with al-Qaeda. While clearly the Foreign Office is the Minister's department, the police and the Home Office are not. But they need to be stimulated into action to put some real pressure on the LTTE so that when we come to reconstruct the east of the country it can actually happen.

I finish on a brighter note. The people I spoke to in the Maldives and Sri Lanka are enormously grateful to the British people for the huge amount of money that was given, both directly by small charities and provided from our taxes through DfID. If people want to do anything else, I suggest they go on holiday. These countries are two of the most perfect places in the world and if people go on holiday there the money will filter down.

4.14 pm

Lord Judd: My Lords, I am sure that the House is grateful to the noble Lord, Lord Naseby, with his deep commitment to the Maldives and Sri Lanka, for having provided an opportunity to review the effectiveness of the response to the tsunami. He has spoken both graphically and convincingly. I should declare an interest, as a lifelong and continuing supporter of Oxfam and, indeed, as a former director of that organisation.

The tsunami was a disaster on a scale and of a complexity never before experienced, with 230,000 dead or missing, 1.8 million displaced, hundreds of thousands of livelihoods lost. Unqualified tribute is due to those in government and NGOs who responded so magnificently and tirelessly. Admiration for the generosity of the ordinary people who dug into their pockets and gave on an unprecedented scale cannot be overstated. This was solidarity at its best. Oxfam alone raised £188 million, 90 per cent of it from the public. The challenges to organisation and co-ordination and the need for co-operation were huge. While, to their credit, government and the NGOs openly acknowledged that some mistakes were inevitably made and some things did not always go as they should, the powerful story of what has been achieved is one of impressively effective humanitarian impact.

I believe that one of the characteristics of government and NGOs alike, which has been greatly reassuring, is their avoidance of complacency and their determination vigorously to evaluate their performance in an endeavour all the time to learn from experience and improve performance. One imperative that has become clear is the indispensability of co-operation and good co-ordination. Another reality is that it is almost always possible to be more effective if an organisation is already established in the affected area and has made its links with partner organisations rooted in the community.

The economic, social and political consequences of the tsunami will continue for many years. For example, it will take two to five years for soil to return to full productivity. If there is any one overriding lesson to be learnt from disasters of this kind, it is that resources and follow-up support are every bit as important in years two, three, four and beyond as the action in the immediate aftermath. The challenges remain acute long after the cameras have moved away.

In the case of Oxfam alone, there is a four-year programme with some £73 million, or 45 per cent, spent in the first year. Despite the incredible public support, funds are far from ample, and I am fairly certain that in the years ahead still more resources will

Vol. 693
No. 115

Monday
9 July 2007

PARLIAMENTARY DEBATES
(HANSARD)

HOUSE OF LORDS

OFFICIAL REPORT

ORDER OF BUSINESS

For column numbers see back page

£3·50

House of Lords

Monday, 9 July 2007

The House met at half-past two: the LORD SPEAKER on the Woolsack.

Prayers—Read by the Lord Bishop of Newcastle.

Introduction: Lord Malloch-Brown

Lord Malloch-Brown—Sir George Mark Malloch Brown, KCMG, having been created Baron Malloch-Brown, of St Leonard's Forest in the County of West Sussex, for life—Was, in his robes, introduced between the Baroness Whitaker and the Lord Hannay of Chiswick.

Introduction: Lord West of Spithead

Lord West of Spithead—Admiral Sir Alan William John West, GCB, DSC, having been created Baron West of Spithead, of Seaview in the County of Isle of Wight, for life—Was, in his robes, introduced between the Lord Drayson and the Lord Ramsbotham.

Terrorism: Tamil Tigers

2.48 pm

Lord Naseby asked Her Majesty's Government:

Whether they have taken any action since June 2006 to curtail or prosecute those persons promoting the activities of the proscribed organisation Liberation Tigers of Tamil Eelam (Tamil Tigers).

Lord Bassam of Brighton: My Lords, the arrest and prosecution for offences related to proscribed organisations is a matter for the police and the Crown Prosecution Service respectively. I understand that the police have recently charged two individuals with offences relating to membership of and support for the Liberation Tigers of Tamil Eelam. It would not be appropriate for me to comment further on such matters, as to do so could prejudice any potential trial.

Lord Naseby: My Lords, is the Minister aware that the action taken by the authorities in arresting Mr Shanthan and Mr Lambert is extremely welcome, Mr Shanthan being the de facto leader of the Tamil Tigers in the UK? In their press release, the police state that,

"a quantity of literature and manuals including Underwater Warfare Systems, Explosive Ordnance Disposal and Naval Weapons Systems"

was found in his home. Does not that, the continuing credit card fraud, intimidation and bogus charities underline the need to ensure that proscription of the Tamil Tigers continues until such time as the leader,

Mr Prabhakaran, comes to the conference table and agrees to have peace and a final settlement in war-torn Sri Lanka?

Lord Bassam of Brighton: My Lords, I entirely agree with the noble Lord and thank him for his support for the police's continued efforts to deal with the LTTE. We have taken action on other fronts. We are clamping down on the group's funds through bogus charities, as the noble Lord will be aware, as part of our work overall to combat terrorism and its funding in the United Kingdom.

Lord Archer of Sandwell: My Lords, does the noble Lord agree that atrocities have been committed on both sides, by government forces as well as by Tamils, and that the real distinction is between the extremists on both sides, who are seeking to escalate the violence, and the moderates on both sides, who are looking for negotiated accommodation? Does he also agree that, in those circumstances, to label one side only as terrorists while condoning the actions of the other is not a helpful solution to the peace process?

Lord Bassam of Brighton: My Lords, the noble and learned Lord is right that we should encourage moderates on both sides of the argument. It serves no good purpose to encourage terrorism in any shape or form. We are completely opposed to terrorist activity, particularly terrorist activity in the United Kingdom. We must make efforts to work with the Sri Lankan Government to ensure that the peace process is reinvigorated, so that peace can be brought to Sri Lanka.

Lord Avebury: My Lords, a few days ago, the Liberation Tigers of Tamil Eelam celebrated the 20th anniversary of its campaign of suicide bombing, which it pioneered long before anyone else took it up. It continues to use child soldiers, and the International Institute for Strategic Studies claims that there is evidence of its commercial links with al-Qaeda. Is the noble Lord satisfied that adequate resources are made available to SOCA to prevent the campaign of intimidation and extortion by which the LTTE raises funds in the United Kingdom for its terrorist activities in Sri Lanka?

Lord Bassam of Brighton: Yes, my Lords, we are content that adequate resources are set aside for anti-terrorist activity. Obviously we must do more to maximise the use of those resources to ensure that our anti-terrorist efforts, whether against the LTTE or the other proscribed organisations, are at their best at all times. We know that we must be ever vigilant, and we encourage the British public to join us in that vigilance.

Baroness Seccombe: My Lords, on proscribed organisations, does the noble Lord have any plans to proscribe Hizb ut-Tahrir? If not, why not?

Lord Bassam of Brighton: My Lords, as the noble Baroness will know, an organisation can be proscribed only if the available evidence meets the test set out in the Terrorism Act 2000, which allows for proscription on the ground that an organisation is concerned in terrorism. For these purposes, that

[LORD BASSAM OF BRIGHTON]
includes promoting or encouraging terrorism. As the Prime Minister made very clear last week, we keep under very careful review all organisations about which there are real concerns.

Africa: Family Planning

2.53 pm

Lord Taverne asked Her Majesty's Government:

What steps they are taking to promote family planning as part of the campaign to reduce poverty in Africa.

Baroness Royall of Blaisdon: My Lords, the Government are committed to improving sexual and reproductive health, including family planning, across Africa. In 2006, DfID provided £25.1 million to UNFPA and £7.5 million to the International Planned Parenthood Federation to support work on sexual and reproductive health and rights. We also work at country level and are funding reproductive health services in the Democratic Republic of Congo, Ethiopia, Sierra Leone and Zimbabwe, enabling women, men and adolescents to avoid unwanted pregnancy and HIV.

Lord Taverne: My Lords, although I welcome and appreciate the Government's efforts, is it not a tragedy that funding for family planning, which has been pretty successful in reducing the birth rate even in some of the poorest countries, should now be reduced and that, because of the lobbying against contraception in the United Nations by the American evangelicals, unfortunately supported by the Catholic Church, the birth rate in countries such as Uganda is now more than seven children per woman—in rural Africa, it is more than six per woman? Does this not mean that any hope of achieving the millennium goals will be frustrated, that no progress can be made in the education of women and, indeed, that making poverty history will be a vain aim? Is it not surprising that there has not been more of a squeak of protest against this moral outrage from Her Majesty's Government, those who organise pop concerts and others who profess their concern about welfare in Africa?

Baroness Royall of Blaisdon: My Lords, in response to the last point, I am slightly outraged at the noble Lord's view of what this Government are doing on sexual health and reproduction. We have been leading the world. It is thanks to this Government that we now have a universally accepted target for sexual health and reproductive rights before 2015. This Government have done an excellent job, although I well recognise that it is important to keep family planning at the heart of development policy.

Lord Kinnock: My Lords, while I endorse the sentiments expressed by the noble Lord, Lord Taverne, on the attitude of the current US Administration, does the Minister agree that the history of our own

society and many others demonstrates that the best inducements to limiting family size are confidence in the future, a falling rate of child mortality and rising incomes? I therefore congratulate the Government on their balanced programme to promote sexual health and family planning while simultaneously addressing assiduously the basic requirements of development throughout the world.

Baroness Royall of Blaisdon: My Lords, my noble friend is right that experience shows that improving health, education and livelihoods, promoting gender equality and rights and addressing sexual health and reproduction all have to be a balanced part of current and future policy. On the earlier question from the noble Lord, Lord Taverne, which I did not answer, I agree that we have some problems with US policy. We firmly believe that policy should be driven not by moral ideology, but by a firm evidence base.

Lord Fowler: My Lords, is there not an important health issue here? Is the Minister aware that worldwide more than 25 million people have so far died from AIDS, mostly in Africa? Can the Government not put it to the leaders of the Roman Catholic Church that the encouragement, not the discouragement, of the use of condoms could preserve life and significantly reduce this toll of death?

Baroness Royall of Blaisdon: My Lords, I am sure that my honourable friends in the other place who have contact with people from the Roman Catholic Church and the Holy See do put it to them. We well recognise that condoms are important for sexual health and reproduction, and as a counter against HIV and AIDS.

Lord Anderson of Swansea: My Lords, is there not a precedent in that one of the major influences on family spacing is the education of women? Will the Minister therefore not give real priority, as the Government have already done, to education generally and particularly the education of women in Africa?

Baroness Royall of Blaisdon: Yes, my Lords. The Government fully recognise that and are making a huge investment in the education of children and especially the education of women in Africa. We recognise that women's empowerment can come only through the education of women and girls.

Baroness Northover: My Lords, does the noble Baroness agree that few countries have risen out of poverty while their birth rates are extremely high? We have heard from other noble Lords about the difficulty and the decline in international support for family planning. Could this be brought more within the current expansion of provision to combat AIDS so that women are better able to control the size of their families, as they clearly wish to do?

APPENDIX IV
11 June 2014 – Review of Sri Lanka post war

4.57 pm

Lord Naseby (Con): My Lords, first, I compliment her Majesty's Treasury on what it has achieved for our economy; secondly, I compliment those associated with welfare reform, in particular, my noble friend Lord Freud, on what his department has achieved.

I wish I could say that I complimented her Majesty's Foreign and Commonwealth Office, but I regret that I am not in a position to do so. I did not support our actions in Libya or our manoeuvrings in Egypt. I was totally against our policy in Libya, and wrote to the Prime Minister accordingly. All those actions have just destabilised that part of the world—and, worse, caused thousands of deaths and millions of refugees. The Syria war was from the start nothing to do with democracy; it was the fourth Sunni-Shia internal war. If we really want peace there, Her Majesty's Government have to find a means of talking to and working with Mr Putin and Russia.

It will not surprise your Lordships that I want to say a few words about Sri Lanka. I have been involved with that country for more than 50 years, and I think I know its ins and outs pretty well. I am the elected leader of the all-party group. I do not support any particular ethnic group, political party or Government. I have no business interests there—but I do fervently support the ordinary people in Sri Lanka and I wish to ask a few questions of Her Majesty's Government.

First, Sri Lanka—a former colony, a founder member of the Commonwealth and one of the few countries that supported the United Kingdom over the Falklands situation—finds today that we, the United Kingdom, are exceedingly unhelpful to it. Why is it that we are so anti the democratically elected Government? Why can we not work with them? Why at every turn must we just listen to the vociferous diaspora, which is usually led by former Tamil Tigers? Why do we not understand that the Tigers were terrorists who murdered every moderate Tamil leader they could find, along with two presidents and thousands of other Sri Lankans—all in the cause of a separate state called Eelam. It was rather similar to Pol Pot.

Can we not understand that after 28 years of fruitless negotiations, it was necessary for a new, democratically elected Government to act to destroy the Tigers? Yes, that meant a bloody war, as the Tigers refused to surrender. However, I know that that Government tried hard to minimise casualties. Why do we refuse to publish the dispatches from our own defence attaché, who was an objective assessor? Why do we think that the Sri Lankan army, which we helped to train, is so different from our own Army? After all, there were allegations against our Army in Iraq, as there were against the Sri Lankan army. I think that in both cases they were highly suspect. Certainly in the case of Iraq, they proved to be bogus.

Do I think that there should be an inquiry into the final days of the war? Yes, I do, but it should be a military inquiry, because all the argument is basically about gunfire et cetera. A retired general should conduct it, perhaps from Australia. There is a wonderful Sri Lankan, Sir Desmond de Silva, who has done splendid work in Northern Ireland. There would need to be a gunnery officer, probably from the UK, and obviously somebody from the UN.

It is claimed that the whole issue is about human rights, but I will take just one aspect. I saw the head of the ICRC in Boossa camp and asked him, "Have you, the International Committee of the Red Cross, ever come across terror as defined internationally?". The answer I got was, "No, I have not and nor have my staff". How is it, then, that this new group called Freedom from Torture can come up and say that it is rife?

I make a plea that we should work diplomatically with Sri Lanka. That may mean a slightly less subservient approach to the Tamil diaspora and the media around the world. It will mean that the reconciliation, which is already happening, will be speeded up. In what way? They have been very brave in bringing forward trilingualism, which is quite an achievement. Thousands of Tamils have gone back from all over the world to Sri Lanka and settled down quite peacefully. There is total freedom of movement in the country and while there is a lot of criticism of the press, there is actually more freedom of the press in Sri Lanka than in Singapore. Certainly, the LLRC inquiry is slow—but not half as slow as Chilcot has been.

I finish on this note. Over the weekend, I sat and listened to the words of President Obama. He said that we,

"waged war so that we might know peace".

Why is it any different in Sri Lanka, where so many thousands of young men and women across all ethnic groups gave their lives to rid their country of terrorism?

5.03 pm

Lord McFall of Alcluith (Lab): My Lords, my speech on the Scottish issue will be vigorous and a statistics-free zone. While I recognise the centrality of the economy—not least the currency, which I have mentioned previously—I want to focus on what we have built together these past 307 years and what we may lose if we wake up as foreigners to each other on 19 September. Have no doubt that both of us will be diminished: Scotland in terms of its trade and investment, prosperity and security, and the rest of the United Kingdom in its global authority and position in the world—not least with multinational bodies—and its leadership role, where it has been a beacon as a liberal and harmonious society to many developing and emerging countries.

My simple message today is that all of us need to engage in the national conversation, where warmth and friendship dominate. Let us minimise the abuse and the bitterness so eloquently expressed by the noble Baroness, Lady Liddell, who mentioned the abuse encountered by JK Rowling and Clare Lally, a former constituent of mine. We need to elevate this discussion to include what is good, valued and treasured in our relationship in which we have worked together for more than 300 years. However, being Scots, reality must prevail. In my view Simon Schama correctly assessed the situation when he wrote in an article in the *Financial Times* a couple of weeks ago that the UK is a,

"splendid mess of a union",

11 December 2014

5.37 pm

Lord Naseby (Con)

My Lords, it is a particular pleasure to join this debate and I thank my noble friend for instigating it. I go back 50 years with Sri Lanka, having worked there in 1963 for the Reckitt and Colman Group as a marketing manager, visiting every conceivable market in the year I was there. When I came back, I wrote a pamphlet in 1967 called Helping the Exporter. It even had to have a reprint, although there are not too many copies left nowadays. Before I came to the House I was a director of one of the major advertising agencies specialising in overseas trade, so I think I have a reasonable heritage to comment on trade between two countries.

The first thing I want to say is that Sri Lanka is very relevant to our country. The population is roughly 30% of the size of our own. I will not cover the same areas as my noble friend, but it is right to re-emphasise that growth since peace in 2009 has been roughly between 6.5% and the 8% at which it is currently running. I congratulate Her Majesty's Government on the trade mission that was put together at the end of November. I think our high commissioner, who I know is on his last few months there, put together a really good programme, and the feedback from the chamber of commerce in Colombo was very positive. Indeed, I shall quote one sentence from the welcome. Thankfully the high commissioner has put "Ayubowan" which is the traditional welcome in Sri Lanka. He says:

"With a Free Trade Agreement with China to be signed shortly adding to the existing FTAs with Pakistan, India, South Asia and Asia Pacific, Sri Lanka could act as a regional hub to over 3 billion potential customers".

That is what it is all about.

I also inevitably did some research into, for me, a relatively new area, looking in some depth, not at the political scene, which I think I know backwards, but at the trade and commerce side. An excellent article appeared by a man called Jon Springer of Forbes Asia. He picks out a number of key determinants why Sri Lanka has such good opportunities for the UK to export there.

First, he picks out government stability. It is true that in 2009, once peace was there, there was stability on the ground. Added to that, there is now a railway system all the way to Jaffna. There are new roads, both up to Jaffna and down to the south-west. There is electricity, without permanent cuts, which was the situation for many years and certainly when I worked there. There is good electricity on tap. I would call that a rising peace dividend.

My noble friends mentioned the stock market. No wonder Sri Lanka is proud if our stock market is using software from Sri Lanka. I would be jolly proud if that happened. A friend of mine, a Tamil, is a director of one of the major companies, MAS, a major clothing manufacturer exporting all over the world. It exports here to Marks & Spencer and other retailers. I went round not only his factories, but the housing developments for some of their people. They are extremely well done. Yesterday, I went to Human Rights Day in the Foreign Office, where there was talk about the need for the corporate sector to show a proper response to its workers and others for whom it is responsible. In passing, I say to my noble friend that I thought yesterday's initiative, Human Rights Day, was very good indeed.

John Springer also picked out a comment that I had also seen from Ceylon Asset Management, which, I admit, is at the far end:

"We expect 25% growth in the equity market on average per year for the next five years. If you think about it, that isn't that much space on 7 to 8% growth in the economy annually. What people don't realise is that on a per capita basis, Sri Lanka is twice as rich as India".

I think that is probably blowing a trumpet a bit, but nevertheless, there is positive note there. Then, of course, next door there is a big brother, but a very much changed big brother. Modi's India is there with a link for Sri Lanka to be the hub for goods and services on their travels eastward to drop in to the brand new port at Colombo city. There is the additional new port down at Hambantota and the revitalisation of Galle harbour, by kind permission of the Dutch. All that means that this is a real opportunity for growth.

I have been a tourist in Sri Lanka on a number of occasions. I was a tourist in the very early days when if you were on the shore you ate fish curry and if you were up country you ate chicken curry. Today, there are wonderful hotels. I looked at the figures, which are astonishing. This year, it is estimated that there will be 1.6 million tourists and there has been a steady increase in the amount of money that tourists spend.

Sri Lanka is really becoming a middle-income country, although there are obviously poor parts of it; I think I know where they are as well. The real estate market is moving in Colombo and surrounding areas and that is a positive move. Are there risks? Of course, in every commercial world—and I was in it for quite a long time—there are risks. There is one simple thing that Her Majesty's Government can take on board, which is supported 100%, I am pleased to say, by our high commission. If we want to do more trade with Sri Lanka, we have to speed up the process of issuing visas to those coming on a short-term visit to do business. Although the Foreign Office claims that it is to save money that visas have to be processed in Chennai, that is a nonsense. We even built a building in Colombo to do the processing. It is sitting there idle. What would be the net extra expenditure for a couple of officers to process the proper visas, maybe just for business visitors? That really needs to be looked at. That is my plea to my noble friend on the Front Bench.

There are some other handicaps. I will highlight three. One is the Small Business, Enterprise and Employment Bill going through your Lordships' House. Parts 7 and 8 and Schedule 3 require that shareholders holding 25% or more, or having some control over a company ownership, have to be kept in a register and that register must be made public. Admittedly, this applies only to UK companies, but I have to tell my noble friend on the Front Bench, as one who has worked and lived in that part of the world, as far as the Middle East and south-east Asia are concerned, nobody wants to have their public or any other public look at a register. That leaves them open to creative journalism and, I am sorry to say, one or two creative NGOs. There is ample provision to check on fraud, money-laundering and other provisions. However, I think my noble friend will have to pass on a message to his noble friends that that will cause a huge problem for trade.

I am sure there are those in the Chamber who wonder why I have not even mentioned politics. I have to mention it on a couple of issues, though. Here in the UK there is a challenge from the part of the Tamil diaspora that just pours out propaganda. I must get one or two things a week, telling me that dreadful things are happening every day, and, more importantly, that Eelam is still on the agenda—that is, the independence of the north and possibly the east. Frankly, that does not help anybody. What I find so disappointing about the Tamil diaspora is that the amount of money and investment that is going into the Jaffna region is so tiny that it is almost embarrassing to record how low it is.

Add to that the news we had yesterday or the day before about torture in Guantanamo Bay. There are allegations of torture in Sri Lanka. On my last visit, I did my level best to check with all the independent authorities whether there was any evidence of torture, particularly the ICRC, which said that there was none. However, we keep getting the odd report, without substantiated evidence, that there is torture. We need to take all those with a pinch of salt.

There are also claims that there is religious intimidation. I say to my noble friend that there is not. There is diversity of faith there. Certainly the Sri Lankan Government are not stirring it up one way or the other. Should we not reflect that mosques were burned down in Luton, Bletchley and Birmingham? We do not know who perpetrated that situation but we know that it is wrong. I believe that the Government in Sri Lanka will be equally keen to find out who is responsible there.

Overhanging it all is the OHCHR situation in Geneva, which, frankly, is not recognised by the Sri Lankan Government. Perhaps more importantly, it is not recognised by a number of Commonwealth countries, including India and Australia. We will have to see how objective it is, but sadly the UN does not have a great history of objectivity in what has happened in Sri Lanka.

I conclude by saying that we have a new high commissioner going from here to Sri Lanka. I hope that he will have really good knowledge of commercial matters and will deal with that with energy. Sri Lanka has a presidential election on 8 January. I do not know who will win; I wish whoever does all possible success. I know those elections, as does the Opposition Whip; I am sure it will be a fair and full election. I thank those who have enabled me to take part in this excellent debate.

Vol. 785
No. 32

Thursday
12 October 2017

PARLIAMENTARY DEBATES
(HANSARD)

HOUSE OF LORDS
OFFICIAL REPORT

ORDER OF BUSINESS

complacency, but I certainly think there is a lot more to do to provide good stewardship of the transition in the world of work in future. I look forward to further debates.

Motion agreed.

Sri Lanka

Question for Short Debate

4.36 pm

*Asked by **Lord Naseby***

To ask Her Majesty's Government what assessment they have made of the progress made by the coalition government of Sri Lanka in meeting the requirements on reconciliation established by the United Nations Human Rights Council.

Lord Naseby (Con): My Lords, I declare an interest: I started the All-Party Parliamentary Group on Sri Lanka in 1975 and am currently its president. I have known Sri Lanka for over 50 years.

I believe the UK has a unique role to play in the future of Sri Lanka, but we need to understand the history behind the current situation. In the 11th century AD Tamil Cholas invaded Sri Lanka and took over the north and north-east. Understandably, the Sinhalese were left with the remainder. Then there was colonisation by the Portuguese, the Dutch and then of course the UK. The British left behind a very good civil service; unfortunately, it was not spread across the two main denominations. It was dominated by the Tamils, who looked after the civil service and indeed the professions. On independence, sadly, this position was somewhat resented by the Sinhalese, and they passed the Sinhalese official language Act.

There remained some smouldering resentment from 1948 right through to around 1973. The Tamil youth have been activated by two people in particular. One is Mr Balasingham, a British citizen after Mr Blair's Government gave him that, and the other is a man called Prabhakaran, a single-minded ruthless activist. In 1973 Prabhakaran killed the mayor of Jaffna, along with six soldiers whose bodies were brought to Colombo. There was a resentful response from the Sinhalese youth; very sadly it was three days before a curfew was brought in, and well over 1,000 Tamils were killed. From then on it has been a situation of Eelam, the independent state, on one side versus the unitary state of Sri Lanka on the other.

Fast forward to 18 May 2009. The Tamil Tiger terrorists are defeated in a military solution, and after nearly 30 years of war there is peace across the whole island, as there is today. This is followed by a presidential election in January 2015 when President Sirisena is elected to head a coalition Government. The platform of that Government was to achieve reconciliation, ensure a durable peace, promote and protect human rights, uphold the rule of law and strengthen good governance and democracy. Out of that flowed UN Resolution 30/1 of 1 October 2015.

I visited Sri Lanka last February. Eight months on it is quite clear to me, from the context that I have, that the Government are addressing all the issues raised in the UN resolution. It may be taking longer than some would wish but that is life, I think. I shall highlight three. The first is missing persons. A massive amount of time and effort was put into the Paranagama commission, set up by the previous Rajapaksa Government, identifying some 20,000 missing persons and actually following up 10,000 of them. To this can be added the superb work done by the ICRC.

The good news is that a commissioner and a department are now set up, and in passing I pay tribute to the enormous hard work putting by Sir Desmond de Silva and his two colleagues. Sri Lanka must be eternally grateful that men of their wisdom and experience have got this task moving in the first place.

On prevention of terrorism, there is acceptance that a new Act is needed—there was in February. I cannot understand why it is taking quite so long to get it on the statute book. The constitution is being debated—the good news is that the leading Tamil party is actively taking part—and the problem of devolution is being addressed. However, the West needs to understand that the East cannot necessarily produce a mirror image of a western structure.

In passing, I pay considerable tribute to Halo and its Sri Lankan operatives, along with the Indians, Canadians and the Sri Lankan army, for clearing a square metre a day of ground, which makes it possible for families to return to the land.

What is not on track and needs urgent attention is the war crimes allegations hanging over the country. These flow from the Darusman report, which, on a best-guess basis, two years after the end of the war, stated,

"there is still no reliable figure for civilian deaths",

but then guessed at 40,000. This figure is bandied about by virtually every human rights organisation and the thousands of Tamil diaspora throughout the world, many of whom were LTTE Tamil Tiger supporters and still are, inflamed by Tamil Net and those ghastly Channel 4 "Killing Fields" films, which so influenced the previous Prime Minister.

I have discovered an unpublished report from the United Nations country team, which stated that from August 2008 up to 13 May 2009, the number of civilians killed was 7,721. The war ended six days later, so it cannot possibly have got up to 40,000. Then I looked at what Gordon Weiss, the former UN spokesman said. He produced an estimate in 2009 of 7,000 civilian deaths. He also made the simple observation that, for the Sri Lankan army, it made no tactical sense to kill civilians. University Teachers for Human Rights is not exactly a right-wing organisation; in fact, it is probably on the far left. It had similar figures, and commented that from what happened it could not say that the purpose of bombing or shelling by government forces was to kill civilians. It also said that ground troops took great trouble not to harm civilians.

The Sri Lankan Government's census department—a very genuine department— issued an in-depth census leading to the conclusion that 7,000 to 8,000 were missing. US Ambassador Blake stated on 7 April that there were deaths of 4,164 from 20 January to 6 April. Major General Holmes in his expert military report of March 2015 concurs with 7,000 to 8,000. Above all, all the people I have cited state that there was no policy to

[LORD NASEBY]
kill civilians—in fact, the opposite. To these I add the British defence attaché, Lieutenant Colonel Anton Gash, who said to me in January 2009 that he was surprised at the controlled discipline and success of the Sri Lankan army and in particular the care that it was taking to encourage civilians to escape and how well they were looked after, and that certainly there was no policy to kill civilians. There could not be a better military man: he is knowledgeable, independent and would be authoritative about what happened in his reports in his dispatches. So I decided to make a freedom of information submission to the UK Foreign and Commonwealth Office concerning those dispatches in the period 1 January to 19 May 2009. The original submission went in on 6 November, but was rejected. Two appeals to higher authorities at the Foreign Office were rejected, so I appealed to the Information Commissioner—with more success. She listened and, as a result of her representations, 26 pages of heavily redacted dispatches were sent me. Obviously, I looked at them with some care. I challenged the lack of dispatches in the last two months. Amazingly, another 12 pages appeared, all redacted.

Still concerned about the lack of dispatches in the past few days, I made a final appeal to the First-tier Tribunal, assisted by my very good friend Amal Abeywardene. We had the sympathy of the judges for the cause, but they accepted the Foreign Office view that if confidential information was given out, nobody in future would give us any more. So I now have the princely sum of 39 pages of heavily redacted dispatches— nevertheless, if you dig deeply, as in life, you find some real gems. For example, on 28 January:

"It is not possible to distinguish civilians from LTTE cadres as few are in uniform".

Then, from 16 February:

"IDPs being cared for in Trincomalee. Welfare appears to be overriding security considerations".

Then on 20 January they say,

"no cluster munitions were used",

and on 26 April,

"civilians killed Feb 1-April 26—6432".

I hope and pray that, as a result of this debate, the UK will recognise the truth that no one in the Sri Lankan Government ever wanted to kill Tamil civilians. Furthermore, the UK must now get the UN and the UNHCR in Geneva to accept a civilian casualty level of 7,000 to 8,000, not 40,000. On top of that, the UK must recognise that this was a war against terrorism, so the rules of engagement are based on international humanitarian law, not the European Convention on Human Rights. The West, and in particular the US and UK, must remove the threat of war crimes and foreign judges that overhangs and overshadows all Sri Lankans, especially their leaders. We in the UK should reflect on the sacrifices of thousands of young Sri Lankan soldiers who died to create peace in that country. Finally, I reflect that Sri Lanka came to our need in two world wars and had casualties, and it was one of just a handful of countries who supported the UK over the Falklands. Now is the time to offer the hand of friendship and act to lead the international community to recognise what the truth really was.

4.47 pm

Baroness Berridge (Con): My Lords, I am grateful to my noble friend Lord Naseby for securing this debate—and I declare an interest as project director for the Commonwealth Initiative for Freedom of Religion and Belief.

The Commonwealth Heads of Government Meeting in Sri Lanka in 2013 helped to focus international attention on the human rights failures of previous Sri Lankan Governments, and the decision of the then Prime Minister David Cameron to attend was, I submit, correct as this international spotlight helped to form part of the driving forces that secured a peaceful transition of power in January and August 2015. Resolution 30/1 of the Human Rights Council came after this democratic transition of power, which saw an alliance of moderates from within the two largest parties, the Sri Lanka Freedom Party and the United National Party, form a ruling coalition. The resolution stresses the importance of protecting the human rights of all Sri Lankans, regardless of ethnic and religious identity. That of course includes the right to freedom of religion and belief, as outlined in Article 18 of the Universal Declaration of Human Rights. The UN Sri Lankan Peacebuilding Priority Plan also stresses the importance of promoting and protecting the human rights of vulnerable peoples.

It is important to recognise the often underappreciated significance of religion to the conflict and the peace process in Sri Lanka. As Dr Rajesh Venugopal of the London School of Economics argues, both Tamil and Sinhalese national identities are bound to Hinduism and Buddhism respectively. Sri Lanka is one of only seven Buddhist majority countries in the world, Cambodia, Thailand, Myanmar, Bhutan, Laos and Mongolia, being the other six. Around 70% of the population identify as Buddhist. However, the country has sizeable religious minorities, with 12.6% identifying as Hindu, 9.7% as Muslim and 7.6% as Christian. Although Tamils are largely Hindu, it is less well known that Muslims and Christians are often seen as outsiders by both the Government and the Tamil militants, thereby suffering at the hands of both. As the Asia Foundation's *Sri Lanka Strategic Assessment 2016* argues, religious violence and hatred serves as a major barrier to securing a long-term peaceful Sri Lanka.

The Sri Lankan constitution currently protects freedom of religion or belief, in Article 10 of Chapter III, and the right to worship individually or as a group, in Article 14(1)(e) of Chapter III. However, under the previous Government, freedom of religion and belief was eroded because of the tacit acceptance by the state of extreme Buddhist sects which propagate an exclusive image of Sri Lankan identity as solely Buddhist, with non-Buddhists as "others", whose loyalty and citizenship should be in question. Ultra-nationalist Sinhalese Buddhist organisations, such as Bodu Bala Sena, were able to spread hatred towards both Muslims and Christians with impunity. In April 2014, BBS raided an interfaith press conference and no action was taken by the authorities. Also in 2014, there was a nationwide BBS anti-halal campaign, which contributed to the toxic environment of religious hatred and, arguably, to the anti-Muslim Aluthgama riots, during which at least

Vol. 795
No. 249

Tuesday
5 February 2019

PARLIAMENTARY DEBATES
(HANSARD)

HOUSE OF LORDS
OFFICIAL REPORT

ORDER OF BUSINESS

[LORD BROWNE OF LADYTON]
How does suspending compliance with a treaty of this nature fit with that commitment, and what steps will our Government take to live up to it? What are we going to do now to "further strengthen arms control" in the light of the deterioration that the noble Lord, Lord Campbell of Pittenweem, has so clearly described? We are heading for strategic problems with the new START because it is an Obama treaty and anything with Obama's name on it is detested by the current President of the United States.

Lord Ahmad of Wimbledon: The noble Lord raises an important point about NATO's previous statement. I specifically draw his attention to NATO's statement of 1 February 2019 on this very issue. It said:

"NATO continues to closely review the security implication of Russian intermediate-range missiles and will continue to take steps necessary to ensure the credibility and effectiveness of the Alliance's overall deterrence and defence posture".

The NATO alliance is important, and we and all NATO partners, including the United States, are committed to it. The noble Lord will know that in April this year the next meeting of NATO will be hosted by Secretary of State Pompeo of the United States. The implication is that non-compliance and compliance have to be a two-way process. However, if from 2014 there is a clearly identified situation in which one side does not abide by the rules and does not comply, it is a tall order to expect the other side to comply. As I said, there is an opportunity for Russia to step up to the mark, and I am sure we hope that it will. However, based on experience, it might be an opportunity that is not taken up.

Sri Lanka

Question for Short Debate

7.23 pm

Asked by Lord Naseby

To ask Her Majesty's Government, following the resignation of the government of the United States from the United Nations Human Rights Council where they co-sponsored with the United Kingdom Resolution 30/1 in 2015 and Resolution 34/1 in 2017, in regard to Sri Lanka, and given the progress made towards many aspects highlighted in the resolutions, what assessment they have made of whether to annul or withdraw those resolutions.

Lord Naseby (Con): My Lords, it is my privilege to introduce this debate this evening. In doing so, I declare an interest in that I started the All-Party Parliamentary Group on Sri Lanka in 1975 and had the privilege of being made its honorary president four years ago.

In a sense, this evening is almost an auspicious day in Sri Lankan terms. Yesterday was the 71st anniversary of the independence of Sri Lanka, so it is no young nation—indeed, it is a very senior nation—and, in democratic terms, it is looked upon as the leading democracy in that part of the world, with regular elections, Governments changing here and there, and so far, thankfully, no sign of any dictator.

The reason for this evening's debate is very straightforward. I thought about this six months ago and realised that the UN Motions on Sri Lanka will be reviewed in March 2019—that is, next month—by the UNHCR in Geneva, and I decided to initiate a debate. It is, after all, nearly four years since the resolutions were passed, having originally been moved by the US and the UK. They were co-sponsored by the Government of Sri Lanka, who welcomed help along the way.

There are two resolutions: one was adopted in September 2015 and the other in March 2017. The key point about them is that they promoted reconciliation, accountability and human rights in Sri Lanka. The cause was really the war in Sri Lanka, and the end of that war has resulted in Eelam being something that nobody in Sri Lanka, other than the Tamil Tigers, really wants. Certainly it is not wanted today and it is not wanted by India. However, unfortunately the UN received the Darusman report, which indicated that 40,000 civilians had been killed.

I have done a great deal of research. Nearly three years ago I made a request under the Freedom of Information Act and secured the publication of Colonel Gash's dispatches to the United Kingdom. I have 40 pages of them here, some of which have been totally redacted, and I shall quote from one this evening. It is the dispatch of 16 February 2009 and concerns 400 IDPs being transferred from the fighting area to Trincomalee. Colonel Gash writes:

"The operation was efficient and effective, but most importantly was carried out with compassion, respect and concern. I am entirely certain that this was genuine—my presence was not planned and was based on a sudden opportunity".

There are many more references in the dispatches to the fact that it was never a policy of the Sri Lankan Government to kill civilians.

I have one other reference that I think is useful. It comes from the University Teachers for Human Rights, which is essentially a Tamil organisation. It says:

"From what has happened we cannot say that the purpose of bombing or shelling by the government forces was to kill civilians … ground troops took care not to harm civilians".

There is a host of other references but I shall quote one more:

"Soldiers who entered the No Fire Zone on 19th April 2009 and again on the 9th and 15th May acted with considerable credit when they reached … civilians. They took risks to protect civilians and helped … the elderly who could not walk. Those who escaped have readily acknowledged this".

Again, that provides proof.

Interestingly, the US has now withdrawn from being a sponsor. My personal guess, following some inquiries, is that the US Government now assess that the Sri Lankan Government have done a huge amount to meet the UN requirements, so they see very little purpose in prolonging what is in effect almost a policing surveillance of the actions of another sovereign state which is now 71 years old. Nevertheless, I think it is right to evaluate what has happened over the last four years.

I pay tribute to Her Majesty's Government for some of the help they have given, particularly in the reconciliation process, through their Conflict, Stability and Security Fund. The HALO Trust has done a wonderful job. I have visited the de-mining operation on two occasions and have seen the very careful work of a Sri Lankan individual clearing one square metre a day. It is very dangerous work and is being done beautifully, so I thank all those involved and look forward to the day in 2020 when the million-plus mines will have been removed.

The UK has also assisted in setting up the Office on Missing Persons. Reflecting on the work I have done, I have noticed that more and more missing persons have reappeared. I received notification three weeks ago of a well-known Tamil activist appearing in the middle of France, complete with wife and children. I believe that this is not terribly unusual, but it is quite some time since the war ended and people are still reappearing.

The Sri Lankan Government have set up their Office for Reparations, which is useful and doing good work. They have also set up a framework for a truth and reconciliation commission. This is absolutely vital in my judgment. It means that all those who were involved have to be prepared to come and give evidence, including members of the LTTE who have disappeared to Canada, the USA or Australia. They must be subpoenaed to attend; otherwise the process will be totally one-sided. Even in the UK, we still have people such as Mrs Balasingham who was a real activist for the LTTE in the recruitment of child soldiers.

I understand why the Sri Lankan Government believe that the judges should be Sri Lankan; I think that they are right. If nothing else, the recent argument in the Supreme Court indicated that the Supreme Court rules supreme in Sri Lanka, whatever the politicians might think. There is a new counterterrorism Act on the way; 90% of the land requisitioned during the war has now been returned to the original citizens; 880,000 displaced people have been resettled, which is a huge achievement, by any yardstick, for any country; and 12,000 former LTTE cadres have been rehabilitated and integrated back into society—I have met some of them, and they are most grateful for what was done for them.

In reality, Sri Lanka has taken positive steps on the four pillars of transitional justice: truth, reconciliation, accountability and guarantees of non-recurrence, which must be taken into account by the Human Rights Council. Add to this the continuing co-operation, almost on a daily basis, with human rights people on the ground in Sri Lanka and the question has to be asked: what is the point of continuing with these resolutions?

It is 10 years, almost to the day, since the end of the war. Surely now is the time for closure and to let this proud country stand on its own two feet. Is it really a good use of resources for Sri Lanka to be monitored by the West almost every day? My view as president of the all-party group is: no, it is not. Frankly, I say to my noble friend on the Front Bench, too easily do we forget what a good friend Sri Lanka has been to the UK over decades. When it was a colony, thousands of Sri Lankans volunteered for the two World Wars. Indeed, the eighth-largest number of people who gave their lives for us in the United Kingdom were from this small island; and, as my noble friend must know, Sri Lanka was one of just seven countries to support us over the Falklands War.

There is a very old adage, "Keep your friendships in repair". Today, there is peace in Sri Lanka. You can go wherever you like. In the north, the infrastructure is repaired—that is pretty crucial—and the trains run on time. They do not run on time on the Peterborough line, I can tell you. The final proof of the normality of life are the 254,176 visitors from the UK who went to Sri Lanka in 2018—up 20%. They voted with their money and feet. I submit that Her Majesty's Government should do the same in Geneva: recognise the good, genuine work done, show some leadership, bring closure to the UN resolution and, in doing so, make it quite clear that there were not 40,000 civilians killed—and, if it helps, I will give all the evidence I have to my noble friend on the Front Bench, so that he can be totally convinced that that is indeed the case.

7.34 pm

Lord Framlingham (Con): My Lords, I start by congratulating my noble friend Lord Naseby on obtaining this most important and timely debate. It is many years since I visited Sri Lanka as part of an all-party delegation led by him. I am not an expert on Sri Lankan affairs and do not pretend to speak with any authority but simply as someone who cares for Sri Lanka and who has watched with great sadness as it has gone from being an idyllic island, through indescribable horrors, and is now in the difficult process of reconciliation and rebuilding.

Our visit gave us an opportunity to undertake a comprehensive survey of the island at that time; I have the most vivid memories of what we saw and the people we met. Everyone was extremely welcoming, the politicians were helpful, the tea plantations were fascinating and the landscape and beaches were beautiful. Even the place names were entrancing: Jaffna, Kandy, Trincomalee. I recall visiting what were called the tea lines: rows of low, whitewashed cottages where the tea pickers lived. We were there to study the workers' welfare and the conditions under which they lived. I will never forget, as we got back on our coach, looking at the somewhat anxious and drawn faces of my parliamentary colleagues and comparing them with the smiling and contented faces of the tea pickers, about whose welfare we were so concerned.

We had, of course, a comprehensive series of political meetings. We were made well aware of the dark clouds that were gathering and the reasons for them. The situation became even more obvious to us, and a little threatening, when we were warned to take great care when visiting the city of Jaffna; the army based there at that time were so beleaguered that they left their barracks only to buy cigarettes and then only under armed guard. Soon after we left Colombo, there was an explosion in the hotel in which we had stayed. I believe that was the beginning of all the tragic events that followed and which are now only too well known by everyone. I still find it hard to imagine the people I met enduring the suffering that ensued.

After such terrible times, the task of rebuilding both trust and structures is huge. Sadly, this is not new to the world. South Africa and Northern Ireland are just two examples that remind us of all that is needed to make it work—to bring people together and rebuild co-operation and confidence.

[LORD FRAMLINGHAM]

In all this, the role of the United Nations—the subject of this debate—is very important. It must of course bring pressure to bear to maintain stability and move the various processes forward. These are the principal reasons for the resolutions that we are debating this evening. But the UN must always be prepared to provide assistance, understanding and an acknowledgement of progress being made. It is surely right at this juncture that, in taking any decision on its resolutions, the United Nations should take account of the progress to date and ask itself what purposes its resolutions are designed to achieve.

It is now 10 years since the end of the conflict, and much progress has been made. My noble friend has listed many of the advances: an independent and permanent Office on Missing Persons has been set up and is working; the Parliament has passed an Act to establish an Office for Reparations; a draft framework on the establishment of a truth and reconciliation commission has been submitted to the Cabinet of Ministers; new counterterrorism legislation is under consideration; 90% of state and private land used by the security forces has now been handed back for civilian use; around 800,000 displaced people have been resettled; and Sri Lanka is due to be declared a mine-free zone in 2020.

Alongside politics and the restoration of civic life, trade helps enormously to get a country back on its feet. The UK remains the second biggest market for Sri Lankan exports after the USA. We account for around one-third of Sri Lankan exports to the EU and are one of the major investors in Sri Lanka.

Tourism of course plays a major role in the life and economy of the country. Sri Lanka was rated by the Lonely Planet guide as a top destination for travellers in the coming year 2019, and in 2017 there was a 20% increase in tourists from the UK. There was an almost 30% increase in the number of cruise ships calling at Colombo port in the first 10 months of 2018, and it is now one of the world's fastest-growing ports. So great strides have been and are being made on all fronts. It is in the light of that progress that we are asked to consider the UN resolutions.

The *Irish Times* described Sri Lanka as:

"A tear-drop-shaped island that's heaven on earth".

In recent years, through civil war and tsunami, it has had its share of tears. The hope must be that everyone who cares for this wonderful island, including our own Government and the UN, will do all that they possibly can to help it to continue on its way to a safe and prosperous future.

7.41 pm

Lord Low of Dalston (CB): My Lords, I too am grateful to the noble Lord, Lord Naseby, for asking this Question for Short Debate.

I first became involved with Sri Lanka shortly after I joined this House, when I was invited to become a patron of DABAL, Deaf And Blind Aid Lanka, a small organisation of highly committed people in this country who raised funds for the support of schools for deaf and blind children in Sri Lanka. I declare my interest as a vice-president of the Royal National

Institute of Blind People. Thanks to the good offices of the members of DABAL, I had the opportunity to visit Sri Lanka last summer and see for myself some of the schools that it assisted. Although the schools were staffed by highly dedicated individuals, it was clear that in all but two cases that had the benefit of private funding, the schools were chronically short of resources. We left hoping that the Government would do more in future to support the education of deaf and blind children in Sri Lanka.

I turn to the matters that are the specific subject of this debate. Like the noble Lord, Lord Framlingham, I am not an expert on the politics of Sri Lanka, so I shall just speak quite briefly. The essential question is how far a peacetime regime has truly replaced the kind of things that go on during war. As we have heard, in September 2015 and March 2017 the UN Human Rights Council adopted two resolutions requesting the Government of Sri Lanka to set up transitional justice mechanisms to address issues of reconciliation. The resolutions were co-sponsored by the Sri Lankan Government. If we look at what has happened since the end of the conflict in 2009, it is clear that the Sri Lankan Government have taken significant steps towards reconciliation, yet I am aware that Sri Lanka remains the object of considerable criticism from the international community. According to Amnesty International, Sri Lanka continues to pursue the commitments that it made in 2015 to deliver justice, truth, reparation and guarantees that crimes under international law will not recur but progress has slowed. There is still evidence of torture and other ill-treatment in police custody, while the Prevention of Terrorism Act is still used to arrest and detain suspects.

However, the positive steps that Sri Lanka has taken on the four pillars of transitional justice—truth, reconciliation, accountability and guarantees of non-recurrence—need to be recognised. We have heard about some of them already. An independent and permanent Office on Missing Persons has been set up. An Act to establish an Office for Reparations has been passed by the Parliament. Proposals have been brought forward for the establishment of a truth and reconciliation commission. New counterterrorism legislation that will repeal the existing Act and bring legislation into line with human rights standards is under consideration by the Parliament. As we have heard, 90% of state and private land used by security forces in the north and east of the island has been released for civilian use. As we heard from the noble Lord, Lord Naseby, around 880,000 displaced persons have been resettled, and around 12,000 former Tamil Tigers have been integrated back into society.

From this, I think it is clear that the Sri Lankan Government have done a great deal. However, there is still more to do and the Government cannot yet completely relax their efforts to bind up the wounds of a society that has so recently been riven by a protracted period of civil strife.

7.46 pm

Lord Sheikh (Con): My Lords, I thank my noble friend, Lord Naseby, for this timely debate regarding Sri Lanka and Resolutions 30/1 and 34/1.

APPENDICES
Section 3:
Significant letters

From: Michael Morris, M.P., Northampton South

HOUSE OF COMMONS
LONDON SWIA OAA

14th June, 1984

Rt. Hon. Mrs. M. Thatcher, MP,
Prime Minister & First Lord of the Treasury,
10 Downing Street,
London, SW1.

I have just returned from leading an all party
delegation of 10 M.P's to Sri Lanka with the
objective of obtaining a balanced view of the
current situation in Sri Lanka.

I understand the President has invited you to
open Victoria Dam which is, as you know, the single
biggest British aid project ever undertaken.

In my report to Sir Geoffrey Howe in January, I
recommended that you should be approached about the
opening, particularly if it could be included as
part of a tour of other parts of S.E. Asia such as
Malaysia.

I do hope you will be able to accept the President's
invitation. It would be a memorable visit for you
and the welcome you would receive is likely to be
something you will never forget. I believe a 48 hour
stopover would be perfectly feasible.

If I can help or advise in any way then I am, of course,
always available.

Yours ever,

Michael Morris

ශ්‍රී ලංකා ජනාධිපති
இலங்கை சனாதிபதி
President of Sri Lanka

The Rt. Hon. the Lord Naseby PC
Chairman
All Party British - Sri Lanka Parliamentary Group
House of Lords
London

My dear Lord Naseby,

I thank you for your letter dated April 30, 2012.

I recall our recent meeting and the useful discussion we had on a range of post-conflict issues which are being addressed by my Government. During the discussion, you had emphasized on the need for Sri Lanka to be given the necessary time and space to address these issues, and that undue pressure from the international community is not helpful. My Government is fully committed to ensuring that all citizens in Sri Lanka enjoy the dividends of peace through speedy resettlement and return to livelihoods.

During your visit to the Northern Province, you would have witnessed for yourself the progress that has been made on resettlement, rehabilitation, demining, and reconstruction of infrastructure. My Government is equally committed to addressing reconciliation issues, including the political aspects, through a process of dialogue with the representatives of various communities.

I particularly appreciate your visit to Hambantota to witness the development programme in the district aimed at the economic upliftment of the people in the Southern Province, and the initiative taken by you in informing the British polity of your views on the ground situation in my country.

ශ්‍රී ලංකා ප්‍රජාතාන්ත්‍රික සමාජවාදී ජනරජය
இலங்கைச் சனநாயக சோசலிசக் குடியரசு
Democratic Socialist Republic of Sri Lanka

Your longstanding political career and experience in government would undoubtedly help you to understand the challenges presently faced by my country. I therefore count on your continued support to counter the disinformation campaign that is being carried out to tarnish Sri Lanka's image by the remnants of the terrorist group's international network.

I thank you for your continued support to Sri Lanka and look forward to your further engagement in the post-conflict developments in Sri Lanka.

With warm regards.

Yours sincerely,

Mahinda Rajapaksa

June 3₀ , 2012

2

ශ්‍රී ලංකා ප්‍රජාතාන්ත්‍රික සමාජවාදී ජනරජය
இலங்கைச் சனநாயக சோசலிசக் குடியரசு
Democratic Socialist Republic of Sri Lanka

වසන්ත සේනානායක (පා.ම.) එල්. එල්. බී. (බකිංහැම්), එල්. එල්. එම්.
විදේශ කටයුතු රාජ්‍ය අමාත්‍ය

வசந்த சேனாநாயக்க (பா.உ.) எல்.எல்.பி. (பக்கிங்ஹாம்), எல்.எல்.எம்.
வெளிநாட்டு அலுவல்கள் இராஜாங்க அமைச்சர்

Vasantha Senanayake (M.P.) L.L.B. (Buckingham), L.L.M.
State Minister of Foreign Affairs

30 /10/ 2017

Rt, Honourable, the Lord Naseby

Caesar's Camp

Sandy

Bedfordshire

SG19 2HD

United Kingdom.

Dear Lord Naseby,

I am writing to thank you formally for the invaluable work you have been doing on behalf of Sri Lanka. We are well aware of your great efforts in the past, but what you have contributed in the last few months is particularly important at a crucial time.

It was very insightful of you to ask for the despatches of the British Defence Attache who served here during the last years of the long conflict from which this country suffered. Though the British Foreign Office appears to have forgotten what are undoubtedly salient elements, what you have brought into the public domain makes it clear that the Sri Lankan armed forces fought a much cleaner war than is often alleged in the international arena. I suspect, that if some of the redaction is removed from the documents already made available to you, the sincerity of the Sri Lankan armed forces will become undisputed.

කාර්යාලය/அலுவலகம்/Office: +94-11-2338676, ෆැක්ස්/தொலை நகல்/Fax No: +94-11-2389484
වෙබ් අඩවිය/வலைத்தளம்/Website: www.mfa.gov.lk, ඊ මේල්/மின்னஞ்சல்/email: vasantha.senanayake@mfa.gov.lk
විදේශ කටයුතු අමාත්‍යාංශය, ජනරජ ගොඩනැගිල්ල, කොළඹ 1, ශ්‍රී ලංකාව. வெளிநாட்டு அலுவல்கள் அமைச்சு, குடியரசுக் கட்டிடம், கொழும்பு 1, இலங்கை.
Ministry of Foreign Affairs, Republic Building, Colombo 1, Sri Lanka

This redaction, according to the explanation given to you is purportedly for securing confidentiality between the British Foreign Office and friendly nations of the international community, however, as far as Sri Lanka is concerned we are quite certain that the original version without redaction will in no way be embarrassing to us. Therefore, we must ask ourselves, why extraordinary lengths have been resorted to, to deprive yourself, one of the senior-most and respected Peers in the House of Lords, of pertinent information? and why indeed what has been given to you subjected to redaction?

It was also very good of you to speak so much more forcefully at the recent debate in the House of Lords. It is particularly important to deal with the various canards that are being spread, and your arguments go to show that the number of civilian deaths was significantly smaller than is being bandied about are clear and irrefutable.

I hope that we in Sri Lanka will be able to build on your work, to ensure that our victory over the terrorists who inflicted such suffering on all our people, Tamils as well as Sinhalese and Muslims, is not traduced.

I look forward to meeting you on my next visit to England, and hope too that you will once again visit this country to which, and to all its people, you have shown such deep commitment.

I fully consent to your using or reproducing this letter, if it will in anyway assist you in your laudable mission of bringing 'real' justice to Sri Lanka.

Yours sincerely,

Vasantha Senanayake (M.P.)

State Minister of Foreign Affairs

25 Courtside Lane

Princeton, NJ 08540

February 18, 2019

The Right Honorable Lord Naseby, PC

Dear Lord Naseby,

As a group of Sri Lankans living in the tri-state area of New York, we wish to express our deep appreciation for your continued support of Sri Lanka over the years. We are particularly grateful for the recent comments you made as the President of the All Party British Sri Lanka Parliamentary Group, highlighting the positive steps taken by Sri Lanka towards reconciliation and for calling to an end to the continued monitoring of our country by some Western countries.

We are fully conscious of the very constructive role you have played with regard to developments in Sri Lanka over the years. They stand out amidst negative and ill-informed criticism made in certain quarters.

It is positive and encouraging comments such as yours that assist our efforts in reconciliation and help our country and our people, move forward towards a future of hope and unity.

We thank you once again and look forward to your continued support of Sri Lanka in the future!

Yours sincerely,

Kevin Jayawardena - USA

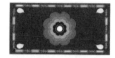

ශ්‍රී ලංකා ජනාධිපති

இலங்கை சனாதிபதி

President of Sri Lanka

The Rt. Hon. the Lord Naseby PC
Honorary President of The All Party UK Sri Lanka Parliamentary Group
House of Lords
London SW1A 0PW

Dear Lord Naseby,

I thank you for your letter of 18th February 2019, briefing me on the debate on Sri Lanka which was held in the House of Lords in the UK on 5th February 2019.

The debate was particularly useful and timely as it highlighted the need for the international community to take note of the tangible progress made by the Government of Sri Lanka with regard to reconciliation, ahead of the recently concluded UN Human Rights Council session in March on the situation in Sri Lanka.

I am particularly appreciative of the content of your statement at the Sri Lanka debate in the House of Lords which registered clearly the positive developments in Sri Lanka as well as the progress made on peace and reconciliation since the last review at the Human Rights Council.

I thank you for taking the interest to update me personally on your efforts and for the Hansard copy which was forwarded to me, which are testimony to your deep and abiding interest in our country as a true friend of Sri Lanka.

I appreciate your continued efforts in positively engaging members of the House of Lords and the House of Commons on matters related to Sri Lanka in your capacity as the Honorary President of The All Party UK Sri Lanka Parliamentary Group. I hope you would be able to visit Sri Lanka again in the near future.

Please accept my best wishes for your good health and personal well-being.

Maithripala Sirisena

April 4 , 2019

ශ්‍රී ලංකා ප්‍රජාතාන්ත්‍රික සමාජවාදී ජනරජය

இலங்கைச் சனநாயக சோசலிசக் குடியரசு

Democratic Socialist Republic of Sri Lanka

GLOSSARY

Sri Lanka Political Parties, organisations and groups:

UNP	United National Party
SLFP	Sri Lanka Freedom Party
JVP	Janatha Vimukthi Peramuna
DJV	Patriotic People's Front
JHU	Jalhika Hela Urumaya, known as the National Heritage Party
UPFA	United People's Freedom Alliance
UNFGG	Front for Good Governance
EPDP	Eelam People's Democratic Party
TNA	Tamil National Alliance
LTTE	Liberation Tigers of Tamil Eelam (The Tamil Tigers) *often referred as 'The Tigers'*
TELO	Tamil Eelam Liberation Organisation
PLOTE	People's Liberation Organisation of Tamil Eelam
EROS	Eelam Revolutionary Organisation of Students
EPRLF	Eelam's People's Revolutionary Liberation Front
TELA	Tamil Eelam Liberation Army
SCRM	Secretariat for Coordinating Reconciliation Mechanisms
TULF	Tamil United Liberation Front
DMK	Dravida Munnetra Kazhagam (Dravidian Progressive Conference – elected in India's Tamil Nadu
PA	People's Alliance (Sri Lanka)

Other abbreviations of organisations, departments and groups:

APRC	All Party Reconciliation Commission
CPA	Commonwealth Parliamentary Association
ECGD	Export Credit Guarantee Department
ODA	Overseas Development Agency
OHCHR	Office of the High Commissioner for Human Rights
DFID	Department for International Development
OISL	Office Investigation on Sri Lanka

SAARC	South Asia Association of Regional Cooperation
CHOGM	Commonwealth Heads of Government Meeting
GSP	Generalised Scheme of Preferences
IDPs	Internally Displaced Persons
ICRC	International Committee of the Red Cross *often referred to as the Red Cross*
FCO	Foreign & Commonwealth Office *often referred to as the Foreign Office*

ACKNOWLEDGEMENTS

In April 1963 I was transferred by Reckitt & Colman from Calcutta to Colombo and there began my fifty-year story with the country of Sri Lanka. I met the late Ananda de Tissa de Alwis and we became good friends through both work and play which took the form of tennis at Queens. In my last two months in Ceylon I was on my own, as Ann and the rest of my family had already returned to England, so Ananda and I played more tennis and in the evenings we enjoyed curry suppers at his home where we discussed his plans to stand for Parliament. This was my first proper introduction to politics and, as the saying goes, 'He lit my lamp'.

The actual catalyst for this book however, occurred one evening in about 2015, sitting with a valued friend at his home at Induwala near Bentota. Royston Ellis, himself an author, said: 'Michael, you should write a book about your involvement with Sri Lanka.' I thought, maybe I will.

Over the next two and a half years the idea began to take hold and so then came the challenge of finding a publisher. I asked around Parliament. One day, I raised the idea with colleagues over my usual lunch of a corned beef sandwich with a glass of spicy tomato juice and one colleague, Lord Baker of Dorking (Kenneth Baker to me), perked up and said he'd send me a note. The next day the note duly arrived and suggested I telephoned Ian Strathcarron, Chief Executive of the Unicorn Publishing Group. I rang and it was not long before a deal was done.

To these four people I owe a huge debt of gratitude.

There are others to thank, as few books can be written without checking on factual data which for me meant calling on the Sri Lanka High Commission and particularly Sugeeswara Gunaratne, the Deputy High Commissioner. There was also the House of Lords Library staff who ferreted out the records relating to all my many questions and debates on Sri Lanka over a period of twenty years. I should like to say a huge 'Thank you' to all the staff who helped in both places.

This book has been a journey for me. Along the way certain individuals have been key but one has been there almost from the beginning: Amal Abeywardene, who became a close friend and kindly accompanied me to the Tribunal Hearing on the Freedom of Information Appeal covered in Chapter 16. He has done so much to brief and encourage me.

There are also the professionals from the publishing world: two authors and an editor who have challenged and encouraged me. Professor Paul Moorcraft who wrote, *The Destruction of the Tamil Tigers* and Professor Michael Roberts whose emails from Australia inspired and informed me to keep going and dig ever deeper.

My editor, Lucie Skilton who bravely unscrambled the twists and turns of life in Sri Lanka as well as the incomprehensible spelling of Sri Lanka names. We both hope we have got them right. Never have I been challenged and questioned in such a way that I actually felt really encouraged.

I must thank my two publishers. The wonderful team at Unicorn who have turned an amateur's recollections and notes into what I hope will be a colourful and vibrant portrait of a beautiful country.

In addition is the team at BT Options publications led by Udeshi Amarasinghe who kindly agreed to print the book in Sri Lanka. I have long admired some of the quite breath-taking images produced in their other books. So to both teams, 'Thanks' from a former advertising man.

Finally, I come to friends and family. A debt of gratitude to the close friends with whom I have shared parts of the book and asked for comments, often over a glass of champagne, and always appreciated. I am particularly grateful to the members of 'The Friends of Sri Lanka' and the 'Cofradia del Vino Chileno', groups, many of whom took a real interest in how the book progressed and were always happy to offer help in any way they could.

And to my family stretched across the world, with cousins in Australia, my younger brother Crispin and Kathy in Canada and my youngest son Jocelyn, Ola, Jan and Maya in the Cayman Islands. Nearer home my eldest son Julian, Hannah, Oliver, Issy and Emma in London and just next door my daughter Susannah with Ciara and Ella. To you all, a heartfelt thank you.

Above all, to my dear wife, Ann, who has read every chapter, improved my punctuation and given me our dining table for a writing desk. She has been the most cherished and special companion on this extraordinary journey.

Thank you

The Lotus flower venerated by both Buddhists and Hindus symbolizes spiritual enlightenment and rebirth; an apt ending for 'Paradise Restored'.

INDEX